food network

STAR

THE OFFICIAL INSIDER'S GUIDE
to America's hottest food show

Ian Jackman

foreword by Bobby Flay

WM

WILLIAM MORROW
An Imprint of HarperCollinsPublishers

HarperCollins books may be purchased for educational, business, or sales promotional use. For information please write: Special Markets Department, HarperCollins Publishers, 10 East 53rd Street, New York, NY 10022.

FIRST EDITION

Library of Congress Cataloging-in-Publication Data has been applied for.

ISBN 978-0-06-208477-4

11 12 13 14 15   ID5/QG 10 9 8 7 6 5 4 3 2 1

CONTENTS

The world of American food has changed out of all recognition since I was a member of the first graduating class at the French Culinary Institute in New York City in 1984. Food had much less bearing on popular culture back then. The emergence of celebrity chefs and hot restaurants and that hip subspecies of the human race, the foodie, lay in the future.

As a young chef, I found inspiration in one type of cuisine and traveled to its source—the American southwest. There I worked with local chefs I knew until I became part of the land. I fell in love with the ingredients and made them mine. I opened Mesa Grill, my first restaurant, in 1991, followed by Bolo in 1993. And then came food television.

There were a few cooking shows on television when I was growing up: Julia Child's, of course, and Martin Yan's *Yan Can Cook* and Graham Kerr's *The Galloping Gourmet,* which I loved to watch as a kid. But as chefs on TV, we didn't have that many predecessors. The Food Network completely changed the landscape. I first appeared on the network in January 1994 when it was two months old. At that point it was called the TV Food Network, and ran in New York City only a few hours a night. I was featured on a show called *Robin Leach: Talking Food,* where Robin interviewed strictly C-list celebrities and for the last fifteen minutes his sidekick, Kate Connelly, did a cooking segment with a local chef—a *very* local chef, like me, because they couldn't afford any travel expenses.

That appearance was a key moment in my life. For one thing, Kate Connelly and I got married and we have a wonderful daughter, Sophie, together. After my first appearance, I taped a tryout show for the network called *Chef du Jour,* followed by my first series, *Grillin' and Chillin'.* These were the early days—I was there with Mario and Emeril. In the years since, I've hosted nine shows on the Food Network in addition to *Next Food Network Star.*

I was a guest on the first season of *Star* in 2005 and I must have made a decent impression, because I was asked back for Season Two with the combined duties of host and judge. My role on the show has never been so defined as to be limiting, so I have the opportunity to act as host, judge, and mentor as needed. As anyone who's watched the show can tell you, I take it very seriously. If you need confirmation, ask any of the finalists.

I cherish my relationship with Food Network. I've been there for so long, it feels like family. It's certainly my TV family. As a judge of *Food Network Star,* I think about the network from a business standpoint. I'm looking for somebody to add to the roster who is going to help make a stronger team. I put my chef coat on for the *Iron Chef* challenges, but what I enjoy the most is evaluating finalists on *Star* when I'm wearing a suit. *Star* kills two birds with one stone. It's a very successful franchise in its own right, and we find talent. The Hearty Boys, Dan Smith and Steve McDonagh; Guy Fieri; Amy Finley; Aaron McCargo, Jr.; Melissa d'Arabian; and Aarti Sequeira are the winners who have had series on the Network. Other finalists didn't win, but got their own shows anyway: Kelsey Nixon is one; Adam Gertler, Jeffrey Saad, and Tom Pizzica did as well.

Now the Season Seven winner has been crowned and there's another whole series of challenges for aspiring finalists to pore over and study. At the start of episode one of each season, these guys are already much savvier than I was when I started my first show. They're students of the network. They know exactly what they need to accomplish, even if they don't have the execution down; talking and cooking at the same time on camera is a lot harder than most people realize.

Their preparedness is one reason why I empathize with the finalists on *Star*, but I don't feel bad for them. Nobody made them do this. While you'll never see me be mean to a finalist, I do push them at times, because I see myself as their coach. "You want to make the team? Then play hard." It's something I feel very strongly about and the finalists realize it pretty quickly. Like any coach, I want everyone to perform well and I don't want anyone to embarrass themselves. *Star* is unique in the sheer volume of advice finalists get from the judges. In this book, one of them compared it to a free university. We have these people under our wings for a few months, and the evaluations last many hours. When we're giving them tips and techniques, we're trying to steer them in the right direction. If you can't perform better on TV after a session with Alton Brown, there's a problem.

To succeed in this competition, you have to manage both elements of the challenge: food and entertainment. You need to produce excellent quality food, but you also need to be able to tell stories to the camera, to have authority in the kitchen. You really need to have it all. We want to find out who is going to light up the camera. The bottom line is that to win *Food Network Star,* you need to live and breathe food. Besides your friends and family, food has to be the most important thing to you. You have to wake up thinking about it; you have to go to sleep thinking about it. If food's number five on your list, don't do this show. This is the best piece of advice I can give anyone who's thinking about trying out for *Food Network Star.* There are some people who do it because they want a job on TV, but they'll never get my vote. Cooking is what I'm most passionate about. I just happen to do it on TV.

★

Food Network Star: The Official Insider's Guide to America's Hottest Food Show demonstrates the passion and commitment of the finalists on our show by telling their collective story through food. Read, cook, eat, and enjoy!

Season ONE

On June 5, 2005, an original Food Network star, Emeril Lagasse, launched the search for the next Food Network star. "Being a chef on TV is the new American dream," said Emeril. Ten thousand aspiring television chefs hoping to realize that dream sent in audition tapes for the new reality-show competition. From these, nine finalists (one a team of two) were selected to compete at the network's studios, located in New York City's Chelsea Market. The prize was a shot at the culinary big time: a show on the Food Network and the golden chance to join the roster of such Food Network stars as Rachael Ray, Paula Deen, Giada De Laurentiis, Bobby Flay, Mario Batali . . . and Emeril. *The Next Food Network Star* host Marc Summers introduced the Selection Committee, whose job it has been over seven seasons to whittle down the finalists week by week.

On the Season One Selection Committee was the Food Network's senior VP of programming and production **Bob Tuschman,** who brought talent like Rachael Ray and Giada De Laurentiis to Food Network. "What we do here," Bob said, "is take great information and make it outrageously entertaining." Second was network VP of marketing **Susie Fogelson.** Susie, responsible for brand advertising, promotions, and events, was looking for someone who would both appeal to the current audience and bring in new viewers. Third: **Gordon Elliott,** host of *Follow That Food* and producer of *Paula's Home Cooking.* He wanted somebody whose "personality fills the room." The judges were ready to find their next star, someone who had equal parts performance, personality, and a culinary point of view.

☆ **"I fell in love with Food Network watching Emeril."**

—Susie Fogelson

"When we first launched the series it was on a more modest basis than it has become. Even then it was a different show than we had ever done before. It was hugely expensive and time-consuming, and we weren't sure if our viewers were going to like it. But *Next Food Network Star* was such a huge hit that every season we have amped it up.

"Food Network came up with the idea. We had been talking internally about it since the day I arrived. Should we do a show like this? We thought it would be fascinating for people to see what it takes to be a food star, but it took a while for food stars to be part of the everyday vocabulary of the nation. Once people saw them as huge celebrities, it was an easy next step to say, 'Let's show them how it's done and what it takes to be a celebrity chef.' "

—Bob Tuschman

THE FINALISTS

1. Brook Harlan. Brook's audition tape showed flash (literally, a pan in flames) and a lot of sizzle. Brook taught culinary arts at a high school and was also an assistant wrestling coach. At age eight he started cooking omelets with his father. What he brought to the show: energy and knowledge.

2. Deborah Fewell. For this Hollywood personal celebrity chef and actress, being on a cooking show seemed like "a perfect marriage between performing and cooking." Trained at the California School of Culinary Arts, Deborah loved to create and develop dishes and show that cooking doesn't have to be overwhelming. Her motto: "Stay cute while you're cooking in the kitchen." Her point of view: "The Spice of Life" found in Caribbean cuisine.

3. Dan Smith and Steve McDonagh. Dan and Steve entered as a couple, which they had been for eight years, as well as caterers working together for seven. "It's time to have a gay couple on TV who have a regular relationship." As "the Hearty Boys," they had a staff of forty to sixty and catering events ranging from affairs for hundreds of people to intimate dinner parties. Their promise: to plan your meal "From Soup to Nuts." They said the benefit of working together was the existing chemistry. The challenge: ensuring that the partnership is equal on the screen.

4. Harmony Marceau. "I like to take an idea and go wild with it," Harmony said. She'd found jobs, like shoe modeling, that allowed her to spend time where she wanted to be—in the kitchen. Harmony's POV: "Adventure of the Senses"—cooking with all five senses.

5. Michael Thomas. The "personal chef and surfer," who dropped pie filling on the floor during his audition, promised to throw himself into the competition, all-out, all-in. "People think that I'm this kind of super off-the-wall guy and just bizarre and weird. Which in many ways obviously I am." When Michael figured out his POV, it was "Where on Earth's My Dinner?" He'd go anywhere, do anything for food—for example, hacking his way through the jungles of Madagascar for vanilla beans.

6. Susannah Locketti. As a working mother of two, Susannah had a schedule that took her out of the kitchen. One day she took back control—and lost eighty-nine pounds over two years. A part-time graphic designer and fitness instructor, Susannah wanted to inspire working Americans with her healthy food under the banner of "Breakfast, Lunch, and Dinner *Thinner.*"

7. Eric Warren. Eric learned how to cook from his mother and grandmother. Now people sit on his stoop waiting to see what he's cooking. Eric was full of love, laughter, and fun. He'd worked in corporate America and now was giving back, working with developmentally disabled adults. Eric's "Mean Cuisine" took traditional dishes way over the top. A fried rib. A lemon icebox pie *this* high.

8. Hans Rueffert. Selected by viewers from ten semifinalists posted online, Hans had been head chef at his family's restaurant for fifteen years and in the kitchen his whole life. His sister's recent passing made him realize that life is short and we have to seize our chances where we can. Hans wanted cooks to boldly go into his "Inhibition Kitchen" and make what they've never made before—feel the fear and cook it anyway.

The First Challenge: Eggs

After Food Network president Brooke Johnson welcomed the finalists, Alton Brown set up the first-ever *Next Food Network Star* challenge. It was fitting because Alton is a Food Network star who'd made his way onto television by sending his own demo tape to the network. Alton's challenge to the finalists was to make their personalities shine on camera while working with eggs. Finalists had twenty minutes to prepare for a five-minute on-camera demonstration of their dish.

The first dish out of the Food Network kitchen on *Star* was an omelet with bacon, sautéed mushrooms, and scallions made by Deborah Fewell.

Alas, Deborah's omelet broke up in the sauté pan.

> "It was exciting, nerve-wracking, and thrilling all at the same time. I was nervous, but I told myself to just dive in and have fun. I came prepared to be challenged, and we were."
>
> —Deborah Fewell

The first challenge set the tone. Some finalists cooked too quickly or too slowly, mumbled or fumbled or forgot to show the camera what they were doing. Others just aced it. Brook thought he talked "way too fast," like the kids he taught would tell him. But he remembered the most important part. "Taste it," he said. "That's *fine*."

> "I make the dish a lot. It's quick and can be made seasonal easily. I tend to just follow the method and use whatever ingredients are in season from the farmers market."
>
> —Brook Harlan

FRITTATA

Recipe courtesy Brook Harlan

Yield: 4 servings ▎ Prep Time: 10 minutes ▎ Cook Time: 20 minutes ▎ Ease of
Preparation: easy

2 tablespoons unsalted butter

½ large onion, finely chopped
(1 cup)

1 large red bell pepper, finely
chopped (1 cup)

8 scallions, white and green parts,
sliced (¾ cup)

8 medium mushrooms, sliced
(about 2 cups)

Kosher salt

Freshly ground black pepper

12 large eggs

½ cup grated Parmesan cheese

2 teaspoons chopped chives, for
garnish

1. Preheat the oven to 350°F.

2. Melt the butter in a large nonstick ovenproof skillet over medium-high heat. Sauté the onion and pepper until they begin to soften, about 2 minutes. Add the scallions and mushrooms and cook until they soften, another 2 minutes or so. Season with salt and pepper to taste.

3. Whisk the eggs in a bowl until they are well blended. Season them with 1 teaspoon each of the salt and pepper. Pour the eggs over the vegetables in the skillet and stir constantly with a heatproof rubber spatula. When the eggs are almost cooked, spread them evenly using the back of the spatula. Cover the pan and bake for 10 minutes. Uncover and sprinkle the cheese evenly over the eggs, and cook until the cheese is melted, about 5 minutes.

4. Carefully slide the frittata onto a plate. Garnish with the chives.

★ NOTE: *Any vegetables can be used. Meat can also be added if it is cooked first.*

☆ **"If you can't handle eggs, you can't really be a cook."**

—Alton Brown

How to Succeed in Television

"One of the things that distinguishes the *Next Food Network Star* from other culinary competition shows is that fully half the requirements and challenges are camera challenges and the other half are cooking. And so it's fun to play along at home. You can judge as well as I can how they're doing on camera. While you are dependent on us to tell you about their food, you are an equal judge of how a finalist has progressed on camera."

—Bob Tuschman

Chef Bobby Flay, one of the biggest Food Network stars, has effortlessly mastered the art of being on camera. He gave Season One finalists the benefit of his experience. The hopefuls had already tried their hands at reading from the TelePrompTer, cooking and talking at the same time, swapping out uncooked and cooked dishes, and not talking two hundred miles a minute. Other challenges: learning to follow the floor manager's stage directions—"Show skewers"—and to adapt to a cue—"One minute left" or "Stretch" and fill dead time.

BOBBY'S SECRETS TO CAMERA SUCCESS

★ Food Network shows are filmed in real time, so the host can't stop the show.

★ Don't say "By the magic of television here's a dish I made already." There is no magic of television. Say "And this is what it's going to look like," and show the camera your food.

★ Learn how to do things in reverse because the front of the food processor is facing the camera.

★ If you're talking about the consistency of a dish like hominy, don't use the word *phlegmy*.

★ If you're talking about food hygiene while cooking, you don't need to say *Salmonella*.

★ Bring energy, have fun, and don't forget to smile.

★ Tell us about yourself, share your personality—we want to get to know you.

★ If something goes wrong, improvise.

★ Be organized.

★ Remember Point One: Never stop. Ever.

Finalists were reminded that they had to find a way to get their personality to pop on camera. Brook Harlan couldn't quite translate the great energy of his audition tape into performance in the camera challenges, and he was the first finalist eliminated.

"Be yourself and be passionate. You can't fake it; no one wants to watch that. Make sure that you're comfortable in uncomfortable situations. The show is twenty percent cooking and eighty percent telling people that you know how to cook and that you know what you're doing."

—Brook Harlan

what is COTIJA CHEESE?

Eric Warren used cotija cheese to make his Cumin-Crusted Chicken for Bobby Flay. Cotija is a town in southwestern Mexico that's the source for this dry, hard cow-milk cheese that can be grated like Parmesan.

SPOTLIGHT ON

BATALI BOOT CAMP

For the next competition, original Food Network star Mario Batali dropped by to make snacks for the newbies: bruschetta (pronounced "broos-*ket*-ta"—take it from Mario). Bruschetta is "a fancy Italian way of calling toast," and Mario simple adorned his with sautéed red onions and red and yellow peppers. Chef Mario has been appearing on the Food Network since its foundation, and he knows what it takes to make it on TV. His Point of View? "Simplicity and Classicism with a Personal Tweak." Which is easy to say when you're Mario Batali.

☆ "The knowledge of food is crucial. [As is] the ability to present it in a way that seems either interesting or intriguing. And then just basically an effervescent, lively personality that makes something fun to watch."

—Mario Batali

Molto Mario

Who better than *Molto* Mario Batali to show finalists how to make a pizza? A pizza is a blank canvas, something on which you can express yourself and the all-important culinary point of view, Mario explained. A pizza shouldn't be a "big *gavonne* [gluttonous] thing with a whole mess of ingredients on it." Mario floured his dough and tossed it expertly, adding marinara, Parmigiano-Reggiano, shaved fennel, and a mess of chiles. The master made it look so easy.

Finalists had thirty minutes to prepare a pizza for a demo. As Susannah Locketti sliced her healthy ingredients, she cut off the nail of her left index finger. She had it treated and returned to the challenge with ten minutes to go.

> "Aside from being cut from *Next Food Network Star,* that was the worst injury I've endured in the kitchen. I'm used to cutting with my old knife at home, and it is so dull compared with the beautiful new Food Network knives, which were so sharp. The first thing I did when I got home from New York was buy a proper set of knives to avoid a take two of that incident."
>
> —Susannah Locketti

In the end, a few of the pies were positively sophisticated—Steve and Dan's Caramelized Onion-and-Garlic Pizza Topped with Goat Cheese and Duck Confit; Hans's Pizza Topped with Calamari, Anchovy Oil, and Cheese. Other dishes were salvage jobs: Eric couldn't roll his dough, so he made a rectangle and called it a sandwich. Was Michael's

what is CONFIT?

A confit is a dish of meat or poultry (duck, goose, pork, turkey) cooked in its own fat and often preserved in a jar. It is a French specialty and a time-honored way of storing food, for months if necessary.

uneven dough a way to satisfy both thick- and thin-crust lovers, or just uneven dough?

Harmony asked us to use our senses, touch the dough, feel it. "Do you need a roller? Can you toss it in the air?" Mario Batali didn't care. "It's beautiful," he said. "And it's perfect."

what is A CHIFFONADE?

Chef Mario Batali made a chiffonade of basil—long, thin strips—to garnish the bruschetta. To make a chiffonade (*chiffon* is French for "rag"), stack leaves of an herb or vegetable, roll the stack into a tight cylinder, and cut crosswise to make narrow slices.

RUSTIC PESTO PIZZA

Recipe courtesy Harmony Marceau

Yield: 1 pie, 1 to 2 servings ▌ Prep Time: 20 minutes ▌ Cook Time: 25 minutes ▌ Ease of Preparation: easy

FOR THE PESTO

2 tablespoons pine nuts, toasted

1 large garlic clove, finely chopped

¼ cup chopped fresh basil

2 tablespoons grated Parmesan cheese

2 tablespoons extra-virgin olive oil

¼ teaspoon freshly ground black pepper

FOR THE PIZZA

1 small red ripe tomato, about 4 ounces

7 ounces prepared pizza dough

All-purpose flour, for rolling

Cornmeal, for dusting

¼ small red onion, thinly sliced (¼ cup)

¼ teaspoon kosher salt

⅛ teaspoon freshly ground black pepper

¼ cup kalamata olives, pitted and chopped

5 ounces fresh mozzarella, sliced ¼ to ½ inch thick

1. **FOR THE PESTO:** Place the toasted pine nuts in a bowl or mortar and crush with a wooden spoon or pestle until they resemble coarse bread crumbs. Add the garlic and combine. Mix in the basil and Parmesan. Stir in the olive oil and season with pepper.

2. **FOR THE PIZZA:** Lay a pizza stone on the floor or lowest shelf of the oven. Preheat the oven to 425°F.

3. Thinly slice the tomato and place the slices between paper towels. Knead the dough on a floured surface, then stretch it into a disk about 8 inches in diameter. Dust a wooden pizza paddle with cornmeal and carefully transfer the dough to the paddle. Spread the pesto over the dough, leaving 1 inch around the edge to form a crust. Add the onion and tomato slices and season with salt and pepper. Scatter the olives over the pizza and top with the sliced mozzarella. Slide the pizza onto the stone and bake until the crust is golden and firm and the cheese is melted, about 25 minutes.

Summer Celebration

After the pizza making, and working on their POVs, in their second elimination challenge, finalists demo'ed a dish to camera for a "summer celebration." One of the many salads was a standout, as was one dessert. According to Eric Warren, "When you go to a picnic, one thing always remains at the end of the day, and that's the potato salad." Not if it's Eric's potato salad. Eric struggled with the TelePrompTer but knocked it out of the park with his dish. The two key ingredients: celery, the "green goddess of potato salad," which brings the flavor to life; and mayonnaise.

> "My godmother gave me that wonderful potato salad recipe and taught me how to make it in 1985. Her recipe had so much flavor and POP that it has become a favorite for so many! I am still making the potato salad the same way, always adjusting the level of mayonnaise so that the finished product has the right amount of creaminess! It sure is good! Oooo Weee!"
>
> —Eric Warren

POTATO SALAD

Recipe courtesy Eric Warren

Yield: 6 to 8 servings (10 to 11 cups) ▮ Prep Time: 20 minutes ▮ Cook Time: 25 minutes ▮ Inactive Prep Time: 3 hours ▮ Ease of Preparation: easy

4 pounds Idaho potatoes

4 jumbo eggs, hard-boiled

2½ cups mayonnaise

4 scallions, white with some green, finely chopped

3 stalks celery, finely chopped

1 tablespoon yellow mustard

½ teaspoon freshly ground white pepper

1 teaspoon kosher salt

Place the potatoes in a large pot, and add water to cover. Bring the water to a boil and cook the potatoes until fork-tender, about 12 minutes. Drain and cool. Peel the potatoes, cut them into small chunks, and place them in a large serving bowl. Peel and finely chop the eggs and add to the potatoes, along with the mayonnaise, scallions, celery, mustard, white pepper, and salt. Mix until just combined. Cover and chill for 3 hours before serving.

Bob: That could be the best potato salad I've ever had.

Susie: It's really good. I'll have another bite.

Bob: I'll just have one more too.

Tofu Is Your Friend

The Summer Celebration Challenge also produced Michael's pie. When cooking, Michael worked hard to disarm everyone, including his ingredients. "Don't be afraid," he said. "Tofu is your friend." Chocolate was also Michael's friend, and he had a conversation with it. "I'm the most delicious flavor in the whole world," said Chocolate. "Well, Chocolate," said Michael, "that's a little presumptuous. There are a lot of flavors . . ." "Yeah. But everybody loves me."

Chocolate and Tofu didn't just talk a good game. "I never thought I would be ecstatic about something with the word *tofu* in it," said Bob Tuschman. "And this is actually delicious."

> "Living in Southern California I am constantly surrounded by tofu-loving, lactose-intolerant, protein-focused folk, so it ends up being a flexible, rich, and decadent dessert for a diverse set of folks. It's great mixed with a bit of orange zest and Grand Marnier, or raspberries and Chambord or thin mints and crème de menthe. . . . Come on, it's chocolate, it goes great with everything!"
>
> —Michael Thomas

TOFU CHOCOLATE MOUSSE PIE
with Raspberry Sauce

Recipe courtesy Michael Thomas

Yield: 8 servings ▮ Prep Time: 10 minutes ▮ Cook Time: 5 minutes ▮ Inactive Prep Time: 2 hours ▮ Ease of Preparation: easy

1 (12-ounce) package semisweet chocolate chips

1 (12-ounce) package silken firm tofu, drained

½ teaspoon vanilla extract

2 egg whites*

1 (6-ounce) store-bought chocolate cookie crust (recommended: Oreo) or graham cracker crust

Whipped cream, for serving

Raspberry Sauce, for serving (recipe follows)

RASPBERRY SAUCE

2 tablespoons seedless raspberry jam

2 teaspoons water

1 teaspoon freshly squeezed lemon juice

1. In a small saucepan, melt the chocolate over low heat, stirring often. Purée the tofu in a food processor. Add the melted chocolate and vanilla and blend, stopping the food processor once or twice to scrape the sides of the bowl with a rubber spatula. Remove to a bowl.

2. In a separate bowl, beat the egg whites until they form soft peaks. Using the spatula, fold the egg whites into the tofu-chocolate mixture. Scoop the filling into the pie crust and refrigerate until set, at least 2 hours.

3. Serve the pie with whipped cream and/or Raspberry Sauce. Don't say tofu, say terrific.

RASPBERRY SAUCE: Whisk all of the ingredients together until smooth.

* Raw-Egg Warning: The American Egg Board states: "There have been warnings against consuming raw or lightly cooked eggs on the grounds that the egg may be contaminated with *Salmonella*, a bacteria responsible for a type of foodborne illness. Healthy people need to remember that there is a very small risk and treat eggs and other raw animal foods accordingly. Use only properly refrigerated, clean, sound-shelled, fresh, grade AA or A eggs. Avoid mixing yolks and whites with the shell."

The Second Elimination

If anyone needed reminding about the importance of on-camera presence in the competition, the judges reinforced the point in elimination. Eric had a charming gift but he needed to be able to get information across; they needed more of Hans's charm and of the real Susannah. And although Deborah's demo had fallen apart, Harmony's nerves on camera were too much for her to overcome and she was eliminated.

> "I seemed so calm and natural on the show because I developed a terrible cold on my trip from sunny Los Angeles to the cold weather in New York. The Food Network staff was there to help me along the way with lots of hot tea and makeup continued to keep me dry between scenes. Typically I am very energetic and full of joy!"
>
> —Eric Warren

Paula Cooks!

Episode four of *Next Food Network Star* brought in network favorite Paula Deen, who showed finalists how to cook and chat at the same time and make it look absolutely effortless. Paula made a Black and Blue Burger and Sloppy Joes—"elbow lickers," she called them. There's a lot of butter. "Butter's my friend," said Paula, even though it killed her grandmother . . . at ninety-one.

Each finalist had to demo two of Paula's peerless southern dishes, such as Fried Green Tomatoes, Country Ham with Redeye Gravy, Tugboat Turnips, and Oyster Casserole. If anyone could cook it like Paula, the real question would be whether that finalist could do it with half as much personality.

> "It was Paula Deen who really pushed us to talk to the viewer at home. Paula immediately put me at ease because she and I noticed that the demo was set up with 'city ham' (boiled ham) instead of the country ham that her recipe called for. Our shared Georgia background made us connect instantly. There are a good number of Paula Deen wannabes, but there's only one Paula Deen!"
>
> —Hans Rueffert

what is RING TUM DITTY?

Paula's ring tum ditty recipe (made by Eric) has been in her family for generations. It's the kind of dish with origins in the mists of time. *Home Science* magazine from 1906 describes "Rink-tum-diddy" with the same basic ingredients Paula uses—tomatoes and cheese—but served on toast. As for its southern heritage, the magazine says the dish was perhaps invented "by a Brooklyn woman."

☆ **"Try not to take yourself too seriously and for goodness' sakes, whoever gets a show, don't become a diva."**

—Paula Deen

"I have never been anywhere in the world where people do not light up when they see Paula Deen."

—Bob Tuschman

In elimination, finalists heard many of the same points again. Michael's demo had never got going and according to Gordon, other finalists were improving faster than Michael. Despite his potential, that was enough to finish his competition.

"I had as much fun as it looked. I try to picture each person watching and try to leave them hungry, interested, and laughing. I hope it worked. I think that everyone is weird and bizarre in their own way. Really. I just happen to wear my goofballness right out front."

—Michael Thomas

Meet and Eat

The remaining challengers had to face the media, demo'ing their dish while answering questions from writers from *Time*, *TV Guide*, *Food & Wine*, *People*, and other magazines. Media consultant Bill McGowan offered this advice: Think of three or four things you

want to say, and don't slavishly follow the question—address what the journalist asks, then bridge back to what you want to talk about.

To the crowd of journalists, Deborah Fewell exuded confidence. "I just took control of the room and I said, You know what? It's about me right now." She fielded questions from Dana Cowin of *Food & Wine* like a pro.

"I first cooked my Trinidadian Stewed Chicken with my dad, who's from Trinidad. He calls it Sugar Brown Chicken, and he taught me how to make it. It represents wonderful memories of special times spent with my family, of comfort and love. I still make it and I'll continue to make it. I've cooked it for a few of my celebrity clients, and the only variation that I would ever bring to this dish would be to change the protein to short ribs, pork, goat, or lamb. This dish really represents the cuisine of Trinidad—it's soul-satisfying food carrying with it taste and a passionate sense of culture.

"I love creating dishes. Recently I've discovered a couple of sauces that give a dish a pop of flavor. First, a bacon, garlic, shallot, sherry, and mushroom cream sauce (served with chicken, beef, or salmon), and a honey chipotle sauce. Crispy prawns tossed at the last minute with this sauce are ridiculously good!"

—Deborah Fewell

STEWED CHICKEN

Recipe courtesy Deborah Fewell

Yield: 6 servings ▮ Prep Time: 20 minutes ▮ Cook Time: 1 hour 15 minutes ▮
Inactive Prep Time: 8 hours ▮ Ease of Preparation: intermediate

¼ cup freshly squeezed lemon juice (about 1½ lemons)

4 scallions, white part and some green, sliced into ½-inch pieces

4 fresh tomatoes, seeded and diced

1 onion, thinly sliced

1 green bell pepper, thinly sliced

¼ cup ketchup

¼ cup cider vinegar

3 tablespoons sesame oil

3 tablespoons ground cumin

1 tablespoon West Indian curry powder

1 tablespoon herb blend (ground oregano, thyme, rosemary, black pepper, and basil) (recommended: My Daddy's Herbs)

3 tablespoons garlic powder

3 tablespoons onion powder

⅓ cup plus 3 tablespoons olive oil

Kosher salt

Freshly ground black pepper

1 (3½-pound) whole chicken, cut into 8 pieces

¼ cup sugar

Rice or mashed potatoes, for serving

1. In a large bowl, combine the lemon juice, scallions, tomatoes, onion, bell pepper, ketchup, vinegar, sesame oil, cumin, curry powder, herb blend, garlic powder, onion powder, and 3 tablespoons of the olive oil. Season with the salt and pepper to taste. Add the chicken to the marinade, cover, and refrigerate for 8 hours.

2. In a Dutch oven, heat the ⅓ cup olive oil and the sugar. Remove the chicken from the refrigerator and brush off and reserve the marinade. Stir the sugar until it caramelizes and turns golden brown, about 10 minutes. (It may smoke some.) Carefully but quickly add the chicken to the pot and let it brown, turning the pieces as you go, for 6 to 7 minutes. Add the vegetables and reserved marinade, cover the pot, and reduce the heat to medium-low. Let the chicken stew until cooked through and tender, 45 minutes to 1 hour. Halfway through cooking, season with salt and pepper to taste.

3. Serve over rice or with mashed potatoes.

Schnit . . . zel

Before the Meet and Eat Hans was crazy nervous, but he quickly settled in. With a name like Hans, he said, he is genetically predestined to like schnitzel. He grew up on the stuff, "which means I'm full of schnit . . . zel."

Dana asked if Hans was really going to do an all-German show. No, that would be six episodes. He was raised in the South and loved southern food. Lori Powell of *Ladies' Home Journal* said Hans was natural and sincere and she wanted to see more.

In the elimination segment, Bob told the finalists, "You are six stars." But only five could move on, so it was good-bye to Eric.

PORK SCHNITZEL with Chanterelle Mushrooms

Recipe courtesy Hans Rueffert

Yield: 2 servings ▌ Prep Time: 10 minutes ▌ Cook Time: 15 minutes ▌ Ease of Preparation: intermediate

2 (3-ounce) pork cutlets, pounded thin

Kosher salt

Freshly ground black pepper

¼ cup all-purpose flour, for dredging

2 eggs, beaten

Bread crumbs, for dredging

2 tablespoons clarified butter or vegetable oil

3 slices smoked bacon, roughly chopped

1. Pat the cutlets dry and season with salt and pepper. Assembly-line style, dredge the cutlets in the flour, then the eggs, and finally the bread crumbs. Heat the clarified butter in a large skillet over medium-high heat. Sauté the cutlets on both sides until they are golden brown and crunchy. Drain on paper towels and keep warm.

2. In a separate skillet, fry the bacon over medium-high heat. Once the bacon has started to become brown and crisp, add the butter and onion. Sweat the onion,

1 tablespoon unsalted butter

½ onion, diced

¾ pound chanterelle mushrooms, chopped if large

1 to 2 tablespoons Dijon mustard

1 tablespoon capers, drained

½ cup heavy cream

then add the chanterelles. As the mushrooms begin to brown, stir in the mustard, capers, and just enough cream to cover the bottom of the pan. Simmer the sauce to reduce slightly.

3. To serve, spoon the sauce over the browned schnitzels.

"The rich, buttery, slightly peppery flavors of the mushrooms meld together with a touch of cream, onion, and bacon to become something celebratory, ephemeral, and just plain magic. My father would serve it with simple salt-water potatoes and a healthy mess of Bavarian-style red cabbage. Any leftover chanterelles would be quickly sautéed with a little fresh thyme and then find their way folded into a simple omelet. Delicious!"

—Hans Rueffert

Lights, Camera, Action

In their next challenge, the last four finalists were given just five minutes to present three budget-minded dishes to Harry Smith at the CBS *Early Show*. Having to cook and answer Harry's questions at the same time threw the finalists.

TV 101
TV VETERAN HARRY SMITH GAVE THE FINALISTS THESE TIPS:

1. The more of your dish you can have prepared ahead of time, the more you can talk about what you want to talk about and the more passion you can put into your presentation.

2. On the air, Harry asked Deborah how long she should cook her pork chops. "Till they're done," she said. "You can't not know the answer to that question on TV," he said afterward.

3. Try not to sound rehearsed—allow for spontaneity, otherwise your performance feels stiff.

Two finalists were let go in quick succession. After the *Early Show* piece, Susannah, to her surprise, went home. Hans left following a market-basket challenge where everyone got the same ten ingredients. Hans made too many dishes—beet salad, spätzle, shrimp, papaya pico de gallo, and salmon—which forced him to race through. "Great food, no doubt," said Bob. "But that did not make for great TV."

what is SPÄTZLE?

Spätzle (pronounced "*shpetz*-leh," which means "little sparrow"), a dish from southern Germany, is small egg dumplings cooked by pressing dough through a sieve, colander, or spätzle maker into boiling water.

ENDIVE AND ROMAINE SALAD

with Walnuts, Pears, and Gorgonzola, and Raspberry Balsamic Drizzle

Recipe courtesy Susannah Locketti

Yield: 4 servings ❙ Prep Time: 20 minutes ❙ Cook Time: 10 to 15 seconds ❙
Ease of Preparation: easy

1 large head Belgian endive

1 head romaine lettuce, leaves torn

1 Bosc pear

2 ounces Gorgonzola, crumbled

¼ cup chopped walnuts

Freshly ground black pepper

2 tablespoons seedless raspberry jam

2 tablespoons balsamic vinegar

1. Clean the endive with a dry paper towel and slice off the bottom to separate the leaves. Arrange the leaves around the edge of a large platter. Fill the inside with torn romaine leaves. Cut the pear into thin slices and arrange throughout the platter. Sprinkle the Gorgonzola and walnuts on top and season with pepper to taste.

2. In a small microwave-safe bowl, combine the jam with the balsamic vinegar and heat for several seconds until just warm. Stir with a small whisk. Drizzle the dressing over the salad and serve.

"To keep the salad lighter yet still decadent I recommend no more than an ounce of the Gorgonzola per serving."

—Susannah Locketti

CHILLED BEETS AND ASPARAGUS
with Garlic Chive Blossoms

Recipe courtesy Dan Smith and Steve McDonagh

Yield: 8 servings ▌ Prep Time: 20 minutes ▌ Cook Time: 30 minutes ▌
Ease of Preparation: intermediate

2 bunches baby beets, peeled and quartered (about 2 cups)

1 bunch asparagus, trimmed and cut on the bias into 2-inch pieces

¼ teaspoon kosher salt

1 cup water

½ cup orange blossom water

½ cup sugar

1 tablespoon freshly squeezed lemon juice

1 small bunch garlic chives with blossoms, roughly chopped

4 ounces goat cheese

8 cups mixed greens, for serving

★ **FIRST, A NOTE ON BEETS:** *They'll stain anything! Unless you want your hands to be vivid magenta, make sure you wear gloves as you're peeling them.*

1. Put the beets in a large saucepan and cover with cold water. Bring the water to a boil over medium-high heat. Immediately lower the heat to medium and cook the beets for about 20 minutes, or just until fork-tender. Drain the beets and run them under cold water.

2. While the beets are cooking, fill a wide saucepan with water and bring to a rolling boil. Submerge the asparagus in the water for about 2 minutes, until bright green and al dente. Drain and immediately run them under cold water. Add the asparagus to the beets and season with the salt.

3. In another saucepan, bring the water, orange blossom water, sugar, and lemon juice to a boil, then reduce the heat to medium and simmer until the liquid is reduced by half and has thickened slightly, about 10 minutes. Toss the glaze with the vegetables and add the garlic chives. Top with the chive blossoms and goat cheese. Serve as a first course on a bed of the mixed greens.

"One of my favorite memories with this recipe is preparing it for a morning news spot. We were very friendly with the anchor. As we were setting up, he mentioned he really dislikes beets and was planning to taste one of the other dishes on set. Of course, as soon as the camera was on live, I pulled a good-sized beet out of the salad and handed it to him to try. He bit in, made a yummy face, and gamely lied through his teeth about how much he loved it."

—Steve McDonagh

The Rachael Ray Mini-Pilot

The Final Challenge was taken by Deborah and Dan and Steve. For this challenge the finalists would shoot a pilot of the show they would star in if they won the entire competition. The pilots were shot on Rachael Ray's set following a demo from the doyenne of the quick kitchen and some of her own cast-iron advice. "No one at the Food Network has asked me to be anything I'm not," said Rachael. "So, be yourself." She recalled being given a great pointer the first day, something she's always lived by.

"Smile all the time for no apparent reason. It's brilliant."

—Rachael Ray

Dan and Steve explained their "soup to nuts" concept: "We bring your party from planning to payoff . . . to take the mystery out of home entertaining." Their Lobster Potpie dated from the time when they ran a café and served it on their menu. "I'm going to make everyone in America jealous when I say I've got two pounds of lobster tail meat here and you don't," said Steve. When Dan and Steve threw to an imaginary commercial, Rachael cheered them on: "That was awesome. Awesome. Awesome. Awesome!" Steve said that if lobster is not in your budget, you can use salmon.

> "The idea for lobster came from my time in Maine but the inspiration for the dish comes from my love of retooled comfort foods. It's one of the staples on our restaurant's menu. I never take it off, even though we change the menu seasonally. It's the same recipe as *Next Food Network Star*—it works well with salmon but it's not as luxurious."
>
> —Dan Smith

For Deborah Fewell's "Spice of Life" pilot, she made Fried Chicken and Country Greens and explained how easy it is to make your food "pop." Deborah was excited and ecstatic with her performance.

LOBSTER POTPIE

Recipe courtesy Dan Smith and Steve McDonagh

Yield: 8 servings ▮ Prep Time: 40 minutes ▮ Cook Time: 1 hour 15 minutes ▮
Ease of Preparation: difficult

FOR THE CRUST

2½ cups all-purpose flour

1 teaspoon salt

12 tablespoons unsalted butter,
cut into small pieces

6 tablespoons ice water

1 egg mixed with 1 tablespoon
water, for the egg wash

FOR THE FILLING

2 tablespoons unsalted butter

2 tablespoons water

1 large Spanish onion, diced
(about 2 cups)

2 carrots, sliced into thin coins

2 teaspoons chopped fresh tarragon

1 cup frozen peas

4 red potatoes, about ¾ pound,
cut into ½-inch dice

Kosher salt

¾ pound cooked chopped lobster
meat

FOR THE BÉCHAMEL

2 cups milk

2 bay leaves

1 teaspoon white pepper

1 tablespoon lobster base

2 tablespoons unsalted butter

4 tablespoons all-purpose flour

½ cup dry white wine

1. FOR THE CRUST: Place the flour and salt in the bowl of a food processor. Add the butter bits and pulse until the mixture resembles coarse crumbs. Pour the mixture into a bowl and add the ice water a little at a time, stirring well with a fork. Transfer the dough to a well-floured surface and knead just until it all comes together; don't work it too much or the crust will be tough. Divide the dough in half, shape into two balls, and flatten each into a disk. Wrap each disk in plastic and refrigerate for 30 minutes.

2. Preheat the oven to 350°F.

3. While the dough is chilling, prepare the filling. In a large saucepan over medium heat, melt the butter with the water. Add the onion, carrots, and tarragon and stir. Lower the heat and cook for 20 to 30 minutes, stirring occasionally. Add the peas during the last 5 minutes of cooking.

4. Put the potatoes in a small saucepan and cover with water. Add salt to taste, and place the pan over high heat. Bring the water to a boil, reduce the heat, and simmer until the potatoes are fork-tender, about 15 minutes. Drain the potatoes and add them to the vegetable mix. Add the lobster meat and set the pan aside.

5. FOR THE BÉCHAMEL: Pour the milk into a medium-size saucepan, add the bay leaves and pepper, and scald (heat but don't boil). Whisk in the lobster base.

6. In another medium-size saucepan, melt the butter over medium heat. Whisk in the flour and cook for 1 minute. Add the wine and whisk until the mixture thickens. Slowly add the milk, whisking constantly, until the sauce is thick and creamy. Remove the bay leaves. Add the béchamel to the lobster mixture and stir well. Set aside while rolling out the crust.

7. ASSEMBLY: Remove the crust from the refrigerator and roll one disk out on a lightly floured surface to about 12 inches in diameter. Line a 9-inch pie plate with the dough and fill with the lobster mixture, and brush the edges of the dough with the egg wash. Roll out the second disk, and place it on top of the pie. Trim the excess dough and crimp the edges. Cut two or three vent holes in the dough and brush the top with the egg wash. Place on a baking sheet and bake for 30 to 40 minutes, until the crust is golden brown. Let cool for 20 minutes before cutting and serving.

THE RESULT

With the country voting on who would be the next Food Network star, we learned a little more about the remaining finalists. About Dan's big Italian family: "If you're Italian you just know how to make your mother's meatballs." And about Steve's English ancestry. "I grew up with a dish that had the meat, had the potato, and it had the vegetable. In the seventies it was a canned vegetable, although my mother would deny that." Dan said, "The joke we have is that I'm Italian so I do the cooking and Steve's English so he does the books."

> "It's very difficult to bring your personality to the screen because you're trying to inject all of your personal experiences and special cooking moments into each segment. You have to know who you are and unlock what you have to offer others from the essence of who you are. Most people haven't tapped into those parts of themselves."
> —Deborah Fewell

From the ten thousand entries and eight finalists, Emeril announced the winner. The first Next Food Network Star was . . . were . . . Dan and Steve.

SEASON ONE	ELIMINATIONS
EPISODE TWO First Elimination	★ **BROOK HARLAN:** "I'm still very passionate about cooking. I'm in my ninth year of teaching high school culinary arts at the Columbia Area Career Center, and I wrote a cookbook called *Cooking with Brook, Appetizers & Hors d'Oeuvres,* which includes of some of my favorite recipes for small plates and finger foods."
EPISODE THREE Second Elimination	★ **HARMONY MARCEAU:** "Susie said that allowing herself to come through on camera was a challenge for Harmony. Harmony reflected: "Obviously I need to work at being comfortable in front of the camera if that's what I want to do with my career."
EPISODE FOUR Third Elimination	★ **MICHAEL THOMAS:** "The key to making a successful show is a specific focus that you can own. I rumbled around for quite a while to find my specific perspective, and what do you know, it ended up being the same thing I've always been focused on—travel, amazing food, and let's be honest . . . minimum effort for maximum deliciousness."
EPISODE FOUR Fourth Elimination	★ **ERIC WARREN:** "I have been blessed with so many of my dreams coming true! I'm expanding the personal chef side of the business since graduating from culinary school and making appearances all over the Los Angeles area doing something dear to my heart, community service. In 2011 I competed against fifteen thousand other finalists to have my own show on The Oprah Winfrey Network. I was thrilled as I was one of the top ten finalists. I am getting closer than ever to having a show on national television."
EPISODE FIVE Fifth Elimination	★ **SUSANNAH LOCKETTI:** "It was a challenge I was not expecting to go home on. . . . I felt that my personality shined through . . . I'll never forget this. Thank you."
EPISODE FIVE Sixth Elimination	★ **HANS RUEFFERT:** "Just two weeks after the finale of the Next Food Network Star, I was diagnosed with stage 3 gastric cancer. I ended up losing over half my stomach and half of my esophagus, then nearly 80 pounds during the chemotherapy and radiation that followed. I'm now officially in remission, and work with charities to help mentor fellow patients. To learn more about the work that I do, visit my website at www.hanscooks.com."
EPISODE FIVE Runner-up	★ **DEBORAH FEWELL:** "It felt very natural to be on TV. I've always dreamed of having my own cooking show. I'm also an actress and love being in front of the camera—it's a comfort zone for me, like the kitchen."

DAN SMITH *and* STEVE MCDONAGH

Dan and Steve's show *Party Line with the Hearty Boys* previewed
on Food Network on September 18, 2005.

Dan Smith *and* Steve McDonagh: A Q&A

What was the hardest thing for you through the competition?

Steve: For me it was feeling confident in re-creating Dan's recipes that may have been unfamiliar to me. Our business had grown so much that we divided it so that Dan was back of house and I was front of house. The competition made me rely solely on my back of house abilities.

Did you have to rework your existing chemistry to make it come across well on camera?

Steve: No, we didn't rework anything. What you see with us on camera is exactly who we are off screen.

You're the only people who have appeared on the show as a couple. Did you ever consider applying separately?

Steve: No, we're much stronger as a unit. Plus we truly enjoy being together. It wouldn't be as fun alone. The Hearty Boys point of view focuses on entertaining as a whole, not just the food segment or the party aspect.

Would you say cooking is a team sport?

Steve: Cooking makes me want to be more Zen. I like to think of a meal as a journey. It's so much more than the dish of food in front of you; it's about how you got there and the process of working with the ingredients. I always say the best date is not having someone over for a meal, it's cracking open a bottle of wine and spending the time together to prepare it.

Steve, your mom is English. What's the best thing in your opinion about English cuisine?

I think English food is in a really exciting place right now and I can only assume that it's due to a new generation of chefs who weren't restricted by the rations and food availability of World War Two. My parents, for example, were raised with a war mind-set that affected both their parents and their own generation and the way they looked at food. It fell to my generation to get excited about cuisine and get in on the global food movement.

That being said, the weather in England calls for warm comfort food. Comfort food has many meanings, as comfort can be found in foods that make us feel secure or nostalgic; but the comfort foods that give us physical comfort as in warming the body are exceptionally vital. A Shepherds Pie with chunks of soft warm lamb in a hearty gravy under a literal blanket of mashed potatoes is a gift from the English.

What is the biggest number of people the Hearty Boys have ever cooked for?

Dan: The catering arm of the company regularly caters a holiday party for one of the largest buildings in downtown Chicago so that's about 5000 people.

Accessible is the word you use to describe your business and your food. How has that concept evolved over the years?

Steve: We look at every item on our menu at Hearty with an eye to accessibility. I've been focusing for years on craft cocktails and have developed an impressive cocktail list. But I'm not looking at it in the same way as some of the elite spots that are making their own bitters and tonic. Everything I serve at Hearty needs to be able to be explained to my guests in such a way that they know they can make this themselves. Education is a very important part of the dining experience for me; I want to open something to you that you haven't had before and make you feel empowered that you could do this as well.

Does one of you cook more than the other at home?

Steve: Hell, yes. And the same one tends to do the dishes too. I'm blessed.

Season TWO

With Season One winners Hearty Boys Dan Smith and Steve McDonagh launched, Season Two introduced eight new finalists and settled on the three-person Selection Committee that has remained in place through Season Seven: Food Network execs Bob Tuschman and Susie Fogelson teamed with network superstar chef Bobby Flay. "The reason that I've had some success in food television is because I am passionate about what is in front of me," said Bobby. "The food is the most important thing. If you remember that, the other stuff becomes easy."

"The judges have good chemistry. We are really respectful and loving to one another, which makes it wonderful for me and quite a unique experience."

—Susie Fogelson

THE FINALISTS

1. Carissa Seward. Carissa grew up on a dairy farm in Washington State. Devastated by her mom's death in 2003, she asked herself, "What do I love?" She applied to the ultra-prestigious Cordon Bleu cooking school in Paris. To her shock she was accepted, so she sold up and moved to France. To Carissa, the kitchen can be fun, sexy, and interesting; her POV: "Simply Delicious, Simply French." Standing in a bikini on the beach, Carissa told us, "I want to bring some of this heat into your kitchen."

2. Andy Schumacher. Once he realized that his true love was cooking, Andy moved to New York to attend culinary school. But with a young family—fiancée Carrie and daughter Sienna—he needed a steady income and left his position as a line cook for a desk job. Andy brought to the show his energy and knowledge. "I can cook a mean steak and make 'em laugh too." His POV: teaching basic techniques of cooking by "Bringing the Restaurant Home."

3. Guy Fieri. Guy's mantra—"I like to live big, laugh hard, and cook wild"—came with the POV "Off the Hook and Out of Bounds." His wife, Lori, was eight and a half months pregnant when the show filmed, and they already had a son, Hunter. Owner of three restaurants, Guy had an "extremely powerful personality . . . like a steamroller. He just makes things happen," said Lori. Guy agreed: "I don't really have an on or off switch. I'm goin' or I'm sleepin'," he said. "If I was food, I think I'd be lasagna. Multilayered, meaty, a little cheesy, a little spicy—and I feed everyone."

4. Evette Rodriguez. Evette was chosen by fans through videos posted on the Food Network website. Puerto Rican, a mom, married with four kids, Evette grew up speaking Spanish at home. "I love to cook with spicy Latin flavor." She hadn't enjoyed being in the kitchen because feeding the family was a serious business—until one day she realized it wasn't a chore at all. Now cooking is her passion.

5. Reggie Southerland. From behind the counter at the Comfort Cafe, presenting his bounty of baked goods, Reggie beamed his positive energy. "If it's cookies or pie, I'm your guy," said Reggie. "I think my personality is going to win me the show." Reggie was bringing to the contest his comfort food, presented in a very chic, modern way: "Southern Boy, City Style."

6. Beth Raynor. Beth, a self-proclaimed food nerd, was shown on TV reading cookbooks. In 2001 she was running her own catering business when the dot-com bust put paid to her dream job. Temporarily. *Next Food Network Star* gave her the chance to get back to cooking full-time, the missing piece in her life. "I'm going to help you get fresh in the kitchen," said Beth. Her mission: "Healthy full-flavor meals with fresh local ingredients."

7. Jess Dang. Born in Vietnam, Jess came to the United States at age two. She attended Stanford and worked sixty hours a week at a consulting firm, cooking when she got home. Jess's view of her strengths: She's a quick learner and receptive to feedback. "I'm bringing spunk into your kitchen," she said.

8. Nathan Lyon. Multitalented Nathan went to culinary school after his mom asked him what he would do if money wasn't an issue. Cooking was his passion. He was also trained as a personal trainer and a stained-glass artist who worked two food-related jobs: at a jazz restaurant owned by Herb Alpert and at a stand at the local farmers market. This informed his POV of seasonal cooking: "From the Market to Your Table." Nathan was forthright and confident: "Food is very sexy. I love food, competing, attention, the camera. . . . I will win this competition."

THE FIRST CHALLENGE

In an uncharacteristically gentle first challenge, new finalists were presented with a brown paper bag containing something they particularly liked to cook with: Guy with an onion; Andy, a piece of pork; Nathan, a bottle of red wine; Reggie, figs; Beth and Jess, shrimp; Carissa, beef; and Evette, potatoes. The task was to make a dish showcasing themselves. Beth quickly won the prize for first knife wound, and the demo revealed her falling prey to other familiar hazards, especially running out of time.

> "I'm a bit of a perfectionist and like to take my time to make sure I understand all the components of anything I'm trying to learn. I think that makes me a good cook, but I wasn't prepared for the fly-by-the-seat-of-your-pants pace in production. I was a communication and media-arts major in college and have done a bit of on-camera work. It was nothing like the frenzied pace of *Next Food Network Star,* which was more like the tornado scene in *The Wizard of Oz.*"
>
> —Beth Raynor

Reggie thought he'd nailed it with his fig salad, and Guy looked like he'd been on TV for years. "He's so strong," said Susie. Nathan's *bulgogi* was way too complicated ("It looks easier on TV"), and Jess didn't enjoy her first experience on camera: "I think I kind of lost my head."

what is *BULGOGI?*

Bulgogi is a Korean dish of thin-sliced marinated beef flavored with soy sauce, sugar, and vinegar and often eaten with rice in a lettuce leaf. As Nathan demonstrated, it takes much longer than five minutes to prepare.

Knife Skills

If the first challenge seemed too easy, it was. In walked the Iron Chefs: Masaharu Morimoto, the original Iron Chef Japan, Mario Batali, and Bobby Flay.

"What's going to happen next, Elvis?"

—Guy Fieri

Masaharu Morimoto's challenge tested finalists' knife skills for accuracy, consistency, speed, and beauty, while Mario Batali wanted them to deconstruct and describe a dish and Bobby Flay judged presentation. Morimoto asked everyone to dice an onion, cut a carrot into julienne, and filet a fish.

Filleting the fish was not a highlight for most finalists. Beth gave up. "Basically, she doesn't have any knife skills," Morimoto commented. To talkative Reggie, Morimoto critiqued: "You are trying to use your mouth instead of your knife." Evette, who had never handled fish before, was lost from the start.

> **"Honestly, I was very green. My husband and I had four children to care for at the time; my budget was always pretty tight and I had not seen such a beautiful fish in its entire, wholesome form. I was taken aback. I did not know how to fillet a fish and I was fearful of destroying it."**
>
> **—Evette Rodriguez**

Chefs Batali and Flay were kinder and gentler to the finalists, even joking around at times. To Guy Fieri, whose hands and wrists were decked out in bling, Bobby Flay said, "We're trying to figure out whether you want to be a cook or a jeweler."

The elimination room was a Season Two innovation, a darker room suited to cutting finalists. But today, after the critiques, there was no drama. "We don't know anyone well enough," said Susie. "We're not going to eliminate anyone."

"CBS Productions knew they wanted at least one Food Network executive on the judging panel, since the person was going to work for the network. So a lot of executives auditioned, and Susie and I were chosen. I was shocked by this development. Sitting with Giada De Laurentiis, Bobby Flay, and Susie on camera is enough to humble anybody's ego. I have been in this business for thirty years now but behind the camera my whole career. I've worked in a lot of jobs. I worked for several years for Diana Ross in several roles, as her assistant, writer, script reader, and in film production. I worked at ABC News as a producer on *Good Morning America,* and I was an agent for a couple of years. So I spent a lot of time making other people look good on camera, and in my thirteen years at Food Network finding people I thought could be stars. It's astounding to me when anyone recognizes me on the street or sends me a fan letter or even cares who I am. I'm like, 'Oh, right, I forgot.' There are millions of people who watch me on TV and know who I am."

—Bob Tuschman

"For me it has been a labor of love to find our next star. . . . The being-on-television part, I think you can probably tell I have no sense of it. I don't focus on it, I barely look at it. I just try to do the job I'm asked to do. I'm originally from L.A. I was a media planner at Chiat/Day advertising agency. Nickelodeon was one of our clients, and I loved the business of television. I went to Nickelodeon as a marketing manager and had a good run. Eleven years ago I came to Food Network."

—Susie Fogelson

"I think Susie is the toughest judge. What makes her such a great marketer is that she is totally driven by her gut. She feels things very deeply, very immediately, and she's very vocal; she'll let you know exactly what she thinks. I am a little more measured in my tone and in putting together where I think someone is in the process."

—Bob Tuschman

"It is the most personal journey a finalist will ever go through. I think it is an unbelievable gift to have people like Bob, Bobby, and me, people who are arguably at the top of our game, doing an intensive boot camp with them. You couldn't buy that. If you like this business, here is a famous chef-restaurateur who has made it on TV. Learn from him. He is here to help you. Here is Bob, who green-lights shows and knows what success looks like, and me, who takes off from the show and hopefully creates the stars. We really are here for you, to make you great."

—Susie Fogelson

Nuts and Bolts

No one is better equipped to show finalists how to do television than Rachael Ray, with multiple shows on the network, more than a dozen cookbooks, and a magazine. Rule Number One for television: Never stop! For their next challenge, in episode two, the finalists had to get comfortable with the off-putting TelePrompTer that scrolls the script. You have to have your head on a swivel, following the stage manager's direction as to which camera to address. Rachael was able to embellish the lines she was given; the finalists struggled to keep up.

Nathan believed that armed with Rachael's advice he would be unstoppable, but she chided him for describing his meat geekily as "protein." Who does that?

Guy got the point and "kept going." When he couldn't find a can opener for his tomatoes, he said he simply didn't use them. Good save.

In the challenge, finalists had thirty minutes to prepare a dish to demo for five minutes on camera. Culinary producer Harriet Siew handed out breakdowns—the recipe instructions plus the chef's movements and actions. Finalists had to set up a mise-en-place—the prepared ingredients they would need—along with any swap-outs. (A swap-out is a finished step in the recipe prepared ahead of time by Food Network cooks.)

Andy said he should have had more ingredients cut up before his demo so he could have spent more time talking. It was Andy's first demo, said Bob, but the food—"It's good."

CURRY CREAMED CHICKEN
with Couscous Salad

Recipe courtesy Andrew Schumacher

Yield: 4 servings ▌ Prep Time: 20 minutes ▌ Cook Time: 25 minutes ▌ Ease of Preparation: intermediate

COUSCOUS SALAD

1¼ cups couscous

1½ cups chicken stock, boiling

½ cup raisins, chopped

½ cup chopped pitted kalamata olives

1 medium shallot, minced (about ¼ cup)

3 tablespoons fresh mint leaves, chopped

3 tablespoons extra-virgin olive oil

2 tablespoons chopped fresh cilantro leaves

Kosher salt

Freshly ground black pepper

CURRY CREAMED CHICKEN

4 skinless and boneless chicken breasts (about 8 ounces each)

Kosher salt

Freshly ground black pepper

1½ cups chicken stock

1 tablespoon curry powder

½ cup heavy cream

8 sprigs fresh cilantro, for garnish

1. COUSCOUS SALAD: Put the couscous in a medium bowl and pour in the stock. Cover with aluminum foil and let sit for 10 minutes. Uncover the bowl and fluff the couscous with a fork. Add the remaining ingredients and stir to incorporate. Season to taste with salt and pepper, and keep warm.

2. CURRY CREAMED CHICKEN: Meanwhile, season the chicken breasts on both sides with salt and pepper. In a wide saucepan, bring the stock to a simmer over medium heat, then lower to maintain the simmer. Add the chicken breasts, cover, and cook for about 6 minutes. Flip the breasts and cook for 6 minutes more. The chicken will be done when it is firm to the touch (you may cut one open just to be sure). Remove from the pan and set on a plate. Cover with foil to keep warm.

3. Turn the heat to high and reduce the stock until 2 tablespoons remain, about 10 minutes. Stir in the curry powder, then add the cream. Cook for 2 minutes, until thickened slightly.

4. Divide the couscous salad among four plates, top each plate with a chicken breast, and coat the chicken liberally with the cream sauce. Garnish each plate with 2 sprigs of cilantro.

Out of Time

Next up was Jess Dang with a dish she said she had prepared a million times but never on camera for a panel of judges. With only five minutes to complete the demo, she ended up with her pound of ground chicken still uncooked. "I felt devastated," she said, and predicted she'd be going home.

> "My Asian Bolognese is a recipe from my mother, and it is absolutely delicious and foolproof (as long as there isn't a timer and cameras around to make you nervous!). My mother's version uses ground chicken (though beef, turkey, or pork are also fine) but I need to find a way to make this dish for my vegetarian husband. . . ."
>
> —Jessica Dang

ASIAN BOLOGNESE

Recipe courtesy Jessica Dang

Yield: 4 servings ▌ Prep Time: 20 minutes ▌ Cook Time: 15 minutes ▌
Ease of Preparation: easy

1 pound ground chicken

1 teaspoon salt

½ teaspoon ground black pepper

2 tablespoons soy sauce

1 tablespoon cornstarch

2 tablespoons cold water

4 medium-size vine-ripened
   tomatoes

½ pound firm tofu, cut into ½-inch
   cubes (1⅓ cups)

1 tablespoon olive oil

2 garlic cloves, minced

1 scallion, thinly sliced

Jasmine rice, for serving
   (optional)

1. Place the chicken in a medium-size bowl and season with the salt and pepper. Set aside.

2. In another bowl, mix the soy sauce, cornstarch, and water and set aside.

3. Bring 2 quarts of water to a boil, and prepare an ice bath. Carve the tops out of each tomato. When the water boils, add the tomatoes and cook for 20 to 30 seconds. Place them immediately into the ice bath and let them sit for about 2 minutes. Drain and peel, then cut into quarters.

4. Place the tofu in a microwave-safe serving dish and heat in the microwave for 1 minute. Drain off the excess liquid and transfer to a serving platter.

5. Heat the olive oil in a wok over medium-high heat. Add the garlic. When the garlic starts to brown, add the chicken. Using a spoon or spatula, break the chicken into small bits. Cook until it is no longer pink and begins to brown. Remove from the wok. Return the wok back to medium-high heat and cook the tomatoes, breaking them up a bit with a spoon, until they are juicy and very soft, about 5 minutes. Return the chicken to the wok, and raise the heat to high, getting the wok as hot as possible. Move the chicken-tomato mixture out to the sides of the wok, forming a donut. Give the cornstarch sauce a couple of stirs and pour it into the center of the wok. Cook for about 30 seconds, until the sauce begins to boil and thicken. Mix the sauce with the chicken-tomato mixture and stir-fry for another minute. Pour over the tofu and sprinkle with the sliced scallion.

6. Serve over jasmine rice, if desired.

Bumps in the Road

While Jess said of Guy: "He's just rollin,' " he had a different view of his pasta demo. "Running in cowboy boots," he said. "It was not smooth." Bob agreed, saying that he made it seem so complicated.

CHIPOTLE PASTA

Recipe courtesy Guy Fieri

Yield: 4 to 6 servings ▮ Prep Time: 10 minutes ▮ Cook Time: 10 minutes ▮
Ease of Preparation: easy

2 tablespoons olive oil

4 hot links, sliced on the bias into 6 pieces

20 (21/25) shrimp, deveined, shelled, and butterflied

1 cup heavy cream

¾ cup Chipotle Sauce (recipe follows)

¾ teaspoon sea salt

⅛ teaspoon ground black pepper

1 pound penne, cooked

¼ cup grated Parmesan cheese, plus more for garnish

¼ cup diced fresh tomato, for garnish

¼ cup chopped scallion, white and some green, for garnish

CHIPOTLE SAUCE

½ cup barbecue sauce

¼ cup canola oil

2 tablespoons freshly squeezed lemon juice

2 tablespoons chipotle paste

½ tablespoon Dijon mustard

½ tablespoon crushed red pepper

⅛ teaspoon cayenne

⅛ teaspoon ground black pepper

1. In a large sauté pan, heat the olive oil over high heat. Add hot links and sear until browned, about 2 minutes. Add the shrimp and cook until pink. Lower the heat to medium. Stir in the cream, Chipotle Sauce, salt, and pepper. Add the cooked pasta and cheese and turn off the heat. Toss to combine.

2. Serve in a pasta bowl, and garnish with the diced tomato, scallion, and more of the grated Parmesan.

CHIPOTLE SAUCE: Combine all of the ingredients in a blender, purée, cover, and refrigerate.

▮ Yield: 1 cup

"Guy was made for the camera. You can't deny it. Guy is really fun to watch. As his friend, I've enjoyed watching his career skyrocket over the years, and whenever he's in L.A. shooting one of his shows, we still make time to meet up. I don't know how he does it. The guy is a machine."

—Nathan Lyon

Thinking on Your Feet

Carissa misunderstood the demo instructions and hadn't prepared any swap-outs. She was impressively fluid, but she was making her dish from scratch and her potatoes didn't cook. Reggie did the best job of improvising. When he couldn't figure out how to get the food processor to purée his Spinach and Sweet Pea Soup, he served it country-style. "It didn't need to be puréed," said Bobby Flay, who had his own issues with a food processor on a show in 1996. "It's good. . . . That's how great things happen—by accident."

Beth had so many ingredients that she thought there was "no way in heck" she would finish her Turkey Wraps in time. She did miss a few items, but unlike anyone else, she managed to taste her own food.

> "This somehow became my signature dish on the show, but it's not something I make that often. I do enjoy the flavors, but I think my cooking has a little more of a creative angle that wasn't necessarily reflected in this recipe. Nonetheless, it's a quick and tasty weeknight dish, and I have a group of friends who swear by it."
>
> —Beth Raynor

"The kindest advice you can give anybody is the most direct, honest advice, and I think the best thing I can do for someone who wants to grow is to be honest with him about his failings. It doesn't do him any good for me to pull my punches.

"I derive no pleasure from tearing someone down. My greatest pleasure is to help people succeed and achieve their dreams. This show gives aspiring chefs an outlet they would never otherwise have, and they are looking to us to help them get through this maze of stardom and TV and the Food Network."

—Bob Tuschman

Now for the elimination room's first victim. Rushing, nervousness, failing to bring personality to a demo are standard *Next Food Network Star* shortcomings. According to Bob, Guy talked about the "set," when there should be an illusion that the chef is taking us into his world. And he talked about "20/25 shrimp" (referring to the count per pound)—but viewers are not all chefs who can understand that lingo. Guy himself noted eighteen points where he felt he went wrong.

But it was Jess, whose stories were endearing but who succumbed to nerves, who went home first.

"It's always tough to take criticism so publicly, but I always tried to take it very literally and make sure that I legitimately worked on everything that they suggested. Any insight or advice they gave, I tried to implement that and put that into practice."

—Carissa Seward

what is A KAFFIR LIME LEAF?

Kaffir limes are a vital ingredient in Thai cooking—the zest is part of the popular Thai red curry paste. For some dishes the leaf, which can be bought fresh or dried, is cut into thin strips, but it is most often used whole, like a bay leaf, as Nathan Lyon did with his Poached Halibut recipe in this challenge.

TURKEY PINE NUT CABBAGE WRAPS

Recipe courtesy Elizabeth Raynor

Yield: 4 servings, 2 wraps per person ▌Prep Time: 15 minutes ▌Cook Time: 15 minutes
▌Ease of Preparation: easy

1 small head red cabbage

1 tablespoon peanut oil

2 garlic cloves, minced

2 tablespoons finely diced fresh
ginger

¼ cup diced yellow onion

¼ cup diced red bell pepper

¼ cup diced yellow bell pepper

½ pound lean ground turkey

2½ teaspoons hoisin sauce

1 tablespoon oyster sauce

1½ teaspoons red chili sauce,
such as sriracha

2½ teaspoons low-sodium soy
sauce

1 teaspoon rice vinegar

1 teaspoon fish sauce

1 teaspoon sesame oil

2 tablespoons cilantro leaves,
plus extra for garnish

2 tablespoons toasted pine nuts

2 tablespoons diced scallion,
white and some green

1. Wash and dry the cabbage and cut off the bottom. Carefully remove about 4 leaves, being sure not to tear them, and cut in half lengthwise. Arrange on a platter or on four plates.

2. Heat the oil in a large nonstick skillet over medium-high heat. Add the garlic, ginger, and onion and cook for 1 to 2 minutes, or until soft. Add the red pepper, yellow pepper, and turkey and sauté until the turkey is almost cooked through and slightly browned, 7 to 8 minutes. Add the hoisin sauce, oyster sauce, chili sauce, soy sauce, and rice vinegar. Let the turkey cook for another 4 to 5 minutes until the sauce is reduced. Remove the skillet from the heat. Stir in the fish sauce, sesame oil, cilantro, pine nuts, and scallion. To serve, place a spoonful of the mixture into each cabbage cup. Garnish with the extra cilantro, if desired.

The Satellite Tour

One of a Food Network star's jobs is to take part in publicity events such as the satellite media "tour" to twenty or more cities from the studio. This involves cooking and saying the same things over and over to a succession of hosts. But most hosts aren't like the ringers provided to finalists for their next challenge: Russ Mitchell and Tracy Smith from the CBS *Saturday Early Show.*

Tracy, as "Ann Walker," asked static-plagued Andy about "dreamy" Bobby Flay, then she called Carissa "Clarissa." Russ as "Brad" called Beth "Carissa," but she was able to run with it. Reggie had terrible interference piped into his earpiece, but he remembered Rule Number One: Don't stop. He did get a little chippy with Russ. Russ as "Miles" told Nathan that his dish sounded "nasty" and asked if Rachael Ray was "hot in person." Evette had "Bruce from St. Louis," aka Russ, who whined about having to do a food segment. She gamely cooked her omelet through the background noise as well as Bruce hitting on her—clumsily at that—on the air.

> **"I grew up with the ubiquitous Spanish omelet or, as we call it, the Tortilla Espanola. It is a favorite for my family and it evolves constantly."**
>
> —Evette Rodriguez

SPINACH, BACON, AND POTATO OMELET
(Tortilla de Papa y Carne de Cerdo con Espinaca)

Recipe courtesy Evette Rodriguez

Yield: 8 servings ∎ Prep Time: 10 minutes ∎ Cook Time: 40 to 45 minutes ∎
Ease of Preparation: easy

8 slices bacon

2 large Idaho potatoes, peeled and diced (2½ cups)

2 tablespoons unsalted butter

1 tablespoon olive oil

1 teaspoon sofrito (recommended: Goya)

½ teaspoon kosher salt, divided

½ teaspoon ground black pepper, divided

1. Preheat the broiler.

2. Arrange the bacon in a single layer on a baking sheet. Cook under the broiler for 4 minutes, flipping halfway through. Remove the bacon from the baking sheet and drain on three paper towels. Coarsely chop and set aside.

3. Add the potatoes to 2 to 3 cups of water and boil until just tender but not falling apart, 8 to 10 minutes. Drain and set aside.

4. In a wide nonstick ovenproof sauté pan, heat the butter and olive oil over medium heat. Add the sofrito

2 ounces fresh spinach, chopped
  (1½ cups)

10 large eggs

Crusty bread or whole-grain toast,
  for serving

and stir-fry until golden brown, about 1 minute. Add the potatoes and cook for 8 to 10 minutes, seasoning with half of the salt and pepper, until the potatoes are golden and slightly crisp. Stir in the spinach, chopped bacon, and remaining salt and pepper.

5. In a separate mixing bowl, beat the eggs until they are fluffy. Pour the eggs over the potatoes and shake the pan a bit while the eggs begin to set. Using a heat-resistant spatula, pull the eggs from the sides of the pan, tipping the pan slightly to one side to allow the eggs to spread over the space. Tilt the pan in another direction to repeat the process, going around the entire pan. Place the pan under the broiler until the eggs are set and the top is golden brown, about 5 minutes.

4. Cut the omelet into wedges and serve with warm crusty bread or whole-grain toast.

Points of View

Every season, finalists have to present and stand by their culinary Point of View—what part of the food map are they going to own? It's a defining element of the show. Giada De Laurentiis is the spokesperson for "Everyday Italian" because that is who she is. Bobby Flay balances big bold flavors with sweeter things for harmony. The take is authentic. "You can't fake it," said Bob.

Sandra Lee, who appeared to introduce the finalists to their episode three challenge, is "Semi-Homemade." She uses 70 percent store-bought and 30 percent fresh ingredients to create dishes that look and taste homemade but don't take much time. Sandra talked about combining a Cordon Bleu education with a saver's sensibility: "Why am I spending fifty dollars on five jars of spices when I can spend a dollar-fifty on this packet?" Her advice: Explore the grocery store and look at what's on the shelves to come up with new dishes.

> "Sometimes people have an idea of what POV they think they want. What they can't know is how many times we might have heard that idea before. When we know it's not going to work, they're stripped naked."
>
> —Bob Tuschman

In this challenge, the finalists had to represent their POV using pasta. Reggie cooked his Macaroni Blanco with Sausages. "Reggie, I love you," said Sandra, "but I felt you were a little scattered." Carissa didn't have a swap-out. Guy was concerned with getting it all done for his "Full-Flavored Bird." "The timing's the hardest part. If you can't launch the rocket, you can't launch the rocket."

Andy, who presented a Shiitake Cheese Ravioli with Brown Butter, Walnuts, and Oregano, felt he demonstrated great techniques but that his POV was weak. Beth tried to get her personality across but Sandra thought she sounded instructional. Nathan talked about cooking his lasagna with his niece. "You're a pleasure to watch," said Sandra. "I think this is yours to lose."

In the elimination room, Susie told Beth that she needed to be bigger. Finally, Bobby let Beth go.

> "I knew what my point of view was—and still is—from the beginning. I can't tell you how many people I heard from after the show asking me to write a cookbook full of healthy, approachable, simple, and flavorful recipes. Hopefully, I'll reach that goal one of these days soon!"
>
> —Beth Raynor

what is CONCASSÉ?

Guy added concassé to his "Full-Flavored Bird." *Concasser* is the French verb for "to chop" or "to crush." Many ingredients can be prepared concassé—for example, tomatoes, herbs, ice, or chicken bones to go in a stock.

The Mentors

In back-to-back weeks, finalists received the best advice from mentors Giada De Laurentiis and Alton Brown. First, in episode four, Giada ran through her TV demonstration techniques in a multi-tasking challenge:

★ Make all the recipes with ten ingredients or fewer.

★ Use simple, fresh ingredients with tons of flavor.

★ Learn multi-tasking, how to make more than one dish at a time.

★ Ask yourself: "Why is my recipe different from the others out there?" That's what you're selling.

★ Give tips: Can I make the dish way in advance?

★ Minimize the number of steps required.

what is A KABOCHA SQUASH?

For the multitasking challenge, Nathan made Salmon Tartare with Roast Kabocha Soup. Originally from Japan, the kabocha is a winter squash with dense, sweet orange flesh.

Right after Evette's elimination in Giada's multi-tasking challenge, finalists had to spend their evening and a lot of the night decorating cupcakes to demo the next morning before a live audience at Sur La Table, the cookware store. To help with the performance, Dave Lieberman, host of *Good Deals,* demo'ed the demo by decorating a sponge cake. "Be natural. Just relax and have fun," said Dave. Finalists should engage the audience while working on their food. While he was grating, Dave asked the audience, "You guys use a Microplane before?"

"What am I going to do with a cupcake? I hate cupcakes. I don't eat them. My kids don't eat them. I'll make you something like Bananas Foster French Toast. That's my kind of dessert. When these kinds of things came up, I'm like, 'All right, here we go.' "
—Guy Fieri

Alton Brown—"the Professor"—took the finalists back to school in episode five and then into Chelsea Market to make a field piece. They were to come up with an idea and a recorded spot for a TV show to present to the Selection Committee. Alton pitched his tips:

★ If you haven't got them in ten seconds, go home.

★ Don't get caught up in how you look: Sexy comes from not being sexy sometimes.

★ Think like Velcro—be very sticky and get them to stick to you.

★ When you're talking about wine, it's very easy to sound pretentious. Don't.

★ Think about how your personality and passion can make your field piece unique.

★ Stop to think if you need to think— your minute-long piece is not the Gettysburg Address.

★ Don't be too rehearsed and stiff or too slick and overconfident.

★ Never say "It's gonna be great!" It's TV: You can't prove it because no one can taste it.

After the pitches, it was Andy, and his idea of "Bringing the restaurant home," that was sent on his way.

★ **"Alton's five times more intense live than he is on the show."**
—**Guy Fieri**

Alton Brown: A Q&A

Has the ability of finalists improved over the seasons?

I've never really been privy to their culinary skills. I've always been brought in to deal with camera-related issues. In general the on-camera skill level has remained the same.

Being on TV is something they have to learn . . .

Well, some people just have the innate ability to perform in that medium. Others have to learn it like a new language. Others just never get it.

So some of them are naturals?

Sure, but it's rare. Most of them, even when they've really polished their act, you can see them turning it on and off. The really good ones, like Bobby Flay or Giada De Laurentiis, just are who they are and it works. They're the same on screen as off and that resonates with people. Sometimes of course you see one of these people and there's a glimmer, just a glimmer of a gem and you think . . . "If I could just get ahold of them, before they get a big head or get polluted. . . ."

What can aspiring Food Network Stars teach themselves?

People pitch shows and ask about the camera. I say, record yourself at home over and over and practice until the person you see on the screen looks like you and sounds like you.

So is the Alton Brown we see the real Alton Brown?

Yep, that's me . . . but polished up and adjusted for the 2-D environment. I move and act a little differently when I'm inside that box. It's different in there.

You don't mind calling it as you see it . . .

You can't have people telling you you are great all the time if you aren't. You need to be honest. These people are young, they are inexperienced.

Still, do you find that you bite your tongue on occasion?

I do bite my tongue. I don't want to beat around the bush and I want to be honest but I don't want to be mean. I have a vested interest in getting a good winner. It's my network too and my stock falls if they're bad. I want good shows.

What do the good ones have in common?

Finalists have strengths and they have weaknesses. The big thing they can do to help themselves is figure out how to play to their strengths and how to fix their weaknesses.

What is the most common weakness?

A lack of confidence and that's fatal. The audience can detect it like a dog smelling fear.

Quite a few finalists seem to get stuck in a rut . . .

Everyone hits a rut. It's those who can't pull themselves out who are doomed.

You've mentored but you haven't judged. Why not?

I haven't done the Selection Committee. I would have a hard time sending people home and ending their dreams.

Are you surprised at the longevity of *Next Food Network Star*?

It doesn't surprise me that it has gone seven seasons. People like to see competition and to see who wins. These are regular people and they are getting a shot. It's the American dream and it appeals to the American spirit.

And the network is still finding willing victims . . .

I'm sympathetic to people who are shoved into that fray. They have guts to chase it. It's a heroic odyssey and it takes gumption.

SPOTLIGHT ON

THE *TV GUIDE* MEET AND EAT

Before Season Two's Meet and Eat, Dave Lieberman tested finalists' ability to think quickly. He asked them to select eight ingredients, and then Marc Summers made the finalists use the food selected by whoever was standing to their left.

Carissa wanted to make a rotisserie chicken . . . without a rotisserie. Guy offered Dave a hundred dollars for an idea to use Nate's "Gnar-ly" pomegranate molasses. Reggie loved Guy's ingredients. With so much to improvise, only Guy didn't run out of time.

> "Of course Reggie was happy, I picked a great basket! I was ready to knock everyone's socks off. Nathan picked this mix of stuff to do his thing with, and I'm like, Come on! I thought, Dead Man Walking: Brussels sprouts and fennel and so on. I remembered the kind of thing I'd handled in the restaurant business. My produce guy would show up at the door and say, 'Hey, man, for ten bucks I got this case of celery root. You want it?' When you're a starving restaurant guy, 'You bet I want celery root.' So this was not that hard."
>
> —Guy Fieri

In Their Element

This season's Meet and Eat was with a roomful of editors from *TV Guide.* Finalists had to pass trays of hors d'oeuvres that matched their culinary style. Guy's dish was a Chicken Avocado Eggroll. "If I had had a beer in my hand, I would have felt like it was one of my parties," he said.

"I was very much in my element," said Nathan, "Because having people come up to me and ask me questions is part of what I do for a living." It showed. Columnist Michael Ausiello said, "Nathan has a lot of energy, and he always seems really happy."

"At home, I design recipes from whatever I have sitting around the kitchen. This was how I created my pork dish. My mom would always whip up delicious meals from the most humble of ingredients, and I was lucky enough to inherit that gift. I look at what I have available, then imagine the way they would taste together: a cup of this, a dash of that—ultimately cooking the dish in my head. If it tastes good in my head, I'll cook it for real. More times than not, the finished dish turns out darn close to what I had imagined. Thanks, Mom.

"While on *Next Food Network Star,* I pitched my show idea, "From the Market to Your Table," a show about sourcing fresh, local, seasonal ingredients whenever possible, just as I do on my shows "A Lyon in the Kitchen" and "Growing A Greener World." So, in the summer months, I'll make a peach chutney to pair with the pork, then a spicy fig spread in the fall. Perhaps even curry the tenderloin, then serve it with goat cheese mashed potatoes and a maple syrup–orange segment reduction during the winter. As I learned from working with farmers for over a decade, when you let Mother Nature guide you, seasonal flavors are always delicious!"

—Nathan Lyon

Basic Elegance

To the *TV Guide* crew, Carissa explained how she made elegant shrimp puffs using pre-made refrigerator biscuit dough, mayonnaise, rock shrimp, scallion, and a little dill. Very basic. Feature director Lisa Chambers said, "I really liked Carissa's hors d'oeuvre. I thought she did a nice job of explaining how that all came together."

"Everyone seemed to like it," said Carissa. "Unless of course they were lying to my face."

SHRIMP PUFFS

Recipe courtesy Carissa Seward

Yield: 8 servings (20 puffs) ▮ Prep Time: 10 minutes ▮ Cook Time: 15 minutes ▮ Ease of Preparation: easy

Spray oil, for coating the muffin tin

1 (7½-ounce) can refrigerator biscuits

1 cup shredded Monterey jack cheese

1 scallion, white and some green, chopped

½ cup mayonnaise

½ pound small shrimp, cooked and peeled

½ teaspoon chopped fresh dill

1. Heat the oven to 350°F. Coat a miniature muffin tin with the spray oil.

2. Split each biscuit in half and place each half into a muffin hole, pressing into the bottom.

3. In a medium-size bowl, mix the cheese, scallion, mayonnaise, shrimp, and dill. Place 1 tablespoon of the shrimp mixture on top of each biscuit. Bake for 15 minutes, or until the puffs are golden and bubbling.

ASIAN-INFUSED PORK TENDERLOIN
with Melted Onions and Herb Goat Cheese

Recipe courtesy Nathan Lyon

Yield: 6 to 8 servings ▮ Prep Time: 35 minutes ▮ Cook Time: 30 minutes ▮ Inactive Prep
Time: 30 minutes ▮ Ease of Preparation: easy to intermediate

2 tablespoons seasoned rice
  vinegar

¼ cup soy sauce

1 tablespoon sesame oil

1 (1-pound) pork tenderloin

Kosher salt

Freshly ground black pepper

4 tablespoons olive oil, divided

2 pounds Spanish onions, thinly
  sliced

1 small fennel bulb, ¾ pound,
  thinly shaven

2 garlic cloves, thinly sliced

2 tablespoons fresh thyme leaves

¼ cup sake

1 loaf French bread

1 garlic clove

Extra-virgin olive oil

1 tablespoon chopped fresh
  chervil leaves

1 tablespoon chopped chives

1 cup goat cheese, at room
  temperature

Crème fraîche, as garnish

1. Preheat the oven to 350°F.

2. In a large bowl, mix the vinegar, soy sauce, and sesame oil and place the tenderloin into the bowl. Marinate for 30 minutes, turning every 10 minutes. Remove the pork, pat it dry, and season with salt and pepper.

3. While the meat is marinating, heat 2 tablespoons of the olive oil in a large pot over high heat. Sauté the onions, fennel, garlic, and thyme until just colored, about 5 minutes. Reduce the heat to low and deglaze with the sake, scraping the solids off the bottom of the pan with a wooden spoon. Cover the pot and cook the vegetables for 30 minutes, stirring occasionally, until the onions are translucent and soft. Remove from the heat.

4. While the onions are cooking, thinly slice the bread. Rub each piece with a halved garlic clove and season with salt and pepper to taste. Lay the bread slices on a sheet pan, drizzle with olive oil, and bake until golden but still soft in the center, about 10 minutes.

5. Heat the remaining 2 tablespoons of olive oil in a medium-size skillet over high heat. Sear the tenderloin until it is evenly colored and transfer it to the oven. Cook for about 15 minutes, or until it reaches the internal temperature of 145°F. Remove from the pan and allow to rest for 15 minutes before thinly slicing.

6. Using a fork, mix the chervil and chives with the goat cheese in a small bowl. Season with salt and pepper to taste.

7. On each piece of crostini, spread a thin layer of the herbed goat cheese. Top with a thin slice of tenderloin, followed by the onion mixture and a dollop of crème fraîche.

Everyone knows the way to a journalist's heart passes through a couple of cocktails, so for the next segment of the Meet and Eat, finalists demo'ed a signature dish with a cocktail. With his Chicken Potpie, Reggie made a Raspberry Lemontini that included Chambord liqueur. "He's like a warm blanket, this guy," said deputy features editor Carol Dittbrenner as Reggie had a lot of sassy fun. Carissa made a Double Double Bacon Quiche and her mom's Spicy Bloody Mary. She felt the press was tough on her, perhaps referring to a question from news editor Matt Mitovich: "You seem like a nice enough gal. Aren't you worried that national TV exposure and fame will turn you into a hardened, bitter woman?" "Take everything with a grain of salt and just have fun," said Carissa, unfazed. "Here's to you, Mom. Thanks for the help."

Nathan paired Chicken Paillard with Olive Tapenade and a Vanilla Rouge—vanilla vodka and pomegranate. Nate named Reggie as his toughest competition, but Nate's unique way of thinking was something that, in his opinion, Reggie didn't offer. "When I cook, I cook with love," said Nate.

In the elimination room, Bobby said that Nate, with fourteen ingredients on a crostini, confused sophistication with complexity. In the Meet and Eat, Nate seemed to knock Reggie. But when it was Nate who left, he was gracious. "I totally understand," said Nate, hugging Reggie. "I love this guy."

> "Too many ingredients can be confusing, true, but sometimes a few extra ingredients can make the difference between a good meal and an amazing one. What about spaghetti with tomato sauce? Good, sure, but arguably more enjoyable with the addition of sautéed fennel sausage, sliced garlic, caramelized yellow onions, dried chili flakes, toasted pine nuts, freshly shaved Parmigiano-Reggiano, torn basil leaves, and finished with a light drizzle of extra-virgin olive oil."
>
> —Nathan Lyon

Out of the Box

Guy's cocktail was a giant glass cauldron of Grape Ape Bowla—grape juice, gin, and vodka. He was asked if he was too edgy for Middle America, but he said no, his true heart was with his family.

> "I can remember down to the second the first time I made this dish. I was in the kitchen at my house and I had a bunch of buddies over to watch a UFC fight. I was prepping some sushi and I'd rolled out the last of the maki rolls. I'd also made some barbecue. I had a little bit of rice left and I thought I'll make some sushi with the barbecue. I was sprinkling the pulled pork into the roll and my buddy Darren comes round the corner. Darren's favorite name for someone is 'Jackass,' as in, 'What you doin' you jackass?' He sees me and he goes, 'What you doin', Guido, you jackass, you can't put barbecue in sushi,' and I said, 'You wanna bet?' I finished rolling and served it to my buddies and everyone was like, 'Whoa, what's this?' and I looked at Darren and said, 'It's the Jackass Roll.' It's one of the number one sellers in Tex Wasabi."
>
> —Guy Fieri

JACKASS ROLLS

Recipe courtesy Guy Fieri

Yield: 6 to 8 servings ▮ Prep Time: 30 minutes ▮ Cook Time: 25 minutes (French fries) ▮ Ease of Preparation: intermediate

8 spring-roll wrappers

2 cups Sushi Rice (recipe follows)

8 ounces pulled barbecued pork butt, warm

32 French fries (crispy)

1 avocado, cut into 16 slices (¼ inch thick)

Spicy Chili Mayo (recipe follows)

Wasabi, for garnish

Gari (pickled ginger), for garnish

SUSHI RICE

¾ cup short-grain Japanese rice

¾ cup water

¼ cup rice vinegar

Pinch of sea salt

1 tablespoon sugar

SPICY CHILI MAYO

½ cup mayonnaise (recommended: Kewpie)

1½ teaspoons mirin

1½ to 2 teaspoons rice vinegar

1½ teaspoons chili garlic paste, such as sambal oelek

¾ teaspoon freshly squeezed lime juice

½ teaspoon tamari

1. Build the rolls one at a time: Gently dip a spring-roll wrapper into a shallow pan of hot water until it is soft.

2. Working quickly and carefully, trying not to tear the paper, place ¼ cup of Sushi Rice on the bottom two thirds of the wrapper, leaving some space at the edges. In layers, add 1 ounce of the pulled pork, 4 French fries, and 2 slices of avocado. Roll the bottom edge of the wrapper into the middle, then fold in the two sides like an envelope. Continue rolling the wrapper to make a tight burrito-style roll. Repeat with the remaining wrappers, keeping the rolled wraps under a damp paper towel.

3. Cut each roll crosswise into 4 pieces and serve with the Spicy Chili Mayo, wasabi, and pickled ginger.

SUSHI RICE: 1. Wash the rice six times, until the water runs clear. Cook the rice and water in a rice cooker, then let stand for 15 minutes. Combine the vinegar, salt, and sugar until the salt and sugar dissolve (this is the *sushi zu*).

2. Place the rice in a *hangiri* or wooden bowl (you can spread on a parchment-lined baking sheet), and pour the *sushi zu* over it. Spread the rice out around the bowl as evenly as possible, being careful not to mash it. Flip the rice over and let it stand for 10 minutes.

Yield: 2½ cups ▮ Cook Time: depends on rice cooker: 50 minutes ▮ Inactive Prep Time: 25 minutes ▮ Ease of Preparation: intermediate

SPICY CHILI MAYO: Combine all the ingredients and mix thoroughly. Refrigerate.

Yield: ½ cup ▮ Prep Time: 5 minutes ▮ Ease of Preparation: easy

"Can they see me sitting next to Paula Deen and Rachael Ray? Can I sit in the middle of that? I'm just trying to show 'em that it's there."

—Guy Fieri

The Early Show

Next up, the three remaining finalists—Guy, Carissa, and Reggie—cooked a romantic three-course meal for Julie Chen of the CBS *Early Show* . . . in six and a half minutes. Guy's dessert was a Ginger-Poached Pear. Julie asked what kind of pear, and Guy was stumped. Julie said she knew more about the pears than Guy. "That's not a good sign because I don't really cook."

Reggie was, for Bob, "electric." Carissa missed her time cues and was time-crunched again. Her nerves had gotten the better of her, and this week it was she who waved good-bye.

> **"Because it was a competition fighting for something that you want so badly I think it's always tough to just be your everyday authentic self so naturally. If we were put into a situation of comfort and support, without being judged so harshly, then I think naturally it would be much easier to be comfortable and show our true selves. In the heat of competition it all just felt really dramatic and over the top."**
>
> **—Carissa Seward**

Miss P

Before Guy and Reggie's final challenge, a pilot presentation in Studio A, Paula Deen dropped by to inspire two fans. "I will put Paula Deen on just to have her voice throughout the house," said Reggie.

"She's intoxicating," said Guy.

"Guy wasn't too far off. He didn't have the confidence he has today but he wasn't too far off. He was something definitely different that Food Network was not offering. He's a worker. You just do what it takes."
—Paula Deen

Guy piloted his Tequila Turkey Fettuccine and Breath Mint Pie. "My show would be a cross between *Jackass, American Chopper,* and *Emeril,*" he said. It was now for America to decide whether that was something they wanted to see. Reggie's pilot presentation was "Simply Spectacular"—Roasted Balsamic-Glazed Chicken with Sweet Fennel and an All-Grown-Up Raspberry Hot Tart. The tart was a classic flavor combo of chocolate and raspberry but all kicked up.

ALL-GROWN-UP RASPBERRY HOT TART

Recipe courtesy Reggie Southerland

Yield: 4 servings ▌ Prep Time: 15 minutes ▌ Cook Time: 25 minutes ▌ Inactive Prep Time: 10 minutes ▌ Ease of Preparation: easy

1 (14.1-ounce) box refrigerated pie crusts (2 crusts)

4 tablespoons lemon curd

8 tablespoons seedless raspberry jam

1 (8-ounce) bag semisweet chocolate chips

½ cup heavy cream, warmed

Ice cream, for serving

1. Preheat the oven to 375°F.

2. Unroll the dough and cut each pie crust into an 8½-inch square. Cut each square in half to form two rectangles. Run a damp finger around the edges of each rectangle to create a small border. Staying inside the border, spread 1 tablespoon of the lemon curd on the bottom half of the square. Top the curd with 2 tablespoons of the jam and fold the dough over. Press the edges closed and crimp. Repeat with each rectangle. Place the tarts on a parchment-lined baking sheet and freeze until firm, about 10 minutes.

3. Transfer the baking sheet from the freezer to the oven and bake until the pastry is browned, 20 to 25 minutes, rotating the pan halfway through.

4. While the tarts bake, melt the chocolate chips in a double boiler. Remove from the heat and whisk in the cream until smooth.

5. To serve, put a scoop of your favorite ice cream on a plate, top with a warm tart, and drizzle with the chocolate sauce.

THE RESULT

The two finalists left standing, Reggie and Guy, teamed up with Bobby Flay to cook a reunion feast for all the finalists. "I look at Bobby Flay like a general in the food army," said Guy.

Back in Silver Lake, Reggie's food had gotten bigger and bolder since *Next Food Network Star*. He now featured an Orange Cinnamon Cayenne/Black Pepper cookie inspired by Bobby Flay. "This is such a turning point for me," he said. Guy, meanwhile, was opening a new restaurant in Sacramento and getting to know his new son, Rider, born eleven days after he got back. His older son, Hunter, said, "I'm really excited. I want to see my dad win."

Once again, Emeril made the big reveal. "The people's choice: Guy Fieri."

> "Knowing Guy outside of TV, he's still that same cool dude. He's got his arm round your shoulder talking about a sports team. He's been able to take his very gregarious personality and take it into a restaurant and talk to someone about the food they make. He's made that transition very smoothly. Guy just makes you want to watch whatever it is he's doing. Whatever he's doing is the coolest thing to be doing because it's Guy doing it."
>
> —Duff Goldman

☆ "The birth of my sons, that's the top. This is right up there."

—Guy Fieri

SEASON TWO	ELIMINATIONS
EPISODE TWO First Elimination	★ **JESS DANG:** "I honestly don't think you can have a very full-time job and be a great chef. You can be a great home cook, but you'll never be able to compete with all the passionate chefs who've made a commitment to the craft. I'll continue to just cook on the side and throw great dinner parties, and that's enough for me right now."
EPISODE THREE Second Elimination	★ **BETH RAYNOR:** "[As a chef at Saffron Lane in San Francisco] I've developed a concept around the kind of food I know and love and want to share with a much larger audience. My formula is based on keeping things healthy yet incredibly flavorful, simple yet elevated, and as organic and seasonal as possible. So far, so good!"
EPISODE FOUR Third Elimination	★ **EVETTE RODRIGUEZ:** "I feel very strongly that one not need have a culinary degree to work in the industry. What is truly needed is to have a strong work ethic. The rest: genius, or otherwise, will come. A thirst for knowledge will ensure you are constantly learning and you must cook all of the time!"
EPISODE FIVE Fourth Elimination	★ **ANDY SCHUMACHER:** "I felt like I was doing good in the competition, I had a good shot . . . a chance to do something I would never do otherwise in my life. It was fun. When I see my family I'm going to give them hugs and kisses."
EPISODE SIX Fifth Elimination	★ **NATHAN LYON:** "The competition taught me how to think on my toes under the most difficult of conditions. Thankfully, on my cooking shows [see chefnathanlyon.com], even though I may cook eighteen half-hour cooking episodes in nine consecutive days, or even twenty-five cooking episodes in five consecutive days (no joke), I always know ahead of time which of my recipes I'll be cooking, and under what conditions I'll be preparing them. On *Next Food Network Star*, we never knew anything, ever."
EPISODE SEVEN Sixth Elimination	★ **CARISSA SEWARD:** "The entire process was really challenging both mentally and physically. I think once you get it, the process gets a lot easier and you're more able to be yourself, to relax and enjoy what is happening to you and around you and take it all in and appreciate the experience. It was tough, but nothing worthwhile comes without a lot of hard work and effort so I didn't mind."
Runner-up	★ **REGGIE SOUTHERLAND:** "People have been incredible, stopping me on the street, stopping their cars while I'm walking the dog. It's been great. . . . I learned so much from so many people."

GUY FIERI

Guy's first series, *Guy's Big Bite*, premiered on June 25, 2006.
Diners, Drive-Ins and Dives premiered on November 4, 2006.

Guy Fieri: A Q&A

☆ **"It's all about the food for me. I woke up this morning and the first thing I said to my wife was, 'Good morning,' and the second was, 'What do you want for dinner?'"**

When did you think you could win *Next Food Network Star*?

I figured out I had a shot to win when Emeril announced that I had won. There was never a time I looked at it and said, "I'm winning." I'm an optimistic person but one of the reasons I might have won was that I didn't go in there having to win. I was very successful in my restaurants and in my life and didn't feel that I had to have this. I don't think I put as much pressure on myself as others did.

So you really felt in danger at certain points?

Every time we went to elimination I went, "Oh boy. Here comes me getting kicked off." Every time it didn't happen I thought, "Well, now the competition's even more difficult, I got to really prepare myself." The competitors were all great chefs, really worked hard, all really wanted it and most of them could have been really successful. I thought I was going to lose a few times. I was packing my stuff.

You weren't confident even in the final two?

I was very grounded with the idea that if Reggie won, I would be very happy. Reggie is a great guy. Again, I was more at ease knowing that whatever happened, I still had a great life to go back to.

So who did you see as your biggest threat?

They were all a threat. The first night they all talked about their accreditations and going to culinary school and I'm sitting there thinking, "I'm just a guy that cooks." I didn't have any classical training. But I didn't really look at them as my competition. The only one who was going to beat Guy Fieri was Guy Fieri. That the only way that I was going to lose was if I couldn't answer the call.

With your wife Lori being pregnant, is it true you almost didn't participate at all?

I did everything I could to not compete. I really didn't want to go on a reality show. I didn't want to go in front of the country and get my ass kicked. But I've always encouraged my friends and everyone around me to live their limits. It was time I walked the talk. I had a good out with Lori being pregnant but she said, "You absolutely have got to do this. You can't keep talking about it." A lot of the right things aligned at the right time to make it happen.

You knew from a young age that you wanted to work with food?

I was always a junkie about food, always really appreciated it. I ran a pretzel cart when I was a kid, that was the beginning. Going to France when I was sixteen was another really influential piece. It's just something that you either have or you don't and I've been bitten by the bug.

Did you used to watch the Food Network before you were on it?

I used to watch the original *Iron Chef* because I enjoyed the eclectic food styles and the different types of prep but that was about it. I never really watched because that's what I do for a living. I knew Emeril's name and I knew Mario Batali and Bobby Flay but I never knew a lot about them. I respected that they were able to be restaurateurs and also do shows, the whole deal.

What about *Next Food Network Star*?

I had never seen the show. I had no idea what I was doing.

From the very first demo, you seemed very comfortable on the air.

Coming from where I have, you have to roll with the punches. My dad did a lot of critical thinking exercises with me when I was a kid. He would put four items on the counter and say. "Make something with that." He was just seeing what my imagination would come up with. And in the restaurant business, do you know how many times I've gone to a catering event and we're serving something that involves tortillas and there are no tortillas? You figure out pretty quickly what the dish is going to be. You learn to adapt. You can't lose it because everybody's counting on you.

And you can't lose it on TV either . . .

I was doing a satellite media tour the other day in New York and here I am on a big station and the burners aren't working and they're making a beeping sound. In the middle of my demo: "beep, beep, beep . . ." Plus the food is not getting hot because the burner isn't working. But I can't look at the camera and say, "Excuse me guys. . . ." You just roll with it. So I was talking for four and a half minutes with the "beep, beep, beep." I was losing my mind when we finished.

Your POV was "Off the hook and out of bounds." Did you always cook like that?

That's not really just my cooking technique, it's my lifestyle. I live life to the fullest. Anything that we can think of we try to do. My family, we dirt bike, we snowboard, we travel. . . . It's the same way with food. Food is unconquerable. It's a gigantic mountain to climb and I look at it as a great journey. There's no structure to it and no rules.

You said if you got a show it would be a cross between *Emeril, Jackass,* and *American Chopper . . .*

That's exactly what it is. That wasn't a prediction, it was just how I was seeing my life. I have a bunch of crazy friends, I've got a big family, we take on enormous projects, things way above and beyond what we should be doing.

Such as . . .

Right now we are building a 25-foot, 10,000-pound pizza trailer. My wife and dad and I were sitting around and he said what in the hell are we doing with this? I said, "Every now and again, I want to have my pizza trailer ready to go," and he said, "You don't have a pizza trailer," and I said, "Exactly. That's why I need one." This is a wood-fired pizza oven—it's a 4000-pound pizza oven from Italy that's going on a trailer. This is badass.

Did you have to hold back on the show?

I had to hold back. They already weren't understanding me. When Bob Tuschman asked me about my culinary POV and I said "Off the hook," he didn't get it. What you are seeing now is what you would have got then if I had let it all out but I held it back. They would just have thought I was full of it!

What's it like being a judge on *Next Food Network Star*?

It's incredibly difficult. I'm not a food critic. When I started doing *Diners, Drive-ins and Dives,* that was one of the things I had to make real clear. I'm not going to critique people's stuff. I'll find the good in anybody, not because I'm afraid I'll call it like it is because I'll do that if I see a friend out of balance but that other side of it is not really my game.

But you have called people out for some bad dishes.

Here's the way I look at food: Is the product being used in the right way? Was it cooked in the right way? Past that, people have different appreciations. If it doesn't agree with me I'll say it. I don't like licorice and tuna fish; chocolate sauce and halibut doesn't do it for me. But as long as they have a premise and a perspective and a reason they are coming from, I'll listen. Someone burning something or taking sushi-grade ahi and cooking it I'll criticize but you can't beat a guy up for trying.

And there's the show-biz, like the red carpet you judged finalists on in Season Six.

People see the tattoos and the hair and the bling and they ask if I got that after I became the Food Network guy and I say no, I was living

this way before that. You have to be comfortable with who you are and how you present yourself. Some people push too hard and think they have to be too over the top. Other people regress and don't give anything and neither is the right way to go. Just be who you are. You might have to dial it back a little bit or you might have to come out of your shell a little bit and that's for people to come to learn.

Does being on TV come naturally to some people?

I think it comes natural to some people but if it doesn't you need to figure out how to make it be natural. Some people are scared to death to walk the red carpet and others make it a big party. However you do it, you have to make it through the red carpet. If it's not in your wheelhouse you need to develop it.

What's your best advice for someone going on a show like this?

Don't sweat the small stuff. It is the little things that create the chain reactions that are going to sink the ship. Stuff is going to happen. It's going to happen on TV, it's going to happen with a recipe, at a demo, with your career even. All these situations, just handle it and move on. Don't let it derail you and don't let it capture your energy.

Were you concerned the look wasn't going to work for Food Network?

I looked at the people that they had on and I thought, "Well, they're not shy about characters." Emeril was the Elvis of food. But I didn't know if mine was going to be acceptable. I'm surprised with how it has gone.

You're surprised at your success?

I did not think it was going to go like this. When I won, my business partner asked me who was going to cover the operations of the company and I said, "Me! I have to go and shoot this six episodes and I'll be back in two weeks." And he said, "No, after that." And I said, "What do you mean after that? Dude, I'm going to be back. No big deal." And he said, "You don't understand. This is going to happen." "They don't need me," I said. That was the ongoing joke.

You've stepped into network TV with *Minute to Win It*. Will you always come back to the food?

Food will always be the center of what I'm doing. We wrapped the end of *Minute to Win It* and for the wrap party I had a couple of my sous-chefs come down to L.A. and we cooked for the cast and the crew. That's what it's always about, My greatest relaxation is to cook and to hang out and cook and then cook some more.

Do you pinch yourself sometimes?

I'm not claiming to be the greatest chef in the world by any stretch of the imagination, and I'm honored to be around anybody that has one badass recipe. And I sit there with Emeril and with Mario, two of the guys that I highly respect, and listen to them talk about different foods I never really had that much depth with, I just go, "You gotta be kidding me!"

You're still involved with your restaurants?

I still work all the menus. I was just there today meeting with my directors. There is still a tremendous amount to do to make it happen with the restaurants. It's my first love and I will go back to it.

What is the best food town in America?

New York. Why? New York has the greatest population in a small area. It's the most diverse food town but it can be difficult to comprehend it all. There are so many great food towns. Minneapolis is a great food town. Portland, Seattle, San Francisco, Los Angeles. And Phoenix. Denver. San Antonio. Austin. The best thing to say is that it's a great food country.

☆ **"My wife asks where will we be when it all ends and I say, 'Probably with a little ten-seat restaurant that I open when I want and I'm cooking what I am cooking.'"**

Season THREE

S eason Three opened with a new look—from inside the carriage house in Greenwich Village in Manhattan, where the eleven finalists would live. Not only were they competing for their own show, but the pot was sweetened with another grand prize—a new Mercury Mariner. With each successive season, challenges have been made harder and more complex. Season Three would open with one of the most chaotic and least well-executed elimination challenges of all.

THE FINALISTS

1. Colombe Jacobsen. Colombe received her formal training at the Natural Gourmet Institute in New York and has worked as a yoga and fitness instructor. She was interested in fresh, healthy, local food that's not complicated—and in hosting her own organic-cooking show.

2. Vivien Cunha. Vivien was born in Brazil but had lived ten years in Los Angeles, where she ran a catering business and taught cooking. Her POV: ethnic food, with a Brazilian twist.

3. Michael Salmon. Salmon ("like the fish") worked as a food-service manager in two New York establishments, one a restaurant, the other a food market. "I've got some of the strongest culinary experience out there," said Michael.

4. Tommy Grella. Tommy, a financial planner, had no formal culinary training but a great deal of experience at home grilling with friends and family. "I think I can bring a new way of thinking to the Food Network," said Tommy. "Going over the top and having a great time. . . . 'Grellacize'—that's what I'm all about."

5. Amy Finley. Amy trained in Paris at the École Supérieure de Cuisine Française, and was now a stay-at-home mom. Her food was grounded in what she learned in France, and her early POV—"Bringing Paris into People's Kitchens"—morphed into "the Gourmet Next Door" over the course of the series.

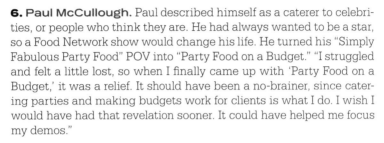

6. Paul McCullough. Paul described himself as a caterer to celebrities, or people who think they are. He had always wanted to be a star, so a Food Network show would change his life. He turned his "Simply Fabulous Party Food" POV into "Party Food on a Budget." "I struggled and felt a little lost, so when I finally came up with 'Party Food on a Budget,' it was a relief. It should have been a no-brainer, since catering parties and making budgets work for clients is what I do. I wish I would have had that revelation sooner. It could have helped me focus my demos."

7. Rory Schepisi. Rory left high school to attend the Culinary Institute of America. In Vega, Texas, she was building a restaurant. "I'm like a scientist in the kitchen, always experimenting and creating new recipes. . . . That's what makes cooking fun!" said Rory. "I make real food for real people. I'm all about blue-collar cooking—turn your backyard into a bistro," hence "Backyard Bistro."

8. Nikki Shaw. Nikki catered weddings, parties, and funerals, all with a hip approach. "I just like to keep it funky and trendy," said Nikki. "I am a little spicy and a little sweet," Nikki said of her food.

9. Joshua Adam Garcia ("Jag"). Known as Jag for his initials, the ex-Marine was working as a chef de cuisine. "I got a passion for food that's unreal," said Jag. His aim: to "Jag it up" and to be one of the first chefs on television to represent Latino Caribe cooking.

10. Adrien Sharp. Adrien hosted a local TV cooking show. He left a job he'd had for seven years at a uniform-rental service to come to New York to compete because he couldn't turn down the opportunity. "My wife, Angie, was very supportive and excited, and that's all that mattered. I'll never forget her reaction when we received that first call from Food Network. Priceless." Adrien wanted to show people that comfort food can be healthy.

11. Patrick Rolfe. Patrick, who had earned a culinary arts degree, worked as a sous-chef. His aim was to introduce new stuff that "ain't no one seen before." His watchwords: "Local, local, local, fresh, fresh, fresh, fresh."

From the Green Market

Colombe came up with a side dish that represented her healthy, fresh POV perfectly. As she explained, "It really looks like a salad that was inspired by a farmers market, and everything's really fresh." Colombe was even-keeled when she found out she had won the challenge. "I don't want to let it get to my head," she said.

"The dish came to me on the fly, under a lot of pressure. Squash was in season. I immediately thought of all of the ingredients I could choose to bring out its naturally delicious flavor. It's a cozy wintry dish that really reflects my seasonal, green market–driven style of cooking. I've also made it as a Thanksgiving side dish. I sometimes throw in spinach or arugula instead of beet greens."

—Colombe Jacobsen

ROASTED BUTTERNUT SQUASH
with Beet Greens, Goat Cheese, Toasted Walnuts, and Mint

Recipe courtesy Colombe Jacobsen

Yield: 6 to 10 servings ▌ Prep Time: 30 minutes ▌ Cook Time: 30 minutes ▌ Ease of Preparation: easy

4 small butternut squash (6 to 8 pounds)

2 tablespoons olive oil

1½ teaspoons kosher salt, divided

3 cups beet greens

¾ cup roughly chopped walnuts

¼ cup roughly chopped fresh mint leaves

1 cup crumbled goat cheese

¼ teaspoon freshly ground black pepper, plus more, to taste

1. Preheat the oven to 425°F.

2. Peel and seed the squash and cut into ½-inch cubes. Place on 2 baking sheets, drizzle with the olive oil, and season with 1 teaspoon of the salt. Coat evenly. Bake until softened and golden, 20 to 25 minutes.

3. Wash, stem, and thinly slice the beet greens. Toast the walnuts in a medium-size skillet over medium-high heat.

4. Remove the squash from the oven and toss with the beet greens, mint, and goat cheese. Top with the toasted walnuts. Add the ½ teaspoon salt and the pepper, or to taste, and serve warm.

SPOTLIGHT ON

WEDDING CRASHERS

"It was a genuine wedding. This was when we stepped up the challenges and made them location-based, real-world challenges as opposed to doing demos in the studio. That was a very difficult challenge. You're not just cooking for TV cameras, you're cooking for someone's biggest day."

—Bob Tuschman

For their next challenge, the finalists arrived at the grand ballroom of the Roosevelt Hotel, where they were faced by a huge, elaborate wedding cake and Duff Goldman, "the Ace of Cakes," or "the bad boy of Food Network," according to Tommy. Duff's showcase cake took three people three days to make; finalists had ninety minutes to decorate theirs. As Bob Tuschman noted, even though they weren't asked to actually bake the cake, this challenge didn't play to anyone's strengths. "It got them off on a very bad foot," he said.

The cakes took shape, often odd shapes, like Patrick's asymmetrical design. (Patrick had practiced with a pastry chef before the show, just in case this kind of challenge came up.) Michael, sticking to basics and hoping for the best, used strawberry leaves, which aren't renowned for taste. Vivien failed to realize that the challenge was for a wedding and made a cake with a Brazilian-flag theme in green, blue, and yellow. "It's fantastic," said Duff. "For a ten-year-old's birthday party." Paul's cake, with a groom and groom on top, looked great, but Duff knew the cut fruit would melt the fondant. Rory's luminescent creation was about half sugar and half cake.

> "I didn't think this challenge was too tough. For some reason I didn't realize the challenge called for a wedding cake, so I had fun with it!
>
> "It's funny; I have had people ask me to re-create that cake on three different occasions. Now I am known to do these wild-looking cakes. So when people are looking for a funny cake that looks like their seven-year-old made it, they call me! Recently I made a red velvet cake with a caramel vanilla custard filling and cream cheese icing. It was bright blue with a blue-eyed horse's head on the top with a yellow mane. Go figure."
>
> —Rory Schepisi

Who won? Amy, whose cake was the most wedding-appropriate. But just when the finalists had wiped their hands clean of icing and fondant, Duff revealed another surprise. In walked chef Robert Irvine from *Dinner: Impossible,* who explained Part Two of the

challenge. Finalists were to split into teams and cater a wedding for one hundred people. In six hours.

As a prize for winning the first two challenges, Amy and Colombe were chosen as the team captains for the wedding dinner. For the Green Team, Amy picked all the caterers: Nikki, Paul, Patrick, Rory; Colombe's Orange Team included Michael, Adrien, Josh, and Tommy. The odd woman out, Vivien, was offered a choice and picked Amy's team.

Chef Irvine: Scared?
Amy: Yes.
Chef Irvine: You should be.

After Vivien chose to be on Amy's team, Colombe got an extra five hundred dollars—twenty-three hundred in all—to spend at the store for cooking one person short. The bride, Jennifer, the groom, David, and their canine ring bearer, Mr. Foo, described what they wanted: a lot of vegetarian food, Indian, Thai . . . When Colombe and Michael shopped, Colombe, who was worried about the budget, ended up spending less than $800. As a result, the team was short of ingredients and seemed to be making too few dishes. "I'm kind of worried right now, for you," said Chef Irvine.

"The wedding challenge was not too stressful for me. After all, I'm a caterer, and cooking a meal for one hundred guests in six hours was pretty manageable. Our Green Team worked well together under Amy's leadership."

—Paul McCullough

Duff Goldman: A Q&A

The cake decorating challenge was maybe the biggest train wreck ever on *Star* . . .

Well, it's one thing to ask someone who's never cooked a steak before to cook a steak—no offense to anyone who cooks a steak—but you can pretty much figure it out. To decorate a cake is such a specialized thing. Finalists are under so much pressure and they're doing something they've never done before. If I was offered a choice, "would you rather dismember a side of beef or decorate a cake?" I'd chose the side of beef. It's easier.

You could see how uneasy some of them were . . .

You're already afraid. Then you have all these TV cameras and people watching you. Then you have all these other people in there doing the same thing so fear is thick in the room. Everyone's looking around to see if there's a ringer. There's always someone who did this before and will shine.

Then you have me standing there. I don't consider myself very threatening at all but I'm the guy with the show about decorating cakes. It was early and they were feeling their way on the show. And it was my first time and I was uncomfortable myself. Bobby came in and introduced everyone and said, "Okay, guys, here's Duff. He knows about cakes. I'll see you later. I'm going to soccer practice." Great, thanks!

So you were nervous yourself?

Every time I've done it, I've been just as if not more nervous than the finalists. You have to run the thing and you have to be the professional. There are these people who want to do what I'm doing and I don't even know what I'm doing.

It helps the finalists feel comfortable because they see me screw up a lot. I'll mess up a line, forget someone's name, say something stupid and have to redo it. They'll see that and say, "Oh. This is television."

Fondant has very specific properties, which some finalists were unfamiliar with.

I worked in a number of different hotels and restaurants before I was a pastry chef and everywhere you work somebody needs to know how to bake a cake, put frosting on it, and put fondant on top. For some reason it fell to me because I had an artistic leaning. I could take something 2-D and wrap it around a cake and make it 3-D and make it look good. So I've worked with it forever.

Even if they didn't know it, the show set them up a little bit because they gave the finalists a lot of fresh fruit to play with. They had star fruit and strawberries and if you stick them on fondant, they'll suck all the moisture out and it will start to melt. I don't know if it was designed like that or the producers didn't know. But it was a mess.

Paul did put the two dudes on the cake and I gave him props for that. Like, man, good for you.

> ⭐ **"They weren't great; they weren't terrible. I've seen worse. I've done worse."**
> —Duff Goldman

in martini glasses, to the Selection Committee. And dropped one on Bobby Flay.

As Susie dabbed at his coat, Bobby said, "It's only Calvin, don't worry." Clearly, this wasn't the impression Nikki was hoping to make.

"Dropping my dessert on Bobby Flay seemed to be a nightmare at the time. I remember holding my breath as I fought back the tears. He looked up at me and whispered, 'Relax, Nikki, it's okay. It's not a big deal.' I really needed that."

—Nikki Shaw

"Nikki dropped that on me and everyone made a big deal out of it. I felt bad for her. I don't care, I've had enough food spilled on me."

—Bobby Flay

PEACH AND RASPBERRY COBBLER-TINIS
with Dream Cream

Recipe courtesy Nikki Shaw

Yield: about 20 heavenly servings ▌ Prep Time: 30 minutes ▌ Cook Time: 1 hour 10 minutes ▌ Ease of Preparation: intermediate

Cooking spray or oil

1 (12-ounce) package refrigerated pie crusts (2 crusts)

3 (24-ounce) cans sliced peaches in juice

1 pint raspberries, plus more for garnish

4 ounces (1 stick) unsalted butter, cubed

3 teaspoons vanilla extract

¼ cup light brown sugar

1 cup granulated sugar

½ teaspoon allspice

1 lightly beaten egg, for egg wash

20 fresh mint leaves, for garnish

1 cup Dream Cream (recipe follows)

DREAM CREAM

1 cup heavy cream

¼ cup sour cream

¼ cup granulated sugar

3 teaspoons vanilla extract

1. Preheat the oven to 350°F.

2. Coat a 9 by 12-inch baking pan with the spray. Roll out one of the pie crusts to make a 13 by 14-inch rectangle. Place in the pan, pressing it up the sides. Prick holes in the crust with a fork or knife and bake for 10 to 15 minutes. Remove from the oven and set aside to cool slightly.

3. Drain the juice from the peaches. Add the peaches and raspberries to the crust. The crust should be three-quarters full. Mix the butter, vanilla extract, sugars, and allspice

in a bowl and spread over the peaches. Roll the second pie crust to 13 by 14 inches and slice into 10 (1¼-inch) strips. Lay 5 strips diagonally across the cobbler and the other 5 diagonally in the opposite direction. Brush the crust with the egg wash. Bake for 45 to 55 minutes, until the crust is golden brown. Garnish with more raspberries and mint leaves and drizzle with the Dream Cream.

DREAM CREAM: In a mixing bowl, combine all the ingredients and beat until well blended. Cover and chill for 1 hour before serving.

Yield: about 2 cups ▌ Prep Time: 5 minutes ▌ Ease of Preparation: easy

Robert Irvine: A Q&A

Was this a particularly difficult challenge?

For the finalists to work together to get this done was difficult from a time standpoint but I do it all the time. You're only as good as the people you surround yourself with in any job and Amy was smart to pick the team the way she did. They're caterers. Hello, that's what they do.

How did they do?

I would not have chosen some of the dishes they chose. You have to pick ingredients that can be multitasked. For example, if you take a tomato you have to be able to make seven dishes with that tomato. It makes the prep so much easier. You have to be creative. A tomato is a tomato until you make it something else. You can do anything with anything. As a chef you do that creating recipes and menus in any environment.

You had a run-in with Nikki over her cobbler . . .

What Nikki made was not what I would call a cobbler. You can do something similar, but don't call it by the original name. My mum used to make one every Sunday so I have this vision of what my mother used to make and what Nikki made was not that. Cobbler is the same wherever you go—a scone-based top with fruit.

Then the team ran out of food . . .

It's a major no-no. It doesn't matter what event you do, you'd better not run out of food. On a buffet you have to triple what you make for a sit-down dinner. An average entrée size for beef or chicken or fish is five ounces for a sit-down event while on a buffet everything is two-and a half to three ounces but you know what people are like at buffets. On average people will eat about a pound of meat on a buffet so you have to take account of that.

But the team that messed up didn't lose anyone . . .

No one was penalized. And if the guests aren't fed that's the first thing they talk about when they get home. It's a bad omen. You can have a great ceremony and everyone's happy and they're not when they run out of food.

Double Elimination to the Carriage House

For the first time, evaluations and eliminations took place downstairs in the carriage house. There were recriminations—the Orange Team had run out of food, and bride Jennifer said she was disappointed that they served only side dishes—potato gratins, vegetarian napoleons, polenta . . . There was a lack of communication from the leader, Colombe, and Bobby wondered why they'd spent so little money. "Why wouldn't you just go insane with the food?"

Amy's team got the plaudits, but Bob told Amy that her Parisian POV could seem pretentious.

> "Amy was maybe the biggest surprise on *The Next Food Network Star*. I didn't like her at the beginning, although I didn't say it on camera. I found her precious with all the talk of France. I had been very wrong. She is a woman of great soulfulness and depth and warmth. She is a fine cook and she was able to make French food very approachable, which is exactly what we are about. I went from being one of Amy's biggest detractors to being one of her biggest fans."
>
> —Bob Tuschman

As the finalists waited upstairs while the committee deliberated, Adrien called out Paul for not telling Tommy about his polenta mistake. Paul apologized but said he was there to win. The judges were down on Vivien's Cabbage Tahini Slaw, the flavors of which Bobby had described as "mismatched." And she and Patrick weren't able to bring it to the camera effectively. To the finalists' surprise, this was a double elimination, and Patrick and Vivien were let go. Jag said he was shocked that Colombe was still around, but the remaining finalists hugged, acknowledging that all but one of them would eventually take that lonely walk down the carriage house steps.

"To make an impression, finalists need a big personality and food that reflects their personality. And if they really really want to continue, they need to play into the drama of the show. It's a reality show after all, and there needs to be conflict. I think in the beginning a finalist can get more attention by creating drama than by creating good food."

—Patrick Rolfe

A New Way to Grill

For this group's first on-camera demo, Giada De Laurentiis broke down one of her recipes into nine parts and each finalist talked one segment through in one minute. After seeing the less-than-smooth results, Giada said, "We don't want to see you sweat. What you need to learn is that confidence and that coolness."

Giada introduced the finalists to Kristine Kidd, the food editor of *Bon Appétit,* who told them that they were competing for the cover recipe of an upcoming issue. The theme: "A New Way to Grill." The dish that the finalists were about to create had to look delicious, be in season, and, most important, be something a home cook would make. To be on the cover of *Bon Appétit* upped the ante in this challenge. "I would kill for this prize," Amy said.

"One of the things I'm known for is doing enormous pieces of meat," said Tommy. "I'm feeling very comfortable [with this challenge]." Tommy introduced his dish to the Selection Committee plus photographer Mark Thomas, Kristine Kidd, and *Bon Appétit* editor-in-chief Barbara Fairchild. Tommy talked up the brown sugar in the rub, which provided the sweet flavor. Outside, he told his competitors, "I have ridiculously mad skills. You can't look at that plate and not want to eat."

GRELLA GRILL RUB with Rabe and Shiitakes

Recipe courtesy Tommy Grella

Yield: 2 to 4 servings ▪ Prep Time: 20 minutes ▪ Cook Time: 1 hour ▪ Inactive Prep Time: 10 minutes ▪ Ease of Preparation: intermediate

FOR THE RUB

1 cup packed light brown sugar

2 tablespoons kosher salt

2 tablespoons black peppercorns, roughly crushed

1 tablespoon paprika

1 teaspoon cumin

1 teaspoon chili powder

1 teaspoon onion powder

1 teaspoon garlic powder

1 teaspoon cayenne

THE GLAZE

1 cup balsamic vinegar

1 tablespoon honey

¼ cup packed light brown sugar

THE VEGETABLES

½ cup olive oil

2 bunches broccoli rabe

Salt

Freshly ground black pepper

8 large shiitake mushrooms, stems removed

2 large red onions, sliced into ¾-inch-thick rings

THE STEAKS

2 large rib-eye steaks, 2 inches thick, with bones (2 pounds)

1. **FOR THE RUB:** Mix all the ingredients in a bowl and set aside. You can store the rub in an airtight container for up to 6 months.

2. **FOR THE GLAZE:** In a medium-size saucepan, over medium heat, combine the vinegar, honey, and brown sugar and simmer until reduced to a syrup, about 30 minutes. Set aside.

3. **FOR THE VEGETABLES:** Preheat the grill to medium-high.

4. Mix the olive oil, rabe, and salt and pepper to taste in a bowl. Season the mushrooms and onions with salt and pepper to taste. Grill the vegetables until tender. (Rabe cooks for 2 to 3 minutes, onions for about 17 minutes, mushrooms for 2 to 3 minutes.) Place the cooked vegetables onto a large plate or platter, cover with foil, and keep warm while you grill the steak.

5. **FOR THE STEAKS:** Preheat the oven to 400°F.

6. Rub each steak, on both sides, with 2 tablespoons of the rub. Grill for about 17 minutes, turning once. Transfer to the oven and continue to cook to the desired doneness (medium rare takes about 20 minutes). Lay the steaks on top of the vegetables and let them rest for 10 minutes. Coat with the glaze and serve immediately.

Don't Mess with Texas

Rory took a gamble by creating her "famous ribs." Normally she cooked them for five hours; here she had only ninety minutes. She knew she had to make a good impression on this challenge. "The only thing going through my head was 'Cook ribs, ribs cook.' " At the presentation Bob asked Rory how this dish represented her POV. "I'm a very simple person, and serving it in the skillet is more me. I like rustic things, especially living out in Texas. It's something that you see out on the ranch a lot."

The winner of the challenge: Rory, with the grilled cantaloupe an interesting twist. Elimination came down to a choice between Nikki and Adrien, and it was Nikki who went home. "The winner's circle feels a little bit better than the chopping block," said Rory. "And I'd really like to stay here a little while."

BABY BACK RIBS AND GRILLED CANTALOUPE with Fresh Parsley Salad

Recipe courtesy Rory Schepisi

Yield: 8 servings ▪ Prep Time: 30 minutes ▪ Cook Time: 1 hour 30 minutes ▪ Ease of Preparation: intermediate

FOR THE RIBS
4 racks pork baby back ribs,
    4 pounds

¼ cup Cajun seasoning

Barbecue Sauce (recipe follows)

1 cup chicken stock

¼ cup soy sauce

FOR THE CANTALOUPE
1 ripe cantaloupe (2½ to
    3 pounds)

1 tablespoon honey

⅛ to ¼ teaspoon cayenne

FOR THE SALAD
2 bunches flat-leaf parsley, leaves
    only, thoroughly cleaned and
    dried (6 cups)

1. **FOR THE RIBS:** Preheat the oven to 450°F.

2. Rub the ribs evenly on both sides with the Cajun seasoning. Place into a roasting pan or a very large baking dish. Mix the Barbecue Sauce, stock, and soy sauce in a bowl and pour over the ribs. Cover the pan tightly with aluminum foil and place in the oven. Cook the ribs until very tender, about 1½ hours.

3. **FOR THE CANTALOUPE:** Heat a grill or grill pan to high. Slice the cantaloupe in half, remove the seeds, then slice into ½-inch-thick pieces. Grill until you see nice grill marks, 2 to 3 minutes per side. Be careful not to overcook.

4. Remove the cantaloupe slices from the grill, drizzle the honey over them, and sprinkle with the cayenne.

5. **FOR THE SALAD:** In a medium bowl, sprinkle the parsley with the vinegar, orange juice, oil, salt, and pepper.

¼ cup red wine vinegar

2 tablespoons freshly squeezed orange juice

1 tablespoon olive oil

¼ teaspoon kosher salt

⅛ teaspoon freshly ground black pepper

Orange wedges, for garnish

BARBECUE SAUCE

2 garlic cloves, minced

1 teaspoon olive oil

1½ cups ketchup

½ cup chicken stock

⅓ cup soy sauce

2 tablespoons light brown sugar

Toss to combine. Serve the ribs with Grilled Cantaloupe and Parsley Salad, and garnish with orange wedges.

BARBECUE SAUCE: In a small saucepan over medium heat, sauté the garlic in the oil until fragrant. Add the remaining ingredients and simmer for 1 hour, stirring occasionally.

Yield: about 1½ cups ∎ Prep Time: 2 minutes ∎ Cook Time: 1 hour ∎ Ease of Preparation: easy

"My ribs are a dish that I've been perfecting since the age of twenty. I love baby backs and always look for ways to heighten the flavor while using simple preparation and execution. The techniques I've discovered over the years enable the precious cut to have that amazing fall-off-the-bone characteristic.

"My Fork 'N' Ribs are on my menu at my restaurant, Boot Hill Saloon & Grill in Vega, Texas."

—Rory Schepisi

The Basketball Challenge

For the next competition, the guest host was Guy Fieri, the previous season's winner. Guy introduced NBA legend Darryl Dawkins, aka "Chocolate Thunder," and the challenge was to make a dish with chocolate that reflected the finalist's personality and to give a tip in the presentation. Oh, and by the way, Guy said, two of you go home this week.

Guy told the finalists they would have to make a crowd-pleasing dish and serve it to fans at a New Jersey Nets game. While shopping for ingredients, Colombe took someone's bag off the conveyor belt, which left Paul without three key ingredients for his Hawaiian burger, so Adrien gave Paul some of his barbecue sauce.

> "When I found out I was missing a bag with key ingredients, it sent my blood pressure through the roof. I was pretty angry when I found out that Colombe saw a stray bag at the store and decided to leave it. But it was not her responsibility either. After all, this is a competition. Suddenly my Hawaiian Barbecued Beef Burger needed a miracle! Adrien saved me by donating a few bottles of the barbecue sauce to my cause."
> —Paul McCullough

The next day, at the Meadowlands in New Jersey, finalists served their dishes to the fans.

Paul was stopped in his tracks by Guy wielding a food thermometer. Guy told him he had to get his burgers up to temperature (165°F.) before he could serve them.

"I felt bad in that situation. I felt like the narc, which is not my style. I would much rather have jumped in and helped Paul rather than have him go through that. How people react to situations is part of the show and he reacted well."

—Guy Fieri

"I had a guest on my local cooking show do a version of Bacon-Wrapped Mushrooms, and I knew I'd keep that with me in the future. I make and bottle my own barbecue sauce for the Mission of Hope Cancer Fund in Michigan—I've always enjoyed making my own sauce. I figured it would go great with the Bacon-Wrapped Mushrooms, and it turned out to be true! I just wish I'd had the time to make my homemade sauce for the show! Glad it still worked."

—Adrien Sharp

At the carriage house for judging, Guy told Jag that his Mexican-Style Tempura with Three-Chile Chocolate Sauce was the winner. As for the NBA Challenge, it was Adrien who won; Bob said he was "relatable, down to earth, warm." In a double elimination, Tommy and Colombe went home.

"I felt incredibly uncomfortable. Tommy Grella and I have stayed friends since the show. He is a really sweet guy who is passionate about life and his family. I'm a softy. I love my family too. I love my friends, I love people, and I love people who are passionate about what they are doing. So that was tough for me."

—Guy Fieri

BARBECUED BACON-WRAPPED MUSHROOMS

Recipe courtesy Adrien Sharp

Yield: 8 mushroom caps ▮ Prep Time: 10 minutes ▮ Cook Time: 20 to 25 minutes ▮ Ease of Preparation: easy

8 medium-size button mushrooms, 1½ to 2 inches in diameter (about 8 ounces)

8 slices peppered bacon, at room temperature, cut in half

4 tablespoons barbecue sauce

1. Preheat the oven to 400°F.

2. To prepare the mushrooms, cut off their stems, rinse briefly, and dry well with paper towels.

3. Wrap each mushroom with 2 of the bacon-strip halves so that the seams overlap on the bottom of the mushroom. The bacon will stick to the mushrooms, so there is no need for toothpicks.

4. In a medium-size ovenproof sauté pan, cook the bacon-wrapped mushrooms over medium heat, seam side down, until the bacon begins to crisp, about 4 minutes. Brush the tops of the mushrooms with the barbecue sauce and transfer the pan to the oven. Cook until the bacon is crispy and the mushrooms are tender, 15 to 20 minutes.

Stadium Food Light

Michael's shrimp rolls were an alternative to the kind of heavy food we're used to at stadiums. Light, no need for a fork, no sauce dripping down your replica jersey. "So different from everything else," said Bob.

"The dish is one I have done for years. Sort of like the poor man's lobster roll, or upscale arena food. 'Perfect,' I thought, and I went with it. They're easy to produce within tight time constraints. Easy for fans to eat, viewers to embrace, and home cooks to execute.

"The name came to me like a vision. Jason Kidd was the captain of the Nets and also the name of a famous pirate, Captain Kidd. The Nets were playing the Atlanta Hawks, so any fan would want to buy into something that knocks the competition. Voilà! Hawk-Crushing Shrimp Rolls were born!

"The fans lined up at my cart, and I sold out faster than everyone else, with people coming back for more. One woman came up to me after her third and gave me a hug and a kiss. Does it get any better than that?

"I had so much fun doing it. Selling my food to the crowd brought me back to my days as a teenager at Shea Stadium selling bags of peanuts in the grandstands. Perfect! 'Hot bag of nuts . . . get your hot bag of peanuts right here! Only twenty-five cents. A mere quarter of one dollar. Hot nuts!'

You can almost smell the crowd! In 1969 I made forty to seventy-five dollars a game and got to see every game. And the Mets won the World Series. Awesome experience."

—Michael Salmon

CAPTAIN KIDD'S HAWK-CRUSHING SHRIMP ROLLS

Recipe courtesy Michael Salmon

Yield: 8 servings as a main dish or 16 servings as an appetizer ▮ Prep Time: 15 minutes ▮ Cook Time: 5 minutes ▮ Ease of Preparation: easy

1 (8-bun) package potato-bread hot dog rolls

2 tablespoons crab boil (recommended: Old Bay)

1 pound shrimp, shelled and deveined, tails removed

2 stalks celery, thinly sliced

About ⅔ cup mayonnaise

1 tablespoon chopped fresh chives, plus more for garnish

1 red bell pepper, cut into small dice, divided

Juice of ½ lemon

1 teaspoon dry mustard (recommended: Colman's)

Kosher salt

Freshly ground black pepper

Baby greens, for serving

1. Open each bun and cut in half crosswise. Lay the buns out on a baking sheet. Cover with plastic wrap and lay another baking sheet pan on top of the buns to flatten them.

2. Heat about 1 quart of water in a medium-size pot until it reaches poaching temperature (the water should start to steam but not actually come to a boil). Add the crab boil. Carefully add the shrimp and cook until they are opaque, 3 to 5 minutes. Drain the shrimp and set them aside until they're cool enough to handle, about 5 minutes. Slice each shrimp in half lengthwise.

3. In a large bowl, put the celery, mayonnaise, 1 tablespoon of the chives, three-quarters of the pepper (reserve the rest for garnish), lemon juice, mustard, and salt and pepper to taste. Toss to combine. Add the shrimp and toss again.

4. Place the baby greens into the base of the buns. Top with the shrimp and garnish with the remaining bell pepper and chives.

Fort Dix

In episode five, the finalists met up with Giada De Laurentiis and Paula Deen at the Fort Dix military base. Their first mini-challenge was to "dress up" an MRE—a military Meal, Ready-to-Eat—so that it was more palatable. Next they were to form teams of two and prepare a home-cooked meal for the troops. Surprisingly, the team who worked best together were the odd couple of Paul and Jag. "Paul is a professional gay man," Rory said. "Jag is a twenty-five-year-old marine who has never had a gay friend in his life. The two of them have linked up like bosom buddies."

Jag and Paul decided to make meat loaf, the great American comfort food, but after thirty minutes they realized that their oven was cold. Jag wigged out but then regained his composure to come up with a solution: Deep-fry the meat loaf.

"We don't get to see each other that much, only on specials. I love seeing these guys. I adore Bobby and Giada. What you see is what you get with them. I always love seeing them."
—Paula Deen

"What folks didn't understand was that I didn't flip out because the oven wasn't working. I flipped out because I knew what I was going to have to do on national television to save that meal, and that was something that I was not happy offering war-dog soldiers and representing myself as a United States marine. We turn and burn and kick ass in the kitchen, period! Those soldiers deserved better than second-rate food."
—Joshua "Jag" Garcia

It was an emotional day for Jag. When he walked into the hangar where the judging was taking place, the smell of the lubricant that the troops use to clean their weapons brought back memories of his days in the service. At elimination, Giada apologized for any discomfort that might have caused him. Amy too was upset, over the blurring of the line between their public and private lives. "I'm starting to understand that there isn't a distinction between the two things, and that's where all of this becomes extremely real."

> "I have to admit, being videotaped while I was going to bed and waking up in the morning, or in the bathroom brushing my teeth—or mic'ed while I was using the bathroom was a little bit odd and made me feel like I was under constant surveillance. I wasn't so excited to be videotaped while I was having my rare personal phone conversation. It's nice to have privacy for certain things like that."
>
> —Colombe Jacobsen

Paul and Jag had the best presentation, and their meat loaf was the most popular food. "To find out that deep-fried meat loaf is the top pick—that's a little bit of God coming down and blessing us," said Paul. "That's the only way it could have worked out."

> "If they favored deep-fried meat loaf over the rest of what the Season Three picks had to offer, then imagine the hamburger bliss they would have gotten from Jag and Pauley Paul's absolute best? And lesson learned! Don't flip out, Jag, you're worrying Paul. And for God's sake, there are children watching. Keep your cool!"
>
> —Joshua "Jag" Garcia

A Few of My (Least) Favorite Things

For the next challenge to camera, Alton Brown asked the finalists to create dishes using strangely matched ingredients. Three ingredients were picked at random: Amy had veal, oyster mushrooms, and popcorn; Paul calamari, fennel, and persimmon; Jag shrimp, snow-peas, and cornflakes; Adrien flounder, Japanese eggplant, and peanut butter; Rory steak, red radish, and prunes. Alton watched as the finalists tried to connect with the camera in their three-minute segment and then critiqued the demos. Explain what you're doing; talk about the ingredients; cook the food.

Alton dramatically introduced the next challenge. As the finalists stood behind a concealed platter of food, he reminded them that they had told the network what their favorite ingredients were. "Lift the dome, go ahead," Alton said, "because that's not what this is." Finalists had also listed their least favorite ingredient and here it was, staring each of them in the face.

Less than happy with this task, the finalists were not afraid to share their feelings about the ingredients they were assigned. Amy objected to the smell of her bok choy and Adrien to his baby corn. Jag was not pleased with the tofu, which he called "high-protein gunk." "Do you have a male billy goat?" Rory asked Alton. To Rory goat cheese tastes like that smell.

"You know what? Prepared correctly . . . cut into smaller pieces . . . firm not silky . . . properly stir-fried in a delicious sauce complemented by black tiger shrimp, hot chiles, garlic, ginger, and soy sauce. . . . Heck, yeah! And yes I have! [Eaten tofu again.]"
—Joshua "Jag" Garcia

Paul's bête noire: the lima bean.

No one aced the demo. Amy was stricken with doubt, Jag was overly complex, Rory said she "bombed," and Adrien lacked expertise and a POV.

This evaluation was the hardest yet. "If these had been your audition tapes, I don't think any of you would be standing here," said Susie. "What happened?" Everyone went

what is A MIREPOIX?

The mix of diced onion, carrot, and celery Paul used to flavor his soup is a mirepoix. It is named for its inventor, the cook of the Duc de Lévis-Mirepoix, a general and ambassador for Louis XV of France in the eighteenth century.

backward; POVs were missing; the viewer was lost. The finalists were obviously feeling the pressure.

> "The worst part was having our cell phones confiscated and not having the opportunity to call home. I had great support from my wife and children. I knew they were safe and in a good place, but not getting to say good night to my babies was very difficult. . . ."
>
> —Adrien Sharp

Amy wondered if she wanted to be there; she was starting to crack under the strain and she missed her family . . . "I'm telling you that if you have a decision to make between me and these other people, I would send me home," she said, but stopped short of saying she wanted to go home. When she was saved, it was not against her wishes. Adrien, who had given up his job to compete, was eliminated.

Allez Cuisine!

> "*Iron Chef* is a gruesome ordeal. I don't envy anyone having to do it. But none of the finalists shrinks from doing it because by the time they make it to the *Iron Chef* challenge they've already been put through the wringer."
>
> —Alton Brown

When episode seven brought the finalists to the Institute of Culinary Education, they had a pretty good idea of what they were in for: Iron Chef.

> "I was so excited to be a part of *Iron Chef*, I actually thought I was gonna pop out of my skin! It was a truly memorable time, and I would love to have another shot at it one day when I'm a little more experienced."
>
> —Joshua "Jag" Garcia

This ultimate *Next Food Network Star* challenge was played out in two hour-long battles in which two finalists would face off against each other in preparing three dishes using a secret ingredient. In the first hour, Rory would go up against Paul; Amy would battle it out with Jag in the second hour. The finalists had help from surprise sous-chefs, the former finalists.

For Paul versus Rory, the secret ingredient was striped bass.

Rory battled with an ingredient she'd never used before, while Alton asked the two noncooking chefs to provide commentary for 50 percent of their score. He asked Jag if Rory was using wild or farmed striped bass. Jag guessed wild. Wrong. Alton asked Amy how they got the light texture on the panko Paul was using, and Amy retrieved the packet, read off the ingredients, and concluded that panko was more of a bread product than a standard bread crumb. "She's good," said Bobby.

In judging, Iron Chef Cat Cora said Rory's Pan-Seared Sea Bass was cooked perfectly. Susie liked Rory's "Backyard Bistro"; her Beer-Battered Sea Bass Wrapped in Bacon was a hit with everyone, but her napoleon, less so. Paul's Ceviche was "summer on a plate" but underseasoned. The Fish Baked with Blackberries was bland; his Panko-Fried Fish was more successful.

> ☆ "The Iron Chefs do bring a whole level of intimidation to the competition."
>
> —Cat Cora

⭐ **"And so it is with an open heart and an empty stomach that I say to you, in the words of our chairman: *'Allez cuisine!'*"**

—**Alton Brown**

"They should be in awe of doing *Iron Chef*. Entering a kitchen stadium is not for the faint of heart. I take *Iron Chef* very seriously too. The people who do *Iron Chef* are hard-core chefs and they're there to crack your head open. This is a softer version of that. They're not really trying out for *Iron Chef*."

—Bobby Flay

Question: "What's the craziest ingredient you've seen on *Iron Chef*?"
Cat Cora: "Barracuda. It's not the best fish to try to make something wonderful out of. It's hard to scale or gut and it's a fin fish so you have to fillet it just right to get the meat out of it and it has an oiliness. Almost like yellowtail but not as yummy. You have to work to get it really nice."

"*Iron Chef* is like a level ten. *Star* is like a level three. If they could make barracuda into something even remotely palatable, they would be onto a winner. It's an idiosyncratic fish, gamey and oily and incredibly difficult to cook well. If the judges could even swallow what they made, it would be a success."

—Alton Brown

" 'Plummy' is what I said . . ."

For Amy versus Jag, the secret ingredient was chicken.

Amy's *Iron Chef* dishes were Casbah Lollipops, Moroccan Chicken Stew, and her stuffed-chicken recipe.

"I made this up after Alton lifted the lid. I had a whole chicken, and I wanted to be able to use the parts that could be used most efficiently in the allotted time. I looked at the breasts. My go-to approaches are to pound it out flat for a paillard or to stuff it. I use goat cheese a lot, and the fresh mushrooms were a logical accompaniment, with the dried mushrooms a good start for a sauce.

"I seldom cook the same thing many times. I enjoy cooking on the fly. I go to the store and buy ingredients that look good and figure out what I want to cook."

—Amy Finley

While Amy was getting into a groove, Paul was intimidated by his role as commentator. When Alton asked what was Moroccan about Amy's Moroccan Stew, Paul failed to mention the spices. Alton asked Rory if Jag was using red pepper flakes or red chili flakes? "A chili is a pepper," she answered. Wrong. Rory looked at the camera: "Kids, stay in school. I dropped out at sixteen. Wrong move."

> Alton: Paul, what's in that can?
>
> Paul: Those are whole plum tomatoes.
>
> Alton: What kind of tomatoes?
>
> Paul: Plum.
>
> Alton: Where are they from?
>
> Paul: Plummy . . .

They were San Marzano tomatoes, an important designation. " 'Plummy' is what I said," noted Paul. "How embarrassing."

"The *Iron Chef* Challenge was a nightmare for me. When we showed up at ICE, I was so intimidated because I had no formal culinary training. Amy, Rory, and Jag all went to culinary school, so I felt at a huge disadvantage and it frazzled me to the core. The cooking part of the challenge went all right, but when it was my turn to commentate I felt so nervous and choked. Rather than staying calm and focused, I started making jokes and not taking it seriously."

—Paul McCullough

Jag's overzealous grilling set off the smoke alarms. "Hey, Jag. Way to grill!" said Bobby.

At the judges' table, Cat praised the cinnamon on Amy's Lollipop but wanted more flavor. Everyone loved the stuffed chicken, and the stew was a "home run" for Cat. Jag's Chicken and Goat Cheese Wonton was overpowered by vinegar. Bobby asked what was Caribbean about the Caribbean Soup, and Jag couldn't say. No one liked his Chicken with Saffron-Lime Cream Sauce. With all of the criticism, Jag found it hard to hold it together. He was distraught and embarrassed over his performance.

But it was Paul, after long deliberations, who was sent home.

"*Iron Chef* was the most fun. Absolutely a riot from beginning to end. It was the most relaxed I was because I felt the focus was not on me. There were other people, the camera was moving around, and it played to my strengths cooking on the fly. The reporting part was fun, a bit like writing. I'm a bit of a food geek, and to be able to do that with Alton Brown, the king of the food geeks, was exciting. And to do well felt good."

—Amy Finley

GOAT-CHEESE-AND-MUSHROOM-STUFFED CHICKEN BREASTS

Recipe courtesy Amy Finley

Yield: 6 servings ▮ Prep Time: 45 minutes ▮ Cook Time: 40 minutes ▮ Inactive Prep Time: 5 minutes ▮ Ease of Preparation: easy

6 skinless and boneless chicken breasts (10 ounces each)

10 ounces cremini mushrooms

2 tablespoons unsalted butter

Kosher salt

Freshly cracked black pepper

6 ounces softened goat cheese

3 tablespoons olive oil

1 recipe Mushroom Wine Sauce (recipe follows)

¼ cup chopped fresh parsley leaves, for garnish

Special equipment: kitchen twine

MUSHROOM WINE SAUCE
1½ cups dried shiitake mushrooms

2 cups boiling water

¼ cup white wine

¼ cup chicken stock

1 tablespoon unsalted butter, cold

Kosher salt

Freshly cracked black pepper

1. Lay the chicken breasts on a piece of plastic wrap, place another piece on top, and pound with a meat mallet or rolling pin until they are each about ½ inch thick. Set aside.

2. Stem the mushrooms and put the caps and stems in a food processor; pulse until finely chopped. Melt the butter in a medium-size sauté pan over medium-high heat and add the mushrooms. Sauté until the mushrooms have released their liquid and the liquid has evaporated, about 10 minutes. This is called a duxelle. Season with salt and pepper to taste. Set aside.

3. Coat each chicken breast with 2 tablespoons of goat cheese and top with ¼ cup of the duxelle. Roll each breast up burrito-style: begin from the bottom, roll into the middle, and tuck in the sides as you finish. Tie the roll with three pieces of twine, securing the ends and then wrapping in the middle. Season with salt and pepper.

4. Heat the olive oil in a large sauté pan over medium-high heat. Cook the chicken roll-ups on all sides, cooking in two batches, until they are cooked through and golden brown, 12 to 15 minutes. Allow the rolls to sit 5 minutes before removing the twine and slicing each one into 4 to 5 slices. Top with the remaining duxelle and several spoonfuls of the Mushroom Wine Sauce. Garnish with the parsley.

MUSHROOM WINE SAUCE: Place the shiitakes in a mixing bowl and add the boiling water. Allow the mushrooms to soak for 15 to 20 minutes, until the liquid gives off a rich, earthy fragrance. Strain, reserving the liquid. Thinly slice the mushrooms and put aside. In a small sauté pan over medium-high heat, bring the mushroom liquid to a strong boil and reduce by half, about 10 minutes. Add the wine and the stock and reduce by half again, 3 to 5 minutes. Add the sliced shiitakes. Remove the pan from the heat and add the butter, swirling the pan until it's incorporated and the sauce is glossy. Season with salt and pepper to taste.

Prep Time: 10 minutes ▌ Cook Time: 15 minutes ▌ Inactive Prep Time: 15 to 20 minutes ▌ Ease of Preparation: easy

Eggs, Dressed Up

For Jag, Rory, and Amy, the last stop was Rachael Ray's studio, where they had to demo a signature dish live in five minutes. The focus would be on the storytelling. For Rory, Rachael was a calming influence. "She gives off this 'Hey, it's going to be okay' feeling."

Amy talked to Rachael about cooking a dish that reminded her of a time before she'd had kids. Eggs, "dressed up, a little chichi, a little fancy-schmancy," or, as Rachael said, "Uptown eggs." Amy talked through her piperade and plated it with lentils and some basil. It was family-style and not too perfect. Amy plugged *Next Food Network Star,* and her time was up.

> "The eggs are a bistro dish, and the piperade often goes on an omelet, so they go with the coddled eggs just fine. The only problem is it can be a little messy with the peppers and the ham. I plated it on *Rachael Ray* and thought, 'This does not look good.' You're either going to dump it on the ramekin so you can't see the egg or spoon it onto the side, where it looks like little worms trailing over the edge. Flavorwise, it works really well.
>
> "You have think about what it looks like. People can't use the normal senses they usually bring to food, so the only things they get are you and your luscious descriptions and what they can see, so it better look good. I'll serve the eggs with a salad or sautéed mushrooms, asparagus, grilled zucchini—however you'd serve an omelet."
>
> —Amy Finley

EGGS EN COCOTTE with Basque Piperade

Recipe courtesy Amy Finley

Yield: 4 servings ▮ Prep Time: 25 minutes ▮ Cook Time: 40 to 45 minutes ▮ Ease of Preparation: easy

FOR THE EGGS
2 cups water
2 tablespoons unsalted butter, softened
8 large eggs
Kosher salt
Freshly ground black pepper
¼ cup heavy cream
½ cup freshly grated Parmesan cheese
Special equipment: 4 (1-cup capacity) ramekins

1. Preheat the oven to 375°F.

2. **FOR THE EGGS:** In a small saucepan, bring the water to a boil.

3. Coat the bottom of each ramekin with the butter. For each serving, crack 2 eggs into a small bowl, being careful not to break the yolks. Carefully slide the eggs into a prepared ramekin. Season each with salt and pepper, drizzle with 1 tablespoon of the cream, and sprinkle with 1 tablespoon of the Parmesan. Set the ramekins into a medium-size glass or ceramic baking pan, allowing at least 1 inch of space between them. Transfer the

FOR THE PIPERADE

2 tablespoons olive oil

3 ounces prosciutto, about 8 slices, cut into ¼-inch strips

1 small onion, finely diced

1 red bell pepper, seeds and ribs removed, cut into 1 by ¼-inch strips

1 green bell pepper, seeds and ribs removed, cut into 1 by ¼-inch strips

1 garlic clove, minced

1 (14½-ounce) can diced tomatoes

¼ teaspoon crushed red pepper (optional)

Salt

Freshly ground black pepper

1 tablespoon chopped fresh basil leaves

pan to the bottom rack of the oven and pour the boiling water into it, being careful not to splash any into the ramekins. Cover the pan with aluminum foil and bake for 12 to 15 minutes, until the whites are set but the yolks are still a bit runny. While the eggs are baking, prepare the piperade.

4. **FOR THE PIPERADE:** In a large skillet over medium heat, heat the olive oil, then cook the prosciutto until it begins to crisp. Add the onion and sauté until lightly golden. Add the red and green pepper and sauté until they just begin to soften. Stir in the garlic and cook until fragrant, 30 seconds to 1 minute. Add the tomatoes and crushed red pepper. Allow the mixture to stew over medium-low heat until the liquid has evaporated and the tomatoes are heated through. Season with salt and pepper to taste.

5. Remove the skillet from the heat and add the basil. Divide the piperade among the ramekins (you will have extra) and serve on a small plate, piping hot.

"The Rachael Ray show was the best time of my life—hands down! That is what I have always wanted to do, what I still want to do, and I won't give up until it happens!"

—Rory Schepisi

Rachael Ray: A Q&A

You seem to enjoy working with the finalists.

I really do, it's a lot of fun. I've always considered myself completely unqualified to be on food television so I am proof positive that in America, anything can happen. And if you have a relationship with the audience, if you're someone who has a story to tell and you love food, anyone can truly be the next Food Network Star. I am the embodiment of that. I enjoy working with the group as it gets smaller, giving them advice on how to loosen up enough to let the story come through. I believe that food television is not really so much about the food as about the storytelling. Engaging a person in your personality is far more important than in technically schooling them on how to prepare a dish.

Guy Fieri is the embodiment of that. It doesn't matter what he's talking about, you just want to listen. He's fun and it's infectious and you just want to be a part of whatever he's got that's making him feel that good.

You don't have to worry about helping them with a Point of View . . .

The hardest trick is coming up with your thumbprint—what is your bag going to be? What is their *30 Minute Meals*? Food Network has got so big that it becomes tougher to come up with something new because it's so diverse. And now there is Cooking Channel too. It becomes progressively harder with each round to reinvent the wheel.

Do you empathize with what the finalists are going through?

Of course. My first time at Food Network I did a pilot of *30 Minute Meals* on Emeril's set and I set a pan on fire. They had been preheating the pan for an hour unbeknownst to me and I poured olive oil in it and the flames shot up as far as I could see. I wanted to throw up.

Now are you able to forget the camera is there?

I am. Everyone is different. I like to know the camera people's names. When I first started it was Camera One, Camera Two and I said, "Can we just call the cameras by the names of the people standing behind them?" I like to have a conversation with my friend Jay or my friend Dante or my friend Hugh. The more I can break down that wall the more comfortable I think the audience will be.

Do you get nervous now?

No, not at all if there is food involved. If I'm at Food Network I'm very comfortable. If I'm on the daytime show and the President or an Oscar winner is coming in, you get a little excited. I don't know if I'm nervous or super-excited to sit down and get to know that person.

The Food Network studio is your office?

It's like hanging out in a really big kitchen. When people come over to my house I invite them so they are there for a lot of the preparation. The kitchen has always been the heart of the home I grew up in and the home I live in. It's great to have work feel like being at home.

How would you have done on *Next Food Network Star*?

I don't think I would have gone in for the competition. I fell into all of this quite by accident so I never perceived myself as belonging with that group of people. I don't think I would have been brave enough to do it to begin with.

Do you think you could be a judge on the show?

I could never make the decisions. I just don't have the heart. I'd like to think that I'm pretty good at making finalists feel comfortable enough to get the best performance out of them but I would be equally poor at breaking their hearts because I know how hard it is. That's what I love about working with the show. They look to me to do the mentoring role and it's all fun and they do all the dirty work. I feel a little bit guilty about it. But not very!

How was *Iron Chef* for you?

The longest most horribly nerve-wracking stomach-curdling experience of my life and I would never be dumb enough to do it again.

Do you have any advice for a finalist on *Iron Chef*?

I have no advice. The day I was on I hadn't slept all night and I was paler than I had ever been in my entire life. I was wearing beat-up jeans and had my hair pulled back and looked absolutely miserable. Gorgeous Giada comes out with her hair done and a beautiful chef coat with embroidery. She looked like a Disney movie, as if animated birds were going to be chirping around her head. Bobby is my good friend but he is very intimidating in that context. My partner was Mario and he's how I got into it to begin with. He said, "Ah come on, it'll be fun." And I got there and I said, "Mario, this isn't fun!"

You said the best advice you were ever given was to smile all the time . . .

Everyone knows the camera puts a couple of pounds on but they don't think about what that really means. Everything you do is bigger on TV except being too big. If you talk in a big booming voice it seems quite normal. If you make a frown you look like the most miserable person on the planet. If you are not smiling you look like you are about to cry. Things get very distorted when you are inside that little box. What feels really over the top comes over as just being in an okay mood. You have to be explosive like Guy Fieri to come across as even an excited or an upbeat person. It is really hard to get that across to people when you are trying to help them be on camera. That is why Sara Moulton's words were so true. You have to smile all the time for no apparent reason. If you catch sight of yourself on a monitor—I never watch myself on TV but you can't help it on set—you look really messed up if you are not smiling. You look really depressed.

So there's almost no such thing as being over the top . . .

Exactly. That's weird. It's tough to get used to that.

What do people mean when they say "be yourself?"

You have to do whatever makes you the most comfortable. You have to look at yourself and ask, "Is my sense of humor the best thing I have going for me?" "Do I know a lot about the history of food?" What was great about Mario's show was that he knew so much about the history and where the recipes came from. Not only was he charming and larger than life but he could teach you a lot without it feeling like you were being taught. Do you love having a party? With Emeril you didn't realize you were learning a recipe because there was a live band and he was telling jokes with people sitting at the counter so it felt like a big cocktail party. Figure out what makes you feel your best.

Are the challenges a fair test?

I'm not sure if anyone should be thinking on their feet how to coat a piece of fish in fruity cereal. I don't want that question answered. It's a classic training technique—the mystery box. And it's television—of course they are going to come up with the most ridiculous thing and no, I don't want to eat it. And I think there is very limited use for marshmallow. But that's just me.

In Season Four, some of the finalists had a hard time working with the kids. . . .

It's the toughest thing of all. I have a children's charity and it's still super-challenging if we have a kid on our show. You are trying to do whatever you can to make the child feel comfortable or attract an audience with children without losing your balance, keeping adults entertained and the food interesting. Any time you layer in animals and children it becomes a lot harder.

What's the hardest thing for the finalists?

It's the whole thing. Being in a studio surrounded by cameras with lots of lights. It's weird and takes a lot of getting used to. It's disconcerting to hear voices in your head too. [Producers talking on an IFB device.] They use them sparingly—if you forget an ingredient they will say, "You wanted tomato in that." Mostly they are time cues. Prompters are hugely distracting and I use them as little as possible. Reading anything on a prompter is ridiculously hard to do without letting people know you are reading, by squinting at it or reading back and forth.

And you have to get the recipe done in the time frame . . .

They tell you day one it is not your job to stop under any circumstances. That's for the directors. I'd only stop if something dramatic happens, like I literally fall down. You just keep going. One time we'd just finished filming *30 Minute Meals* and it was my birthday and they brought out thirty little cupcakes. I leaned in to blow out the candles and I set both sides of my hair on fire. I wish the cameras had been running for that.

Some of the women are cooking in heels, which would seem to make it harder . . .

It's tough to do anything in high heels. Women are more conscious of their look and they have every right to be paranoid because it matters more. Unfortunately it is still not an even playing field. I do forget the camera's on; I never forget when I am in high heels.

The show asks a lot of the winner . . .

Finalists don't consider that they are going to become in one way or another a celebrity. I think it's a small and fairly reasonable price to pay for all the fun and great opportunities it affords you. Being on food television, they have to be very open about themselves. You're in somebody's home, in the kitchen and they have to trust you. You have to give them more of yourself than you think or they're not going to believe it.

So people feel that they know you . . .

You have to allow them to to some extent.

In Season Six you directed finalists' pilots—how was that?

I loved it. It was so fun. I loved being on the other side of the camera and I'd love to do that again. That's something I am definitely qualified to do: directing food television.

With a Twist

Rory had a great time with her Blue-Collar Texas House-Fire Steaks, Chuck Wagon Potatoes, and Grilled Asparagus.

Off the bat Jag wielded his achiote oil, or "Evoo Red," as he called it. He played to the crowd: "How many you guys like lobster?" "The Italians say that it is taboo to add Parmesan cheese to seafood. But I'm not Italian, guys, so you know what? Let's have a good time."

"Jag did something on *Rachael Ray* that no one else has been able to do—he just took the crowd. He has an incredible energy."

—Bobby Flay

LINGUINI AND LOBSTER CARIBE

Recipe courtesy Joshua Adam Garcia

Yield: 4 servings ▌ Prep Time: 40 minutes ▌ Cook Time: 20 minutes ▌ Ease of Preparation: intermediate

¼ cup plus ½ teaspoon kosher salt, divided

1 Spanish onion, halved

4 lobster tails (2 pounds), shells reserved, meat cleaned and roughly chopped

½ bunch culantro or cilantro, 10 sprigs left whole, 3 tablespoons leaves, chopped

3 tablespoons achiote oil (recipe follows), annatto seeds reserved

2 tablespoons unsalted butter, divided

12 ounces linguini or your favorite pasta

¼ teaspoon freshly ground black pepper

2 cloves garlic, thinly sliced

2 Roma tomatoes, seeded and roughly chopped (⅔ cup)

1. Bring a large pot of water to a boil. Stir in the ¼ cup salt until dissolved. Add half of the onion, the lobster shells, the culantro sprigs, and the annatto seeds. Reduce the heat and simmer for 30 minutes. Pour through a fine-mesh strainer into another pot and return to a boil.

2. Heat a large sauté pan over medium-high heat. Add the achiote oil and 1 tablespoon of the butter. Drop the pasta into the seasoned water. Thinly slice the remaining half onion and add to the pan. Cook until slightly caramelized, about 3 minutes. Add the lobster meat and sauté until it begins to firm and turn opaque but is not completely cooked through, about 2 minutes. Season with ¼ teaspoon salt and the pepper. Add the garlic, tomatoes, and 2 tablespoons of the chopped cilantro and sauté lightly for 1 minute. Stir in the wine and crushed red pepper. Cook for 1 minute, until reduced by one quarter. Add the broth and simmer until slightly thickened, about 2 minutes. Remove from the heat and add the remaining 1 tablespoon of the butter,

¼ cup white wine

¼ teaspoon crushed red pepper

¼ cup high-quality chicken broth

ACHIOTE OIL
3 tablespoons extra-virgin olive oil

½ teaspoon annatto seeds

stirring to incorporate. Drain the pasta and add it to the skillet with the lobster sauce. Toss lightly and season with the remaining ¼ teaspoon salt. Top with the remaining 1 tablespoon of the chopped cilantro and serve immediately.

ACHIOTE OIL: In a small skillet over low heat, warm the olive oil and annatto seeds until the seeds begin to release small bubbles and the oil turns a rich orange color, 15 to 20 minutes. Remove from the heat. Strain the oil and reserve the seeds.

"I first learned this dish while working as a sous-chef at a little Italian ristorante called Marcello's in Suffern, New York. For sit-down staff lunches, chef Marcello Russodivito often gave me the opportunity to add my own spin to whatever we had lying around the kitchen. One day I was interested in upgrading his spicy Lobster Fra Diavolo by adding Spanish saffron and the peppery smokiness of fresh culantro. So I tweaked a little pot of his tomato pomodoro, sautéed some shrimp and lobster in butter and achiote oil, deglazed with some leftover white wine I found, and introduced the Jag'ed-up tomato sauce. I tossed in some fresh ribbon noodles and Pecorino Romano cheese, and the rest was history!

"I think the chef may have been less upset with breaking the taboo about adding cheese to seafood than with the fact that I used lobster meat for a staff lunch!"

—Joshua "Jag" Garcia

THE RESULT

At elimination, the Selection Committee said Rory was inconsistent and Amy was less relatable on *Rachael Ray*. Jag was unpredictable. He'd been captivating, but it was so hard to get information out of him. But after Rory was asked to stay, the second finalist was . . . Jag, which meant that Amy was sent home.

what is CULANTRO?

Not to be confused with close relation cilantro, culantro is a leafy herb used in Puerto Rican and other Caribbean cuisines as well as in Southeast Asia. It has a much larger leaf than cilantro but a similar taste, so the two can be interchanged.

The *Next Food Network Star* finale is taped live, a few months after the finalists' second-to-last challenge. In Season Three, during these few months, the Food Network learned that Jag had misrepresented facts about his military service and his culinary training. After talking with Susie and Bob, he resigned from the competition. "I can't in good conscience continue, knowing what you guys demand of a Food Network star. I can't continue knowing that I'm not mature enough yet to meet those requirements," he told the judges. "And I'm sorry."

The Food Network flew Rory back to New York to tell her the news. Jag had withdrawn and she had a new opponent for the finals: Amy.

In the season finale, the Food Network traveled to the hometowns of the finalists. Before *Next Food Network Star*, Vega, Texas, with a population of 936, didn't even *get* Food Network. In Vega, we met Rory's boyfriend, a cowboy who trained horses and took care of cattle while Rory was working to open the Boot Hill Saloon & Grill. Amy's home visit was spent on the beach with her children, Indiana and Scarlett. Her whole big family lived together under one roof, and cameras taped her grilling for them.

Once more, Emeril had the envelope with the result of the popular vote.

The winner: Amy.

SEASON THREE	ELIMINATIONS
EPISODE TWO First Elimination	★ **PATRICK ROLFE:** "I didn't know it was a double elimination until Vivien came up the stairs and said she had also been eliminated. I was very sick that day, had a high fever, and it all was a hazy blur. I spent the next two days after the elimination in bed. Vivien brought me soup. I do remember that."
EPISODE TWO Second Elimination	★ **VIVIEN CUNHA:** "I'm not angry, I'm not sad, I'm just disappointed. I did everything I could. They didn't see fire. Too bad."
EPISODE THREE Third Elimination	★ **NIKKI SHAW:** "My life has drastically changed since appearing on *Next Food Network Star*. Incredible opportunities come my way regularly. I'm currently working with the L.A. Lakers, Kraft Foods, Kaiser Permanente, Anthem Blue Cross, the *Foxxhole* (Jamie Foxx's Sirius XM radio show), and the California Department of Public Health. I'm certainly indebted to the Food Network for believing in me."
EPISODE FOUR Fourth Elimination	★ **COLOMBE JACOBSEN:** Colombe's dry brioche and store-bought chip and dip were her downfall. "Disappointed," Colombe said. "Maybe this isn't the right path for me."
EPISODE FOUR Fifth Elimination	★ **TOMMY GRELLA:** "I'm not sure where this next point in my life takes me, but I can tell you it won't be away from my family again."
EPISODE FIVE Sixth Elimination	★ **MICHAEL SALMON:** Michael exited after the Fort Dix Challenge. "When I allowed myself to be nervous, happy, proud, stressed, whatever the moment called for, being myself came much easier. . . . I said to myself, 'Do the best you can, enjoy *The Next Food Network Star* experience, and simply have fun.' And that's what happened. I had fun, enjoyed a once-in-a-lifetime experience, and did my best."
EPISODE SIX Seventh Elimination	★ **ADRIEN SHARP:** "It was a huge gamble to give up my job, but you only live once. An opportunity like *Next Food Network Star* doesn't come twice, and there was nothing that would stop me from participating! . . . I am now executive chef at a hospital in Hillsdale, Michigan, and I'm starting culinary school. . . . I would always encourage others to follow their dreams. It just doesn't make sense not to. Why live with regret? I'll never live my life that way."
EPISODE SEVEN Eighth Elimination	★ **PAUL MCCULLOUGH:** "*Iron Chef* ended up being my last challenge. Though it was sad to leave, I understood the judges' decision. It was a tough pill to swallow."
EPISODE EIGHT Ninth Elimination	★ **AMY FINLEY:** "Who knows what the future will bring. I still think 'the Gourmet Next Door' is a great idea. We'll see if it pops up again someplace. . . . We just wait and see."
EPISODE EIGHT Withdrawal	★ **JOSHUA "JAG" GARCIA:** "There's always going to be that what-if thing, but I ultimately believe I made the right decision, and we'll see where it takes me in the future."
Runner-up	★ **RORY SCHEPISI:** "Being one of the finalists from my season was huge, but due to the drama that occurred, I felt a lot of opportunities for many people were taken away. After seeing subsequent seasons, and all of the shows that have been given to several of the finalists, it makes you think, 'Why have they not called? Am I not a good enough chef to have my own show?' Then I snap out of it and tell myself, 'Wait, I am a great chef and love what I do! My time will come.' "

WINNER

AMY FINLEY

Amy's series *The Gourmet Next Door* premiered on October 14, 2007.

Amy Finley: A Q&A

Tell me about your book.

How to Eat a Small Country covers the period in my life following *Next Food Network Star* and moving to France.

What is it with you and France?

I've always been enchanted by the idea of France. I went for the first time as a high school student and appreciated none of it, except maybe the view from the top of the Eiffel Tower. In 2000, I'd just been introduced to my now husband, who lived in France at the time, and I went off to France and enrolled in culinary school and fell in love with the food. I learned that French techniques are the backbone of good cooking. With the repertoire of skills, you have access to thousands of different recipes. France was the first place I'd really seen a connection between how people lived and what they ate.

Some Americans find the idea of French food off-putting.

There is the French food that is very fancy and fussy and composed of intricate and layered steps, but what I learned in Paris is that the French are just like us. They don't have time. They want to make the most of what they have. Some of my favorite food comes from country cooking—it's really simple. A handful of techniques plus the imagination of the cook.

So it's not difficult to cook?

Some recipes take twenty to thirty minutes up front in preparation and then three hours, but it's three hours on the back of the stove and it's ready when you're ready. Cooking is not just something that begins and goes on furiously and continuously until you put the food on the table. . . . We too are less mystified by food and getting more involved in preparation. It's not brain surgery. Anyone can cook, they really can.

What's harder—writing about food or cooking it?

Writing about food is harder. Writing is a painful process, and I'm much less judgmental of my cooking than I am of my writing. When you get through the mystery and fear, cooking is easy. The hardest part is organizing your schedule so you're not doing it rushed or stressed, because that makes everything unenjoyable.

Who are your favorite food writers?

Waverley Root, Mark Kurlansky—writers who realize that it's about people.

Shows like this blur the line between private and public life . . .

It becomes a growing realization for finalists. The more time you spend in front of the camera and with the crew, the more real the idea of what this would be like later on becomes. This is a job that is going to be very hard and demand things not just of me but of the other people in my life. It's something you should go into very clear-eyed. It sounds very simple to go on TV and become a celebrity, and then you start to think critically about how that's going to feel and whether or not it's something you would enjoy. You have to ask yourself some really hard questions.

Were you relieved to get eliminated?

There was a mixture of real true regret and relief. It was a relief not to have to make the decision myself.

How did you feel when you were reinstated?

I was elated. I thought, "Maybe this could work." . . . I had gone in with the intention of winning, so it was exciting to go all the way. I felt bad for Jag. And for Rory. There was no way that it was going to feel great to her unless she won. Even though she had a fifty-fifty chance against me, losing to someone who had already lost must have stung.

At what point did you think you could win the competition?

I arrived in New York thinking I was going to win. Everyone probably does. At the first challenge, we presented our dish and our Point of View and they did a critique and I was told my entire Point of View was off-putting and snobby, and "When you talk like that we all hate you . . ."

Oh. That was my whole game plan right there. I have no idea what I'm going to do now. It was probably good to get a smack-down right off the bat because you need humility to keep your ears open. If you're really listening, they're giving you great feedback, and you have to integrate that. Whether or not you like what you're hearing, you have to respect the expertise.

So you adapted.

I had to find a way to do that food without putting the veneer on it. We were lying in our bunks at night, and Rory and I were talking. I think of myself as an average person . . . the girl next door . . . the Gourmet Next Door. Okay! They did like it.

Do you ever forget the camera is there?

You never forget the camera is there. What's worse, you get comfortable with it being there. They set up situations. You're sitting around and the producers say, "Why don't you talk about . . ." Their job is to find things that are interesting. They hold all the cards. But the representation of me was fair.

You're going to keep writing?

Absolutely, about the place cooking has in our lives and how it can be transformative. I'd like to think I'm someone who is helping the Food Network brand by going off and saying some interesting things about food. I think that's what they're looking for. They're not just looking through tapes and saying, "This girl is pretty and this guy has buff arms." They really are looking for people who can make a contribution. You just never know what forum it's going to come out in.

Season FOUR

Ten new finalists gathered in New York to compete for the prize: their own show on Food Network plus a special feature in *Bon Appétit* magazine. For the first time, this edition would yield, in addition to the winner, two other finalists who would go on to earn a series on the Food Network or Cooking Channel. This bonus was emphatically not in the cards as finalists gathered in New York for the first challenge.

"In walks Bobby Flay. And that's when I wet my pants."
—Kevin Roberts

"Alton Brown walks out and I'm giddy like a little schoolgirl."
—Adam Gertler

THE FINALISTS

1. Kelsey Nixon. To Kelsey, a recent culinary school graduate, cooking was not intimidating. She started her own cooking show, *Kelsey's Kitchen,* in college. If *Kelsey's Kitchen* was going to make it to Food Network, Kelsey outlined its mission: "I'm going to teach you to be comfortable in the kitchen with classic tips and techniques with an innovative twist."

2. Kevin Roberts. Kevin was a restaurant owner, radio host, and author of a couple of cookbooks—*Munchies* and *Kissing in the Kitchen.* The second of these informed his mission statement: "Let's bring romance back into the kitchen by eating well, drinking well, loving well, living well."

3. Shane Lyons. At nineteen, Shane was the youngest-ever finalist. When he was sixteen Shane weighed 250 pounds and lost weight by using cooking as his outlet. He graduated from the Culinary Institute of America at age eighteen. His Point of View: "French Technique Without the Fuss." "I take timeless techniques and modern ingredients to make easy, at-home, French-inspired food without the attitude."

4. Jennifer Cochrane. Jennifer described herself as an executive chef and single mom of daughter Lyric, age four. Her Point of View: "Keep It Simple," said Jennifer. "I don't have all day."

5. Cory Kahaney. A stand-up comedian with an advanced culinary degree from France, Cory had been a catering manager for hotels in New York City. To Cory, this was a chance to marry her two loves—comedy and food. She'd find the hip, trendy items and save you the legwork.

6. Jeffrey Vaden. Jeffrey, a caterer, described his loves as soul food and French food, which he'd work to combine. "My food is all about my classical French training combined with soul food. There's going to be a lot of pig."

7. Adam Gertler. Adam, a restaurant server with fifteen years' experience in the business, also did improvisational theater. *Next Food Network Star* looks for a performer and a cook, and Adam was both. "Using a little bit of humor and a little bit of culinary chaos, I make fun, full-flavored comfort foods that you can make at home."

8. Lisa Garza. Lisa owned a fine-dining restaurant with her husband in Dallas. She portrayed herself as a Renaissance woman. "There is a place for style on the Food Network," said Lisa. Her adjusted Point of View: "I'm taking you on a journey through the art of fine dining with 'Beautiful Basics.' "

9. Aaron McCargo, Jr. A hospital catering executive chef, Aaron wanted to let America know that he'd come from nowhere and he'd arrived. "It's like a modeling audition," said Aaron. "The women are gorgeous. The men are handsome. I said, 'I'm lost, I'm in the wrong room for real.' " His Point of View: "Take herbs and spices that are used every day, and with love turn out a great delicious meal."

10. Nipa Bhatt. A marketing manager and self-taught cook, Nipa was born in India and immigrated to the United States at age five. "No one knows how to cook like me," said Nipa. "I want to teach the world that ethnic food is approachable."

First Challenge

The finalists were introduced to Bobby Flay and Alton Brown. When they regained their composure after meeting network stars, they started their first challenge, presenting their Point of View to Alton Brown. Then they split into teams of two for the Main Challenge: to make three dishes for a table of even more stars: Chef Morimoto, Sandra Lee, the Neelys, and Giada De Laurentiis. Lisa and Kevin were hardly on the same page. "I'm thinking degustation," she said. "What?" said Kevin, who called Lisa "the Diva from Dallas." Shane's pork for the "beauty plate" for the judges was undercooked and not fit for human consumption, according to Morimoto.

> "I had been a big fan of *Next Food Network Star* and knew how important it was to come in with a strong Point of View. With that said, it was still challenging to keep my Point of View in focus throughout the entire season. The challenges where I did best were when I was very focused on the Point of View and my recipes supported it."
>
> —Kelsey Nixon

Adam and Jennifer tried to cook meat loaf in nine minutes. To achieve this, they threw the meat onto a flattop and cut off the well-done pieces after it was finished cooking. Adam was afraid of what Morimoto might say. "He stares with eyes that pierce the back of your soul, and I'm about to serve a Frankenstein meat loaf. Dear God, help me."

Shane was upset—he wasn't proud of his food. "A little piece of you goes on that plate, and you're saying, 'Judge me.' " Gesturing to Bobby Flay, he said, "Chef, you know. It's a huge deal." For Cory, it was her shaky presentation of her Salmon with Herbes de Provence Glaze that helped seal her fate, and she was sent home.

what is DEGUSTATION?

In the context Lisa used with Kevin, degustation is a selection of small plates, something like a chef's tasting menu. It can also mean the act of tasting food itself, especially in a series.

GRILLED BEEF with Buckwheat Soba Noodle Salad

Recipe courtesy Cory Kahaney

Yield: 4 servings ▌ Prep Time: 25 minutes ▌ Cook Time: 20 minutes ▌ Inactive Prep Time: 1 hour ▌ Ease of Preparation: intermediate

FOR THE BEEF
1 cup rice vinegar

½ cup soy sauce

¼ cup dark sesame oil

¼ cup sweet chili sauce

2 tablespoons hot chili oil

1 tablespoon freshly squeezed lime juice

2 pounds skirt steak

2 teaspoons finely chopped garlic

½ cup light brown sugar

Kosher salt

Freshly ground black pepper

FOR THE SALAD
8 ounces soba noodles

¼ English cucumber (2 ounces), cut into thick matchsticks, ¼ by 1 inch

1 small daikon radish (½ pound), cut into thick matchsticks, ¼ by 1 inch

3 scallions, white and some green, thinly sliced

2 tablespoons chopped Thai basil leaves

¼ cup chopped cilantro leaves

5 to 6 red-leaf lettuce leaves

1 hard-boiled egg, sliced with an egg slicer, for garnish

1 cup store-bought kimchee (optional)

Black sesame seeds, for garnish

1. **FOR THE BEEF:** In a glass bowl, whisk together the vinegar, soy sauce, sesame oil, chili sauce, hot chili oil, and lime juice. Set aside 1 cup of the marinade for the noodle salad. Put the skirt steak in a glass bowl with the remaining marinade and chill for at least 1 hour.

2. Preheat a stovetop grill pan or outdoor grill over medium-high heat. Right before grilling, take the meat out of the marinade and rub the garlic and the brown sugar on both sides. Season with salt and pepper. Grill the steak for 5 to 6 minutes on each side for medium rare. Remove from the grill and let rest for 5 minutes. Slice thinly across the grain.

3. **FOR THE NOODLE SALAD:** Fill a medium saucepan with water, bring to a boil, and add salt generously.

4. Cook the noodles until just tender, about 3 minutes. Drain and rinse under cold water. Using your hands, toss the noodles with the cucumber, daikon, most of the scallions, the basil, cilantro, and reserved marinade. Chill until you're ready to serve.

5. To serve, arrange the lettuce leaves on a platter. Mound the noodle salad in the center. Arrange the steak slices so that they overlap slightly on the noodles and one side of the platter. Slightly overlap the egg slices on top of the meat. Place the kimchee, if using, on the other side of the noodles. Sprinkle the remaining scallions and sesame seeds on top.

SPOTLIGHT ON

THE RAW AND THE COOKED

At 3 A.M. on the day of the next challenge, Chef Robert Irvine woke up the carriage house guests to get them started. Finalists were divided into teams (Blue: Lisa, Nipa, Shane; Green: Jeffrey, Kelsey, Kevin; Gray: Aaron, Adam, Jennifer). The winning team would be featured in *USA Weekend.* As part of the challenge, teams had to move from one specialty-food store to another, answering questions at each stop. Each correct answer earned the team an ingredient of their choosing. But if they got an answer wrong, they had to perform a penalty task. The Blue Team started the challenge with a bit of a handicap—they had to wait for Nipa to get ready.

STAR TRIVIA

1. To make white flour, what two parts of whole wheat grain are removed?
Jeffrey's answer: The hull and the husk.

2. What does it mean when baking powder is double-acting?
Adam's answer: It rises once when water is added, again with heat.

3. What ingredient helps give pumpernickel bread its dark color?
Nipa's answer: Molasses.

4. How many pounds of milk does it take to make one pound of cheese?
Jennifer's answer: Ten.

5. What is the name of the method in which cheese curds are piled on top of one another, cut up, pressed together, and piled again?
Shane's answer: Cheddar.

6. What is the main dietary requirement of pigs used for Iberico ham?
Adam's answer: Acorns.

7. What seed produces the vegetable dye for orange Cheddar cheese?
Kevin's answer: Annatto.

8. Name these cuts of meat. [Not shown.]
Lisa's answer: Shoulder. . . .

9. What are the four primary cuts of beef?
Kelsey says loin . . . but runs out of steam.

1. Wrong: Bran and germ. 2. Correct. 3. Correct. 4. Correct. 5. Correct. 6. Correct. 7. Correct. 8. Two of four were wrong, including a boneless leg of lamb. 9. Chuck, rib, loin, round.

After they collected their ingredients (including some strange combinations: Green's duck breast, mozzarella, and raisin semolina bread; the Blue Team's lamb, blue cheese, and baguette; Gray's strip steak, ricotta, and brioche), the finalists headed for Whippany, New Jersey, where Chef Irvine met them at a train halt. There the teams found out that they would be cooking brunch for the Selection Committee and thirty others, all while trying to keep their balance on a moving train.

First up was the Gray Team. Adam wanted to put eggs on Jen's rounds of French toast and planned to keep the yolks runny. Aaron advised him to scramble them.

"Trust me," said Adam. There was no agreement.

"We're doing things backward," Aaron said. In the end, Adam got his way—and undercooked his eggs.

To present their brunch, Adam wanted to create a train-robbing skit. "Hell, no. I'm from Camden," said Aaron. "I'm black and I'm not robbing no train." Aaron's presentation was strong and his steak the committee's favorite. But the guests struggled with Adam's eggs.

> "The sunny-side up eggs were a bad idea. That was a tough challenge. I get very stubborn and can't get past an idea sometimes. I'd like to think that if I did it again today, I'd do better. I'd like to think that anyway."
>
> —Adam Gertler

> "From the moment Adam talked about the eggs I knew it wasn't going to work. You have to let someone learn for themselves and I didn't want to be a know-it-all and a big mouth."
>
> —Aaron McCargo, Jr.

☆ **"Those eggs will never leave me. What's more disgusting than undercooked eggs?"**

—Susie Fogelson

The Blue Team had problems with plating. "Being a Food Network star is a high-stress situation," said Nipa. "I don't know if I'm ready for this." Shane was nervous; his salad was overdressed and Nipa's lamb was very spicy. The Green Team's troubles were numerous: Kevin left behind the extra olive oil they needed, so they were short; they made twenty plates of food but needed thirty; and they couldn't agree on anything. "I think the crostini is sexy," Kevin said. But Jeffrey had "no idea what was romantic about a crostini." And to Bobby, Kevin's POV didn't say anything and his crostini was way too sweet.

The carriage house evaluation was the most dramatic yet. The Green Team discussed their plating issue. Chef Irvine said the figs and honey made the crostini too sweet, and Bob said the romance wasn't resonating. On the Blue Team, after critiquing her lamb, Bobby asked Nipa, "Are you enthusiastic about this? Honestly. Really." Nipa's response: "I dunno." Bob tried to light a fire under her by complimenting her on being charismatic and warm, with a unique POV. "But you're not engaged," he continued. Nipa couldn't take it anymore, and she left the room midway through the judging. She didn't want to cry or quit on the spot. She decided she wanted to continue, so she returned and apologized for losing her temper. "I want to introduce Indian food to Food Network viewers, and I want to relate to everybody my immigrant story. . . . I want to stay and win."

"When Nipa walked out she was within inches of being pushed out the door. We had a long combative conversation among the judges as to whether we would let her come back. She came very close to being sent home."

—Bob Tuschman

Chef Irvine said the winners of the *USA Weekend* spread were Lisa and Aaron. For Kevin, it was the end of the road. "Nipa, you're on warning from us," said Bob. "If a star had done that, it would probably be her last show."

"It's weird, all the Food Network shows I watch have one host/chef, yet in their pursuit to find a new one, they team you up with people you would never usually work or cook with.

"I really wanted to make my salmon pitas on the show—they are very tasty! The flavors work perfectly together, so I hope you enjoy."

—Kevin Roberts

SALMON PITAS
with Olive Tapenade and Wild Field Greens

Recipe courtesy Kevin Roberts

Yield: 2 servings ∎ Prep Time: 10 minutes ∎ Cook Time: 10 minutes ∎ Ease of Preparation: easy

2 (4-ounce) salmon fillets

Kosher salt

Freshly ground black pepper

Vegetable oil, for grilling

2 medium pitas

1 small (8-ounce) jar olive tapenade

2 cups wild field greens, rinsed and dried

1 avocado, diced

2 tablespoons balsamic vinaigrette

1. Preheat a grill to medium-high. Sprinkle the fillets with salt and pepper. Once heated, brush the grill with an oil-soaked rag. Grill the fillets, turning once, until they reach the desired doneness, about 8 minutes for medium. If you're stuck indoors, you can bake or pan-roast them.

2. Cut the pitas in half and warm them gently on the grill or stovetop. Spread the tapenade on both inner halves of all the pitas. Mix the field greens, avocado, and vinaigrette in a large bowl. Season with salt and pepper. Halve the fillets. Place one piece of the salmon in each pita, then stuff the pitas with the greens mixture.

Robert Irvine: A Q&A

The train challenge was one of the hardest *Star* challenges ever . . .

You couldn't swing a cat in the galley and they had three people in a team in there. That was a very interesting meal. And everyone was changing what they did. They all wanted to do their own thing but there has to be a consensus and there always has to be a leader.

Whenever you are doing an event you have to plan for what equipment you have and K.I.S.S. Let the flavor of the food come out. If you're going to do a sauce make sure it's a great sauce. Make sure the meat is cooked the way it is supposed to be cooked. They were trying to impart so many flavors and they didn't have to.

Aaron did a good job . . .

Yes, the one guy who did stand out was Aaron. His presentation was awesome. He could sell sand in a desert. You have to make the guests feel great and you sell them something and it's all about the delivery. He had the delivery down. He nailed it. I've worked with him on a couple of things and he hasn't changed since I first met him. And that's why he has been successful.

What about Adam's eggs?

If you were in a body-building competition in the seventies, yes, eat raw eggs. Not made on a train by a guy in a cooking competition.

These challenges are all about the timing?

You take your time to plan. I have a plan of action and a timeline for everything. If it's a banquet for 1000 people, at seven o'clock, the first course goes out. At eight, we clear. Everyone has to be on the same page. Things go wrong and things change but at least you have a rough guideline.

Most people, if you're doing a dinner party at home, you have that feeling too. If people are coming at six you want to be done by four so you can clean up and get ready. In a competition, it's so intense and there are so many things happening that you forget the timing and the consequences can be very different.

Are some finalists intimidated by you?

When they first meet me and they haven't seen the shows, I've had people say, "Wow what a jerk!" But when they spend some time with me and watch the shows and get the premise, they understand it. People ask, "Why are you so intense, why are you so angry?" I'm not angry. I have a time line of things to do and if I don't get them done, there are those consequences. In *Restaurant: Impossible* they can be very bad.

I'm tough and intense but I never want to see somebody fail. There are two sides to me. I was in the Royal Navy. We're like that, you know.

Martha!

☆ **"It's not a mirage, everybody; it is Martha Stewart."**

—Bobby Flay

For the next challenge, finalists had to put themselves into a jar—they would be creating a packaged food product and handing out samples to food store buyers plus one very special guest. Adam wanted to make a smoking rub and smoke some chicken, but he couldn't find any wood chips. Using a trick he saw on *Good Eats,* he used corncobs.

> "Smoking with corncobs is something I know people do, but I had never done it before. When we shopped for the challenge, I looked for hickory chips, but it was winter when we taped and there were none available. So I had to adapt. I think it made for some good drama."
>
> **—Adam Gertler**

Nipa's Sweet and Spicy Peanut Seasoning was a simple mix of cayenne and sugar; Kelsey made All-in-One Sauce for Sloppy Joes to impress the buyers; Jeffrey, a Seasoned Salt for Fried Catfish, and Shane, Cherri-Gac Steak and Meat Sauce.

After the buyers tried the products, the special guest arrived. In walked Martha Stewart.

Lisa: Everyone knows I'm about to explode.

Martha: Why?

Lisa: Because I love you!

Something Fishy

Chef Tyler Florence, host of *Tyler's Ultimate,* came to work with the finalists for the fourth episode's first challenge, teaching skills and information in sixty-second technique videos. Unfortunately, Shane and Aaron forgot Tyler's main focus—"Cook and talk at the same time." They both ran out of time. Nipa was having her own set of difficulties because she had "no idea" how to clean a squid. "You've got to figure it out," Tyler told her. "You've got to come across as an authority."

Jennifer apologized for not being able to shuck an oyster. "If I can't do an oyster, I can't do anything." Most of the finalists felt defeated, except for Kelsey. Tyler liked Kelsey's energy as she Frenched lamb chops, and she was also the best communicator of the bunch.

"I have always been someone who thrives under pressure and almost gets an adrenaline rush when that red light comes on. Being in front of the camera does get easier and more comfortable with experience. The camera and I have become good friends."

—Kelsey Nixon

In the Main Challenge, Iron Chef Michael Symon, with Michael LaDuke of the seven-hundred restaurant chain Red Lobster, told finalists that they would have to prepare a fish dish showcasing freshness and culinary expertise.

what is *BEURRE BLANC?*

Kelsey made beurre blanc to accompany her cod. *Beurre blanc* means "white butter," a French sauce for fish made of warmed butter and an acid such as vinegar, white wine, or lemon juice.

To sweeten the pot, the winner would be featured on the menu at Red Lobster. The catch: They would have to make a seafood second dish, using an "uncommon" ingredient—something sweet like marshmallow, caramel, white chocolate, or that multicolored fruity breakfast cereal . . .

> "The competition is about testing mettle. I know that some of the scenarios are ridiculous, but you might be put in a situation on your own show where you have to be fast on your feet. It might not be making mahimahi with fruit cereal, it might be that you think you have three minutes for a segment and it turns out you have thirty seconds and you've got to think. That kind of stress is very real.
>
> "We're asking, 'How clever are you?' If you can hide the crazy ingredient in the sauce. What kind of person are you? They are coming into our family, and it's a marathon. You can be awesome the first three episodes and then fall off a cliff. It's a very hard job."
> —Susie Fogelson

Finalists prepped their dishes in the Food Network kitchens. Kelsey coated her Tilapia in Macadamia Nuts and made a White Chocolate Beurre Blanc to serve over Coconut Rice. Jennifer prepped "Beer-Battered and Coconut Cereal–Crusted Mahimahi. Nipa, working with trout and grape jelly, cut a tiny piece from her fresh fish and threw the rest away.

The finalists climbed aboard the U.S. Coast Guard cutter *Escanaba* to serve their final creations to thirty Coast Guard men and women. Kelsey was up first and presented her Tilapia Fish Cake with Chipotle Mayonnaise and her other tilapia dish with the chocolate. Susie liked her personality; the chefs liked the sauce.

Adam staged a pratfall into the mess deck for his presentation. No one laughed.

"I so wish he hadn't done that," said Bob. To add insult to injury, Adam's fish was over-cooked. "It was a train wreck," said Chef Symon.

It didn't get better with the other finalists. Nipa, while presenting her Tandoori Trout and her Trout Marinated in Grape Jelly with Cilantro and Mint, did a Bollywood dance that raised some eyebrows. Aaron's cod was dry; Jennifer's cereal crust tasted too sweet. Lisa, who always cooked in her heels, took a hard fall in the kitchen and ended up covered in her sauce. Although she was worried about her Pucci shoes and three-hundred-dollar shirt, all she truly cared about was her food.

Michael Symon: A Q&A

Was this challenge a decent test of a chef's ability?

I am a chef who does television in that order so for me it's interesting to see how quickly someone adjusts to something that isn't natural. It shows you what kind of person they are and how they are going to do on TV. You will do live appearances and you have to be quick on your feet because things happen.

You were upset that Nipa threw away her fish . . .

I have been a chef for twenty-five years and have spent a lot of time on farms and with the product and I know we're killing something to eat it. You need to respect that. You see how hard farmers and fishermen work to get us this great product. Forget television—as a chef and someone who loves food it was a slap in the face.

Kelsey did a good job in that challenge.

I thought it then and I think it now, there were a lot of talented people on that run and Kelsey was my favorite then and she's still my favorite. Everyone thought she was a little bit young. She had the personality and she had the cooking chops and I think she is very good at what she does now.

When Lisa presented her arctic char dishes, she mentioned that her brother, who was serving in Iraq, would be proud of her. "It was the most charming I've ever seen her," said Bob. In evaluation, Chef Symon told Nipa that her discarding of the trout offended him as a chef. Shane made Dover Sole with Orange Liqueur Sauce and also with Parsnip Roasted Garlic Puree with Marshmallow Cream and Panko-Crusted Sole and Michael Symon liked both dishes very much. "Thank you, chef," said Shane, "that means the world." Aaron's food was disappointing, and he hadn't shared who he was in his presentation. When he was safe from elimination, Aaron said that his son had run away from home right before the show started. He wanted his son to come home to the next Food Network star. Kelsey was the winner of the Red Lobster challenge, and for her off-the-wall white-chocolate dish rather than the more conventional offering. It was good-bye to Nipa.

> "The challenge I was most proud of and could have walked away at the end of feeling great was cooking Dover sole and marshmallow in a galley of a ship. Chef Michael Symon gave my food the highest marks of the challenge and after that I could have left feeling at ease."
>
> —Shane Lyons

DRY-RUBBED SHRIMP
with French-Cut Green Beans and Steamed Basmati Rice
(Jhinga Masaledar)

Recipe courtesy Nipa Bhatt

Yield: 4 servings ▌ Prep Time: 20 minutes ▌ Cook Time: 35 minutes ▌ Ease of Preparation: intermediate

FOR THE SHRIMP

1 teaspoon chat masala

Kosher salt

1 pound (16/20 count) shrimp, peeled and deveined, tails removed

2 tablespoons canola oil

¼ cup chopped fresh cilantro leaves, for garnish

FOR THE GREEN BEANS

¼ cup canola oil

1 teaspoon mustard seeds

½ teaspoon dhanna jeeru powder

¼ teaspoon turmeric

½ teaspoon chili powder

2 (9-ounce) packages frozen French-cut green beans, thawed and drained

1 teaspoon salt

STEAMED BASMATI RICE

1 cup basmati rice

2 cups water

Pinch of salt

1. **FOR THE SHRIMP:** Rub the shrimp with the chat masala and salt, and set aside for 5 minutes. Over high heat, heat the oil in a large skillet until it shimmers. Add the shrimp and stir-fry until they turn pink and start to curl, 2 to 3 minutes. Transfer to a serving platter and garnish with the cilantro.

2. **FOR THE BEANS:** In a medium skillet, heat the oil and mustard seeds over high heat. When the seeds start to pop, add the dhanna jeeru powder, turmeric, and chili powder and cook for 30 seconds, then add the green beans and salt and toss to coat. Lower the heat to medium, cover, and simmer for about 7 minutes. Serve with the shrimp and Steamed Basmati Rice.

STEAMED BASMATI RICE: Rinse the rice two or three times. In a small pot, add the rice, water, and salt. Bring the water to a boil over high heat and cook, uncovered, until most of the water has evaporated, about 6 minutes. Turn off the heat, cover the pot, and let the rice steam for 10 minutes. Fluff with a fork.

Yield: 3 cups cooked rice ▌ Cook Time: 20 minutes

Bon Appétit

In the first challenge of the next episode the remaining finalists—Aaron, Adam, Shane, Jennifer, Lisa, and Kelsey—lined up, each behind a basket. In the Food Network kitchen, chef Cat Cora instructed them to create a dish from the ingredients in the basket and describe it on camera. But once they'd finished, she switched things up a bit. Now they would have to describe a dish made by one of the other finalists. "If you're going to be on camera, you gotta be able to talk about anything," Cat explained.

"She is striking and she wields a powerful knife," said Shane of Cat. "That's a hell of a combination."

> "Cat Cora was one of my favorite judges. She had such a welcoming, natural chemistry with all of us."
>
> —Shane Lyons

Shane talked about "aromas of saffron" and the "Mediterranean, sea-inspired" elements of Kelsey's Pan-Seared Cod with Saffron Polenta. Cat liked his energy and his description. She reminded Adam to tell viewers his POV and to anticipate the wrap-up—but he took a huge bite of food with ten seconds to go.

Aaron wanted to describe his own dish. Jen mistook udon for linguini. "You don't really know your food," Cat told her.

The winner was Shane, whose victory gave him a leg up in the Main Challenge.

> "That salmon dish is all about technique. Pan roasting a piece of fish or meat, caramelizing onions, and of course the sautéed greens are all very basic cooking methods that can be applied well beyond those ingredients. I run specials of bowls of fresh greens from my restaurant's garden during the summer (anything from spinach to collards to Swiss chard), sautéed with caramelized onions, mushroom dashi broth, Amarillo chili paste, and shiro miso paste, finished with fresh basil, cilantro, and lime."
>
> —Shane Lyons

PAN-ROASTED SALMON
with Caramelized Cipollini Onions, Sautéed Greens, and Fines Herbes Truffle Butter

Recipe courtesy Shane Lyons

Yield: 6 servings ▮ Prep Time: 25 minutes ▮ Cook Time: 25 minutes ▮ Ease of Preparation: intermediate

FOR THE TRUFFLE BUTTER
¼ pound unsalted butter, at room temperature

2 tablespoons chopped fresh fines herbes mix (parsley, chives, chervil, tarragon)

1 to 2 teaspoons white truffle oil

Kosher salt

Freshly cracked black pepper

FOR THE ONIONS AND GREENS
18 medium-size cipollini onions

2 tablespoons unsalted butter

5 cups (8 ounces) prewashed baby spinach

3 cups (8 ounces) prewashed arugula

Kosher salt

Freshly ground black pepper

2 tablespoons canola oil

6 (5-ounce) skinless salmon fillets, patted dry

1. **FOR THE TRUFFLE BUTTER:** In a small bowl, combine the butter, herbs, and truffle oil and mix well. Season with salt and pepper.

2. **FOR THE ONIONS AND GREENS:** In a large saucepan, bring 2 quarts of water to a boil. Trim the onions, drop them into the water, and boil for 2 minutes. Drain the onions and plunge them into a large bowl of ice water. Once the onions are cool, peel and dry them.

3. Heat a large sauté pan over medium-high heat and add the butter. Once the butter is melted, add the onions and sauté until tender and golden brown, 3 to 4 minutes per side. Add the spinach and arugula with a large pinch of salt and pepper. Cook until wilted. Adjust the seasoning.

4. **FOR THE SALMON:** While the onions are cooking, prepare the salmon. In a large sauté pan, heat the canola oil over high heat. Making sure there is no excess moisture on the fillets, salt and pepper them liberally on both sides. When the oil begins to smoke, lay the fillets in the pan, making sure they are not touching one another—cook in batches if needed. Cook 4 to 5 minutes per side, for medium.

5. To serve, place a spoonful of the onions and greens in the center of each plate. Top with a salmon fillet and a dollop of the truffle butter.

Reinventing the Classics

In addition to her *Iron Chef* duties for Food Network, Cat Cora, also the *Bon Appétit* Executive Chef, introduced the Main Challenge: The three teams of two had to reinvent a classic dish for the modern home cook, in forty-five minutes. The winners and their dish would be featured in the magazine. Because Shane had won the previous challenge, he chose the dishes for each team: Beef Wellington for himself and Kelsey, Coq au Vin for Aaron and Adam, and Turducken for Lisa and Jennifer.

These are dishes that take hours or days to make, and Lisa and Aaron weren't happy: "This is impossible," said Lisa.

Aaron agreed. "I'm not a French-food dude," he said.

When presentation time came, Adam and Aaron's plating was less than perfect. Chef Cora asked them if they had intentionally plated their pasta over the edge of the bowl. What's more, the dish didn't reflect the original.

Lisa and Jen's dish was missing components at presentation time because Jen accidentally smashed a bottle of apple juice on the stove. With glass everywhere, everything on the stove had to go in the trash.

Shane and Kelsey presented their No Nightmare Beef Wellington and were declared the winners.

> "You don't often see Beef Wellington on menus these days. If you have the urge, I'd make sure you're at a well-respected eatery with cooks who can execute it properly, otherwise you might find yourself gnawing on burnt puff pastry, underseasoned pâté, and raw beef tenderloin."
>
> —Shane Lyons

It was time for elimination. Bobby said that Adam was on "very, very, very thin ice" because his food was not up to par. The judges all agreed that Adam was having issues getting comfortable with the camera and gave credit to Lisa for not being a perfectionist.

It was Jennifer who was going home; she did not describe the dish well in the first challenge, and in the Main Challenge she had missed a side dish.

what is TURDUCKEN?

The turducken is a boned chicken stuffed in a boned duck stuffed in a boned turkey. Although we've been stuffing animals into other animals for centuries, the origins of this dish are obscure. It's now thought of as a Cajun, or at least a southern, specialty.

CHICKEN PARMESAN with Vodka Sauce

Recipe courtesy Jennifer Cochrane

Yield: 4 servings ▐ Prep Time: 30 minutes ▐ Cook Time: 30 minutes ▐ Ease of Preparation: easy

FOR THE SAUCE

4 tablespoons unsalted butter

3 tablespoons extra-virgin olive oil

½ red onion, diced (¾ cup)

3 garlic cloves, minced

½ cup vodka

1 (28-ounce) can whole peeled Italian tomatoes, with juice, crushed with hands

1 cup heavy cream

10 large fresh basil leaves, torn

½ teaspoon kosher salt

¼ teaspoon freshly ground black pepper

FOR THE CHICKEN

¾ cup all-purpose flour, for dredging

2 eggs

½ cup panko

½ cup seasoned Italian bread crumbs

4 (6- to 8-ounce) skinless and boneless chicken breasts, split, pounded flat, ¼ to ½ inch thick

¼ teaspoon kosher salt

⅛ teaspoon freshly ground black pepper

⅓ cup canola oil, for frying

8 ounces thinly sliced fresh mozzarella

1 pound pappardelle, cooked

Grated Parmesan cheese, for garnish

1. Preheat the oven to 400°F.

2. **FOR THE SAUCE:** In a medium saucepan, heat the butter and oil over medium heat until the foaming has subsided. Add the onion and garlic and cook, stirring frequently, until tender, about 5 minutes. Pull the pan away from the stove and add the vodka. Return the pan to the heat and continue cooking until the vodka is reduced by half, about 2 minutes. Add the tomatoes, cream, and basil. Cook over medium heat, stirring occasionally, until slightly thickened, 15 to 20 minutes. Season with the salt and pepper.

3. **FOR THE CHICKEN:** Place the flour in a shallow dish. Whisk the eggs in a separate shallow dish. Mix together the panko and bread crumbs in another shallow dish. Season the chicken with the salt and pepper. Dip the chicken first in the flour, then in the eggs, then in the crumbs.

4. In a large sauté pan, heat half of the oil over medium-high heat. Fry the chicken, in batches, until golden brown and just cooked through, 2 to 3 minutes on each side, adding the remaining oil as needed. Place the chicken in a 13 by 9 by 2-inch baking dish, then top evenly with the sliced mozzarella. Bake until the cheese is melted, about 5 minutes. Toss the pasta with three-quarters of the sauce and place on a plate. Top with the chicken, and pour the remaining sauce over the chicken and pasta. Sprinkle with the Parmesan.

Cat Cora: A Q&A

Are you surprised how well the finalists have done on the Iron Chef challenges?

Being under that kind of pressure, being that tired, some have been fantastic. It's amazing what they can do when they are exhausted and been put through the ringer and they have the time crunch and they know we're going to be judging them. If you can get through that and do well, then you have great potential for the Food Network.

What would you have chosen in the reinvention challenge?

I'd do the Beef Wellington. You don't have to cook it that long and it uses puff pastry, which they didn't have to make. You can make that easily in 45 minutes. I would never have chosen Coq au Vin or a Turducken, which I have only made one time. It's hard to cook it well, almost impossible in the time. Even to do the turkey in 45 minutes is tough. The only way to do a Coq au Vin would be if I had a pressure cooker.

Do you enjoy the mentoring process?

I love teaching and mentoring young chefs. A lot of young chefs come to my dinners and I get to touch their lives a little bit. It's something that Julia Child did with me when I was first starting out many years ago and I have paid it forward since then. If someone comes to ask advice, anyone should take the time and help out even if it's for five minutes.

You've got four kids—does that affect how you cook professionally?

Having kids helps so you think on your feet and be more patient and helps you cook from the hip and on the fly. You just have to get dinner on the table at a certain time.

What do finalists need to succeed?

They have to have a finesse about cooking. They have to be good at it innately. You can learn proper seasoning and techniques but to be a Food Network star you just have to have *it*.

Do you ever get the jitters on camera?

If I'm doing something brand new. The first time I went on *Oprah* was a big deal. I cooked for the president last year and that was a big deal too and I got nervous then. Being on camera, not really. I've been doing it however many years.

Short-Order Cooks

For their first live demo, the final five had to make an innovative and delicious meal and demo it on *Rachael Ray* assisted by a personal sous-chef—a Brownie. Finalists met with their helpers: Aaron with Mikayla; Kelsey with Dimitra; Lisa with Hailey; Adam with Shynashia; Shane with Francesca.

Shane was nervous about it. "Working with kids is not fun. . . . An eight-year-old is not going to win or lose this competition for me."

But Adam was in a comfort zone. "Some people might think that Lisa and Aaron have an advantage because they have children," he said. "But I have an advantage because I still am a child." He prepared a barbecued chicken sandwich he made at the restaurant he opened with his brother. (When it closed, Adam went from being a business owner to waiting tables.)

At the studio, Rachael reminded finalists to tell a story and to remember to include the kid. "We have a whole organization called Yum-o, and that's what it's about—getting kids to eat a little bit healthier."

Aaron started out his demo with his back to the audience, then he relaxed and got into cooking his pizza with Mikayla.

> "Watching Shane with the kid, I laughed like I have never laughed before. I'm looking at Shane and he's asking, 'Do you like chocolate?' 'No.' 'Do you like milk?' 'No.' He said, 'What should I ask her?' and I'm like. 'Smile!' It was hilarious. I had the advantage because I have kids and love being around kids and Shane's a kid himself."
> —Aaron McCargo, Jr.

CASSOULET

Recipe courtesy Lisa Garza

Yield: 6 to 8 servings ▮ Prep Time: 30 minutes ▮ Cook Time: 2 hours ▮ Ease of Preparation: intermediate

¾ cup olive oil, divided

10 garlic cloves, minced

1 medium-size white onion, diced

2 carrots, diced

4 stalks celery, diced

1 herb bouquet: 4 stems rosemary, 8 stems fresh oregano, 10 stems fresh thyme

1 bay leaf

2 (15.5-ounce) cans cannellini, undrained, or 3 cups cooked white beans

2 quarts chicken stock

6 links spicy Italian chicken sausage

½ cup Spinach Pesto (recipe follows)

Crostini, for serving

SPINACH PESTO

4 ounces spinach leaves

2 garlic cloves, smashed and minced

¼ cup toasted pine nuts

6 tablespoons grated Parmesan cheese

¾ cup extra-virgin olive oil

½ teaspoon kosher salt

Freshly ground white pepper

1. Heat ½ cup of the olive oil in a medium-size stockpot. Add the garlic, onion, carrots, and celery and cook, stirring frequently, until lightly browned around the edges. Add the herb bouquet, bay leaf, cannellini, and stock, and bring to a boil. Reduce the heat and simmer, uncovered, for 1½ to 1¾ hours, until thickened.

2. Heat the remaining ¼ cup of the olive oil in a large skillet over high heat. Add the sausages in a single layer and reduce the heat to medium-high. Cook until the sausages are browned on one side, 3 to 5 minutes. Turn and repeat on the opposite side. Remove the sausages from the heat and cut into ¼-inch slices. Add the sausages to the thickened cassoulet and cook for 10 more minutes.

3. Ladle the cassoulet into bowls and top with the pesto. Serve with crostini.

SPINACH PESTO: Combine the spinach, garlic, pine nuts, and cheese in a food processor and pulse to combine. Add the olive oil, salt, and pepper, and purée until smooth.

▮ Yield: 1 to 2 cups

"In my opinion, Lisa is the biggest star that got away. I think she would have been a breakout talent."
—Bobby Flay

Adam's Mac and Cheese included Parmesan, Cheddar, Fontina, and processed American cheese. To kick it up, he added some lobster, while Lisa added goat cheese and poblano peppers. When Dayna interviewed him, Adam kept cooking and didn't even look at her, while Lisa engaged and answered the questions.

Paula Deen: In upscale restaurants I've had lobster macaroni and cheese before and I didn't like it. But that is delicious.

Adam: Really, Paula Deen?

Paula: I might borrow that panko crust.

Adam: We'll talk.

Paula: We ain't going to talk, I'm just going to take it.

As for Lisa's Mac and Cheese, Paula said, "I have to be honest. I do not like it at all. Not at all. In fact I hate it." But Lisa's Cassoulet was, in Bob's opinion, "a masterful dish." Paula said the flavors were wonderful. Bobby chimed in: "Honestly, this could be the best Cassoulet I've ever had."

Adam's was not successful.

"As much as I love Bobby, it was blowing away Bob Tuschman that made me feel like a success. He said it was better than the Cassoulet he had experienced in France."

—Lisa Garza

"I am a tough critic for Macaroni and Cheese. Down South we make the best and we don't muck it up with a lot of different ingredients. As far as I'm concerned, ours ain't broke so I don't try to fix it."

—Paula Deen

Vegas Throwdown Round Two

Next up: Aaron's Stuffed Pork Chops versus Kelsey's Chicken Parmesan.

Aaron decided to stack his pork high, Vegas-style, while Kelsey went petite and dainty, counterintuitively referencing Vegas's reputation for fine dining rather than all-out excess.

Aaron had some time to talk to Dayna, but until Lisa gave him a meaningful look with about eighteen minutes to go, he'd forgotten to cook the Chicken Parmesan.

> "I was always a 'stuff the chop'-type guy, but with this recipe it all happened on the spot. It really surprised me but also confirmed that with pressure . . . and the pig . . . you can get a prize, which was that recipe. I definitely change up the stuffing in the chop by using broccoli rabe and provolone, crispy pancetta, butternut squash, and dried cherries. There are so many ways for me to funk this recipe out."
>
> —Aaron McCargo, Jr.

Paula thought Kelsey's Chicken Parmesan was small enough to be an appetizer, while Aaron's piled-high version was heartier. Kelsey had told Dayna that her pork was overdone and it was overpowered by the scale of Aaron's dish. Paula declared that the sweet and the heat in Aaron's dish was delicious.

PAN-ROASTED FILET
with Fried Shallots

Recipe courtesy Kelsey Nixon

Yield: 4 servings ▮ Prep Time: 15 minutes ▮ Cook Time: 30 minutes ▮ Ease of Preparation: intermediate

1 cup olive oil

1⅓ cups thinly sliced shallots, separated into rings, plus 1 large shallot (¼ cup), minced

½ teaspoon plus a pinch of kosher salt

¼ teaspoon plus a pinch of freshly ground black pepper

4 (8-ounce) filet mignon steaks

2 tablespoons extra-virgin olive oil

2 tablespoons balsamic vinegar

½ cup beef stock

2 tablespoons unsalted butter, cubed

1. Preheat the oven to 425°F.

2. Heat the oil in a heavy 1-quart saucepan over moderate heat until it's hot but not smoking. Fry the sliced shallots in two batches over medium-high heat, stirring occasionally. Cook until golden brown, about 3 minutes. Using a slotted spoon, transfer to paper towels to drain. Season with a pinch each of the salt and pepper. They will crisp as they cool.

3. Heat a large, heavy ovenproof skillet over medium-high heat. Sprinkle the meat generously on both sides with the remaining ½ teaspoon salt and ¼ teaspoon pepper. Add the extra-virgin olive oil to the pan and heat until glossy. Place the steaks in the skillet and sear until browned, about 3 minutes. Turn the steaks and transfer the pan to the oven. Cook until done, 10 to 15 minutes for medium rare.

4. Transfer the steaks to a plate and loosely cover them with foil. Let them rest while you prepare the sauce.

5. Heat the skillet over medium-high heat, and sauté the minced shallots for 2 minutes, stirring frequently. Add the vinegar and scrape the pan with a wooden spoon to loosen the browned bits. When the vinegar is almost completely evaporated, pour in the stock and cook until reduced to a glaze, about 4 minutes. Turn off the heat and add the butter, stirring until melted. Spoon the sauce over the steaks and top with the fried shallots.

> "When I was first married, my husband was convinced that steak at home was never as good as steak at a great restaurant. We've always lived in apartments without access to a grill, and he was convinced that apartment living was not suitable for cooking a steak. I was determined to prove him wrong. With the right cut of meat, a well-seasoned cast-iron skillet, and simple ingredients, I knocked his socks off.
>
> "Needless to say, we have steak at home at least a couple of times a month. This recipe has seen many variations. When you stick to the essential technique of preparing it, the possibilities are endless. Most recently I served this steak with blue-cheese butter and grilled grapes. A little out there, but oh so delicious!"
>
> —Kelsey Nixon

Leaving Las Vegas

In evaluation, Adam and Aaron lost credit for performance—Adam was ungracious with Dayna; Aaron wasn't able to talk and cook. Lisa's Cassoulet was so good, but she didn't bring out her big guns with the Mac and Cheese. Kelsey's attempt at the Vegas twist had failed. Sure, she mentioned her culinary school background, but did she have the life experience yet? Of Adam and Kelsey, it was Kelsey who had to leave.

> "I was talking to Kelsey recently, and she said, 'You know, Bob, you were right. I really wasn't ready for TV. I didn't know it at the time, but I really did have more living to do and needed more experience.' Every now and again it's nice to be told you're right by somebody whose dreams you crushed. But now she has her show and her life has caught up to her dreams."
>
> —Bob Tuschman

> "Getting an opportunity to share my approach in the kitchen on a national level was always the dream. I stayed very focused on my goal, and it became part of who I was. Each job I took was taken with the mind-set that it would prepare me to share with people what I love about cooking. This dedication made a difference."
>
> —Kelsey Nixon

> "Kelsey's show [*Kelsey's Essentials* on Cooking Channel] is terrific and it does really well. She's resonating with the viewer. Kelsey is a professional, completely prepared. She knows where she's going, she's not flighty. If you ask her to do something she does it 120 percent and that's what I love about her."
>
> —Bobby Flay

Showtime

The final three—Aaron, Adam, and Lisa—were met by Bobby Flay and Guy Fieri, who arrived at the Venetian by gondola. For their next challenge, Guy asked finalists to deliver a thirty-second promo, on location. At Charlie Palmer's Aureole at Mandalay Bay, Lisa had to rappel as a "Wine Angel" up and down the restaurant's vertiginous wine tower. Lisa couldn't do it to her satisfaction and it was extremely frustrating.

> "Anytime you put the camera in front of somebody and say, 'Do this, do that, say this, say that,' it can rattle anybody's cage. Lisa hung in there—she had great energy and she didn't quit on it. There is a lot of pressure on these folks."
>
> —Guy Fieri

On the casino floor at Planet Hollywood, Aaron eventually nailed his walk-and-talk. At Bally's, with the Jubilee showgirls, Adam didn't get a perfect take. For the Main Challenge, "the Ultimate Vegas Buffet" at the Wynn, the three were asked to create an over-the-top monster buffet for the Wynn's chefs and a collection of Vegas entertainers. They had six hours and one thousand dollars. At the Tryst nightclub, they met their sous-chefs, their past competition. Lisa chose Kelsey, Adam picked Shane, and Aaron teamed up with Jen.

To smoke his meat for his pork chops, wings, and portobello mushrooms, Adam bought some hickory and built a smoker out of woks. "If I gotta go down, I gotta go down smoking." Aaron included three pasta dishes to go with his Sirloin Bruschetta and Crab Cakes. Lisa had mislaid half her fish at the market, so her Monkfish Piccata was short, and she also burned her pork chops.

> "We've smoked some interesting things—bologna, salt. Maybe apples are the most interesting. The craziest smoked dish I've eaten is smoked sea urchin. Actually not that bad. Creamy, briny, and delightfully smoky. I just love smoked foods. Since *The Next Food Network Star* I've had the chance to eat great food all over the country. I still get more excited about great smoked barbecue than almost anything."
>
> —Adam Gertler

The guests were chefs from the Wynn, pirates, gondoliers, showgirls, the cast of Spamalot, Tony and Tina, Joan Rivers, Cher, and a six-foot-four Diana Ross. Lisa revealed a new layer: She sang her presentation—and she could really sing.

☆ "I knew I had to do something to set myself apart. I'm an old pageant girl, so I made up the song in the shower that morning and just went for it."

—Lisa Garza

Aaron would rather have paid someone to do his presentation, and he was a little goofy. Adam introduced his "Vegas Smoketacular."

The evaluation was to decide which two chefs would go back to New York. Aaron's table was a little thin, but the crab cakes worked. Lisa's food was incredibly elegant, but some of her pork was overcooked. Adam's presentation was boring, but he took a risk with the smoker and it paid off: His food was good. "You settled all questions this week about whether you can cook or not," said Bob.

ROOT BEER AND BACON BAKED BEANS

Recipe courtesy Adam Gertler

Yield: 6 to 8 servings ∎ Prep Time: 10 minutes ∎ Cook Time: 2 hours ∎ Ease of Preparation: easy

½ pound applewood-smoked bacon, diced

1 cup diced white onion

1 (1-inch) cinnamon stick

½ cup tomato paste

1 (12-ounce) bottle microbrew root beer (recommended: Virgil's)

½ teaspoon minced canned chipotle peppers in adobo

2 tablespoons molasses

2 tablespoons dark brown sugar

1 tablespoon apple cider vinegar

1½ teaspoons Worcestershire sauce

½ teaspoon kosher salt

½ teaspoon freshly ground black pepper

1 tablespoon Creole mustard (recommended: Zatarain's)

4 cups cooked, drained pinto beans (canned is perfectly acceptable)

1. Preheat the oven to 350°F.

2. In a heavy 4-quart saucepan or Dutch oven, sauté the bacon over medium heat until it just starts to brown, 10 to 12 minutes. Add the diced onion and cinnamon stick and cook until the onion is translucent, about 5 minutes. Add the tomato paste and slowly whisk in the root beer to combine—you are essentially creating root beer ketchup. Add the chipotles, molasses, brown sugar, vinegar, Worcestershire sauce, salt, pepper, mustard, and beans and bring to a simmer. Cover the saucepan and transfer to the oven. Bake until the beans are a uniform color, about 1 hour. Remove the cinnamon stick and serve.

"These baked beans came out of a happy accident. I was trying to come up with a recipe for beans in my mother's kitchen and was getting frustrated that I couldn't come up with a unique way for them to pop. In my frustration and half jokingly, I grabbed a can of root beer out of the fridge and dumped it into the pan. To my shock, it worked. I had never heard of root beer being used like that before, and I was very proud of the discovery."

—Adam Gertler

Surprise Twist

The committee debated the talents of the three. Who could be a star? As Guy said, perhaps a composite—have Adam open the show, have Aaron prepare the menu, and have Lisa cook it. "I don't know who to kick off," said Bob. It was the committee's hardest decision so far.

Bob: Now we are going to do something that we have never, ever done before.

Susie: Aaron, Adam, Lisa. We're going to bring all three of you back to New York.

"We'd only planned on bringing two back. I never like to have an episode where nobody gets eliminated. Each of the three of them were so different in their culinary skills, their Point of View, and their performance and what they could offer. We literally could not make a decision, and rather than spend the rest of our lives in Vegas locked in a room, we decided to bring all three back and let them battle it out for real."

—Bob Tuschman

FINALE

The final three finalists took viewers back to their homes. Lisa wore so many different hats—mother, wife, designer of aprons, restaurant owner, and apprentice to executive-chef husband Gilbert for the previous sixteen years. She wanted to prove she could stand on her own two feet.

On the site of his former restaurant, the Smoke Joint, Adam said he had a lot to prove. He didn't mind serving food as long as it was his food. It had been a struggle for Aaron too. He wanted to say to young people, "You know what, guys, if I can make it, you can make it. It's about self-esteem. . . . You got to believe in yourself."

> "Aaron was genuine to me. I loved the fact that he stepped onto the stage to do this."
> —Bobby Flay

The Final Challenge: Create a pilot presentation of their show on Rachael Ray's set under the direction of executive producer Gordon Elliott. His question: What do you bring that is unique?

Lisa pitched three multi-themed shows, of which Gordon liked *Beautiful Basics.* Gordon suggested *Big Daddy's Kitchen* for Aaron, and Adam pitched *I'm Always Hungry in Philadelphia,* including a live web chat to give a twist to classic American dishes. As Lisa demo'ed her Black Cod, Gordon told her to connect more with the viewer. Adam chatted online as he prepared his Smoked Dancing Beer Can Chicken and felt amazing, while Aaron wasn't happy with any of his takes. But Gordon said he did a great job.

The pilots were shown to a live audience. Gordon said he believed that each of the finalists could execute a very successful show. Bob was impressed by Lisa's confidence

and culinary knowledge; Bobby said she was unpredictable in a good way. Bob said Adam was a joy to watch, and Susie said he nailed it. "This was the Aaron we love," said Bob. "You were funny, generous, big, and bold."

Deliberating, Bob said that they had the right three people: They were all incredibly likable and very intriguing, but who had that extra drive and dedication to start work tomorrow? The winner's show would air in just one week's time. Bobby announced the winner, and the next Food Network star was Aaron McCargo, Jr.

"Aaron embodies everything you want a Food Network star to be: somebody who would never have had a chance to get on TV otherwise but who actually has the warmth, the humor, the skill, the passion, the interpersonal connections he makes with viewers. He had it all and he was really just waiting for a chance for it to come together. And he is an amazing cook."

—Bob Tuschman

SEASON FOUR	ELIMINATIONS
EPISODE ONE "Star Quality" First Elimination	★ **CORY KAHANEY:** "The committee said I can't mix the comedic personality with the cooking personality. I don't feel that I have to be funny all the time."
EPISODE TWO "Food Network on the Go" Second Elimination	★ **KEVIN ROBERTS:** "I'm still in shock walking up the stairs. I didn't think it was my time yet. . . . Obviously I'm super-bummed. But I guarantee you haven't seen the last of Kevin Roberts."
EPISODE THREE "You . . . in a Jar" Third Elimination	★ **JEFFREY VADEN:** "This experience has been awesome. . . . You're going to get knocked down . . . but that's why we get up. Sometimes we get up bigger and stronger."
EPISODE FOUR "Being an Expert" Fourth Elimination	★ **NIPA BHATT:** "I'm not so sure whether or not I wanted to win this. I think that whatever happens always happens for the best in life—I really believe that."
EPISODE FIVE "Enticing and Easy with *Bon Appétit*" Fifth Elimination	★ **JENNIFER COCHRANE:** "I gave up a lot to be here, but life is like a big book and I'm going to start a new chapter. I'm still going to continue to be a wonderful mother and a great chef."
EPISODE SIX "Into the Studio" Sixth Elimination	★ **SHANE LYONS:** "Age has never been a deterrent for my success. I just turned twenty-three years old and am the Executive Chef at a very busy small plates restaurant in Colorado. I was very proud that I did as well as I did. Did I make mistakes during the competition? You know it. Did I have some successes? Absolutely. My mind-set is to acknowledge and own my failures and successes and not focus too much energy on one side or the other, understanding and accepting that success and failure are both important for a balanced life."
EPISODE SEVEN "Vegas Throwdown" Seventh Elimination	★ **KELSEY NIXON:** "I have a lot of work ahead of me, and I can't wait to get back. This is so just the beginning for me. How lucky am I to have had such a big experience like this at the beginning of my career? I know more than ever that I have to be cooking on television." Kelsey's show *Kelsey's Essentials* premiered on Cooking Channel on November 6, 2010.
EPISODE EIGHT "Ultimate Vegas" No Elimination	★ **LISA GARZA:** "This has been one of the most incredible experiences of my life. . . . You stay with all these people and you bond with them and they become your family. It's been awesome."
EPISODE NINE "Finale" Runners-up	★ **ADAM GERTLER:** "I learned so much about my weaknesses as well as my strengths. To have come this far really just confirmed that this is the life I want." Adam's show *Will Work for Food* premiered on Food Network on January 19, 2009.

AARON MCCARGO, JR.

Aaron's show *Big Daddy's House* premiered on Food Network on August 3, 2008.

Were you always the Big Daddy?

I've always been someone's Big Daddy, Big Willy, or Big Poppa, but I've never been known to so many people as the real Big Daddy! It rocks!

What made you apply to the show?

My wife was watching TV and she saw the commercial for *Food Network Star* and she thought it was a great fit for me. She got the application and filled it out, my brother-in-law was excited about me entering and he taped a demo video and sent it in. A few months later we got the call to come to New York.

Had you ever watched the show?

Everyone else had watched it but I was lost about what was going on. I didn't know about the evaluation process. The first night we had evaluation and they said, "Someone's going home," and I was like, "What do you mean?" Shane and Lisa and the other guys told me what was going on. I was just this guy from Camden going in there asking, "Hey, what do I have to do next?"

Maybe that took the pressure off you?

Many of the other guys were nervous and really wanted their TV show and I was just doing the best I could.

Did you watch your own season?

It was hard to watch myself on TV when they aired the episodes. Never in a million years would I have imagined myself in a cooking show competing with people I never met before. I was more weight-conscious than anything else. I looked about five hundred pounds. I still laugh about that final moment when I jumped in the air when they called my name. I didn't know what to do. Kissing Bobby Flay was not going to be my number one move.

You said at one point "I am not a camera person" but by the Finale you certainly were. How did you come to master that aspect of the job?

I'd never been in front of a camera and never understood the madness of looking directly into the lens and knowing that millions of people are seeing you from inside out. I will always thank Shane for taking the time once, at three o'clock in the morning, in the bathroom at the house, to tell me not to be scared of the camera. I said, "Shane, it's looking at me, man!" He said focus on something that makes you happy. He said, "Dude, you're going to win."

He was eliminated and I was in Vegas shooting the promo and Bobby said, "Walk like you have confidence and look at the camera like you own it," and I took that approach, and sure enough now looking in a camera is like looking in a mirror to me. I love looking into the lens.

You took a while to open up and share your stories. How difficult was that for you?

It was very difficult to open up because where I come from and how I was raised, you were always told to keep your guard up and stay out of other people's business. So to be with ten people I'd never seen in my life and to be told to open up and share something about me wasn't the easiest thing for me to do.

I was focused on the food and in evaluations I was hearing people talk about their personal life and I was like, "Are we on the Food Network or are we on *All My Children*? I don't want to be standing next to Erica Kane." That's not how I roll. You don't put your business out on the street. That's how my father and mother raised us. It was tough.

What was the hardest part for you?

The challenges were so far from what I imagined. You don't have a cookbook. You don't have a phone. You don't have a laptop. You just have your skill and you don't know what's coming every day. Bobby or Bob or Susie says, "Your challenge is . . ." and you have two minutes to think about what you're going to create and I'm working with someone I never cooked with before. That was the most stressful part.

At what point did you think "I have a shot at this!"

I always believed I had a shot from the first day I received a call saying that I was one of the ten finalists to come to New York to compete for the *Next Food Network Star.* I believed in God, in myself, and in my food.

Bobby Flay loved your Bacon-Wrapped Potatoes—how gratifying was that?

It's always good knowing that a chef such as Bobby Flay appreciates your creativity and can appreciate the flavors that work together to make something pop. The fact that he also happens to be one of the judges doesn't hurt one bit.

In the show, you had to create a branded product, and now you have a line of signature products out yourself. How cool is that?

It's a great feeling knowing that I have my spice line out. I never thought that I would brand anything on this level. It's a great accomplishment and blessing. I was rocked out of my socks when we had to brand a product as part of the competition and to have Martha Stewart dig what I thought was a hot product . . . Cool Beans!

What about that Apple Cider Vinaigrette?

I am looking forward to putting out a line of vinaigrettes and funky dressings in the near future and hope that they will be as exciting and as creative as my Apple Cider Vinaigrette in the competition.

How much has your life changed since you won?

Not as much as you might think. People notice me a lot more, which is exciting because I just

want to be an encouragement and tell people to just go after their dreams. I travel a little bit more but it's still the same at home. I still have my chores to do.

You were born and raised in Camden. There are some hard times there now.

It's been hard times since I was born. It has a cloud over it. I hope that me winning this competition is something to get other people in Camden to have hope. I think that what we lack in Camden is hope. We have good talent and we have great people but often the crime outweighs the good with people that don't believe in themselves. Hopefully something will change.

I started a foundation called Play to Win and dedicated my first cookbook to my son. He's been getting a lot of help and prayer and I started this foundation to help people like him. It's hopefully going to reach a lot of homes and people and it's all about the kids.

It still shocks me that I came out on top because the day I came into the competition was the day he ran away and so really during the competition and hearing people complain about their situations and I felt all their pain I really did and kept my mouth closed about my situation. My wife was at home with three kids and my son out there in the streets living homeless.

Season FIVE

S eason Five finalists competed for his or her own series, an exclusive feature in *Food Network Magazine,* and a spot at the Food Network New York City Wine and Food Festival.

"After Season Four we realized there were people who were really interesting personalities but they didn't have a high enough level of technique to be in it for the long run. So we raised the culinary bar and started administering harder tests in the Food Network kitchens for the final twenty-five. If they make it in the food world and have cookbooks and products and appearances, they are going to be creating thousands of recipes in their lifetime, so they need to have a deep well of cooking knowledge."

—Bob Tuschman

THE FINALISTS

1. Jen Isham. Jen was a sales manager in a hotel. "I'm the modern housewife: Housewife version 2.0." Jen said that she worked, then came home and cooked dinner for her husband, the most important person in her life.

2. Jamika Pessoa. With a Jamaican dad and a Trinidadian mom, Jamika called herself a true Island girl. Her aim: to bring Caribbean cooking to the network.

3. Katie Cavuto Boyle. Katie had watched the Food Network since she was a kid, and appearing on it had always been a dream for her. She worked as a dietician and personal chef, and her mantra was "Healthy, Healthy, Healthy."

4. Brett August. An executive sous-chef at a hotel restaurant, Brett described himself as full of energy and high-powered. "And when I get out in front of the cameras, it's going to be even more."

5. Michael Proietti. "Food Network needs to pizzazz it up a bit, honey. I bring entertainment and fun and great food." An executive chef at a hotel, Michael was living with his parents. He described his Point of View as "Global A Go-Go: from Bed Stuy to Bangkok, honey, we do it all."

6. Eddie Gilbert. Sous-chef Eddie said, "What would you attempt to do if you knew you could not fail? For me the answer is 'Being the next Food Network star.'" Eddie had stepped off the corporate route for a while. "You can't really keep a tiger in its cage if it doesn't want to be caged," he said.

7. Melissa d'Arabian. A stay-at-home mom, bringing up four girls, age three and under, Melissa described herself as the ultimate home cook—doing "home cooking at its best." Melissa's final Point of View: "Kitchen Survival Guide."

8. Teddy Folkman. Teddy, the executive chef at his own restaurant, said, "No matter what I set forth for myself, I succeed." His style: Take dishes you find in a bar and bring them up to restaurant quality. His Point of View: "Gourmet Bar Food."

9. Debbie Lee. Debbie worked as a restaurant consultant. Her Point of View was southern cuisine kicked up with the spices and flavors of Korea: "Seoul to Soul." "I think I'm going to win this competition by, number one, being myself."

10. Jeffrey Saad. Jeffrey had worked in restaurants from the age of thirteen to thirty-two. He owned a real estate firm and cooked at home, bringing the chile and the spice. His POV evolved into "Cooking Without Borders" and then "Ingredient Smuggler."

First Challenge: Sweet Sixteen

Immediately, it was game on. The Selection Committee reminded the finalists what they were looking for. "We are inviting a new person to be part of our Food Network family," said Susie. "Integrity really matters." Then Bobby Flay set out the challenge: They would split into two teams and cater a party to celebrate the network's sixteenth anniversary. The seventy-five guests would include a battery of stars: Ted Allen, Alton Brown, Anne Burrell, Giada De Laurentiis, Duff Goldman, "Big Daddy" Aaron McCargo, Jr., and Chef Morimoto.

Brett took the lead on the Green Team with Teddy, Jamika, Jen, and Melissa. Debbie said she liked to lead and took on the Red Team: Eddie, Michael, Katie, and Jeffrey.

> **"I think you are always putting yourself at risk when you choose to lead. Especially when it's a cooking competition. I have no regrets and am glad I took the initiative first. It was a lot of fun!"**
>
> —Debbie Lee

Each team had twelve hundred dollars to shop with. At the register, Debbie and Michael were way over budget, so they removed bagloads of items. The ingredients weren't there for Eddie's beignets, so Debbie bought angel food cakes to make a dessert. Back at the kitchen, Jeffrey was missing the achiote, onions, and dried chiles for his Pepper-Grilled Zucchini. He also wondered if the angel food cake was going to cut it with the crowd they were cooking for. When Bobby Flay visited, he asked Jen if she thought her green bean dish was fancy enough. "You'll see," she said.

On the Green Team, Brett organized with a lot of energy. Melissa was getting worried as she made trays of apple tarts. "I'm a home cook. I don't make seventy-five tarts."

At the party held at chef Alex Guarnaschelli's Butter restaurant, the finalists felt the heat of celebrity.

"Cooking for the anniversary was great. I thought it would be my chance to shine! I wasn't nervous at all."

—Brett August

"It was very intimidating but more exciting than anything. Coming face-to-face with these food icons was one of the most memorable moments of my life."

—Teddy Folkman

"It was my thirtieth birthday so, truthfully, my mind was elsewhere. I missed my girlfriend and my friends. I definitely wasn't myself that day."

—Eddie Gilbert

Alex Guarnaschelli asked Brett if he would have liked to serve his Butternut Squash Soup piping hot, and Brett said he would, but "We're working with circumstances in the kitchen a little unique."

"I know," said Alex. "I'm the chef here. Don't talk smack about my kitchen."

Melissa's tart, and her presentation, were favorites. Chef Morimoto said of Jen's beans, "You can buy them round the corner at the grocery." Duff said the mushrooms on Brett's

what is ACHIOTE?

Achiote paste is used in Mexican cooking for flavor and color. It is derived from seeds of the achiote (or annatto) plant, which is a bright red and is used around the world to color cheese, smoked fish, and other foods. It has had hundreds of other uses, from sunscreen to war paint.

tenderloin were "like wet snails. . . . I felt like I was either in jail or in the army."

Debbie, presenting the Red Team, said she wasn't the normal Asian girl. She was raised southern. "My mom did not know how to make kimchee, and I don't speak any Korean." "She has a really great personality," said Giada. But she didn't take ownership of the dessert. When she saw Duff taste it, she said she should have thrown it into the garbage. "The cake was an embarrassment," said Susie. "My daughter could have made that, and she's three."

"Had I known that we wouldn't have been penalized for not serving the dessert, I would have definitely forgone the angel cake debacle! I think it's always better to serve nothing than a bad dish. Unless you have time to remake it!"

—Debbie Lee

In evaluation, Debbie was called out for saying that her team came in under budget at the store (they hadn't, at first) and that everyone had what they needed. Jeffrey said he missed his first-, second-, and third-choice ingredients. "I just want to emphasize," said Bob, "character matters." Debbie admitted she'd made the wrong decision about the cake and also won praise for her crab cake and for her storytelling. Jeffrey described his dish very well and won the challenge.

Jen was the first to leave.

GREEK SHRIMP SALAD

Recipe courtesy Jen Isham

Yield: 4 servings ▮ Prep Time: 25 minutes ▮ Cook Time: 5 minutes ▮ Inactive Prep Time: 20 minutes ▮ Ease of Preparation: easy

16 large shrimp, shelled and deveined (about 12 ounces)

1 small bunch oregano, leaves chopped (¼ cup), divided

2 garlic cloves, chopped

4 tablespoons plus 2 teaspoons olive oil

1 lemon, zested and juiced

¼ teaspoon kosher salt

⅛ teaspoon freshly ground black pepper

1 (8-ounce) bag mixed greens

1 pint grape tomatoes

½ red onion, sliced

½ cup pitted kalamata olives

½ cup crumbled feta cheese (2 ounces)

1. In a medium-size bowl combine the shrimp, half the oregano, the garlic, and 2 teaspoons of the olive oil. Allow the shrimp to marinate, at room temperature, for up to 20 minutes. Remove from the marinade.

2. Heat 2 tablespoons of the olive oil in a sauté pan and add the shrimp and the lemon zest. Season with the salt and pepper. Cook until the shrimp are just opaque, about 3 minutes. Remove from the heat and transfer to a plate.

3. In a large bowl, toss the mixed greens with 2 tablespoons of the lemon juice and the remaining 2 tablespoons of olive oil. Add the shrimp, tomatoes, onion, olives, and the remaining oregano and toss again. Serve on four individual plates, topped with the feta.

Cooking for the *Esquire* Man

In episode two, Bobby Flay and Ryan D'Agostino of *Esquire* challenged the chefs to make a sophisticated dish for the *Esquire* reader, who might be sipping a martini while grilling. "I can sleep at night knowing I'm not the *Esquire* man," said Michael. Finalists received a hunk of meat with a sidekick: pistachios or whiskey, maple syrup or peanut butter. The winner's recipe would be featured in the magazine.

Michael's presentation fell short, but his Coffee-Rubbed Pork Chops combined flavors well. Katie was almost apologetic for the healthiness of her Bran-Crusted Rack of Lamb, and the meat was too rare. Teddy (Rib Eye with Butternut Squash) was pumped up; and Brett's dish (a Blue Cheese Burger with a Pickle) was coming from a place Bob described as "Planet Brett."

Eddie said his New York strip steak was "the perfect blend of fat and flavor for the sophisticated modern man." "Using Brussels sprouts in a hash is a really innovative idea," said Susie, and Ryan agreed—this was the winning dish: "The flavors are hearty, bold. This is something we could include."

"Winning the *Esquire* challenge was a huge thrill. I didn't start off very strongly, so winning a challenge made me know I belonged in the competition. At the finale, Bob Tuschman told me it was his favorite dish of the whole competition, which was awesome to hear!

"The hash was created one night with friends in college. We got back from a night of drinking, and we were all hungry. My friends always made me cook late night food and all we had in the fridge were Brussels sprouts, bacon, onions, mustard, beer, and a few steaks (it was a college fridge!). I went to school in the South and hash is such a staple of the regional cuisine but I wanted to put my own spin on it. Onions, mustard, and bacon are the key to making Brussels sprouts delicious!"
—Eddie Gilbert

GRILLED NEW YORK STRIP STEAK
with Tennessee Drunken Braised Brussels Sprouts and Bacon Hash

Recipe courtesy Eddie Gilbert

Yield: 4 servings ▮ Prep Time: 40 minutes ▮ Cook Time: about 20 minutes ▮ Inactive Prep Time: 10 minutes ▮ Ease of Preparation: intermediate

8 strips bacon, diced

4 tablespoons unsalted butter, divided

2 medium-size shallots, diced

2 leeks, white and light green part only, cut in half lengthwise and thinly sliced into half circles, well cleaned

4 tablespoons thinly sliced scallions, white part only

2 pounds Brussels sprouts, outer peels removed, trimmed and chopped

Kosher salt

Freshly ground black pepper

2 (11-ounce) bottles Jamaican lager, divided, plus more for serving

1 tablespoon whole-grain mustard

2 New York strip steaks (about 16 ounces each)

1. Heat a grill or grill pan to medium. Preheat the oven to 350°F.

2. In a Dutch oven over medium-high heat, cook the bacon until crisp, 4 to 5 minutes. Transfer to a paper-towel-lined plate.

3. Melt 2 tablespoons of the butter and add to the pot, along with the shallots and leeks, and cook until translucent, about 3 minutes. Stir in the scallions and Brussels sprouts. Season with salt and pepper to taste. Pour in about 8 ounces of the lager, so that it covers half the hash mixture. Continue to cook, reducing until almost all the liquid is gone and the sprouts are tender, about 7 minutes. Stir in the mustard and bacon and remove from the heat.

4. Smear about 1 tablespoon of the butter on each steak, then season with salt and pepper. Grill the steaks just to sear the outside, about 3 minutes per side, then place them on a baking sheet or in a pan large enough to fit. Brush with the rest of the lager and bake until they reach the desired doneness. Transfer the steaks to a cutting board and let them rest for about 10 minutes before serving.

5. Divide the hash among 4 plates. Cut each steak in half widthwise, and place one half on top of the hash. Serve with chilled glasses of lager.

Good Housekeeping Holiday

For the Main Challenge, at the *Good Housekeeping* Research Institute kitchen, Giada and *Good Housekeeping* editor-in-chief Rosemary Ellis wanted a holiday celebration dish. Eddie assigned the holidays. Some were easy: Mardi Gras for Debbie; Valentine's Day for himself. On the other hand, Jeffrey was given Groundhog Day.

☆ **"I remember thinking, 'Groundhog Day!? This is going to be interesting.' I can usually identify any holiday or event with a typical food, but Groundhog Day stumped me for sure!"**

—Jeffrey Saad

Melissa, with Mother's Day, made breakfast in bed: Oven Scrambled Eggs and Orange-Scented French Toast. Teddy and Brett offered to help her plate. "She's great for cooking for her kids," said Brett. "But she has no culinary background like we do."

"Melissa's inexperience might eventually lead to her downfall," said Teddy.

Melissa was grateful for the assistance, but Jamika saw the guys giving her a hard time.

"This is just aces," said Bob of Melissa's food. And Rosemary Ellis said approvingly, "The idea fell right out of *Good Housekeeping*."

Jamika took a risk by making two sides for her New Year's Day dish but Bobby said it was "delicious. This is the kind of food I love to eat."

And Rosemary: "I'm southern. I hate collards but this is delicious."

Bob felt like a long-lost family member at Jamika's New Year's Eve table. "To me it was the essence of a Food Network star."

New Year's Day, said Jamika, is a time to be with family. In southern tradition, you eat certain foods to bring you good luck for the new year. "The spicier you make collard greens, that's how spicy your sex life will be. . . . I got a little pepper for you, Bobby." And the gold color of the corn bread symbolizes prosperity.

"The first time I made collard greens was in culinary school. I was experimenting with different flavors, then added the corn bread for a magnificent blend of spicy and sweet. After an overwhelming response from my classmates, I began to perfect it to what it is now. I make collard greens for special family meals and holidays, especially for New Year's, to bring good luck."

—Jamika Pessoa

"I want food with flavor and I don't want someone to get lucky feeding me something good. I want to know that the person who made this knew what they were doing and I can tell right away. It has depth and foundation and tells a story and is well seasoned and delicious. It doesn't happen a lot but it did with Jamika's dish."

—Bobby Flay

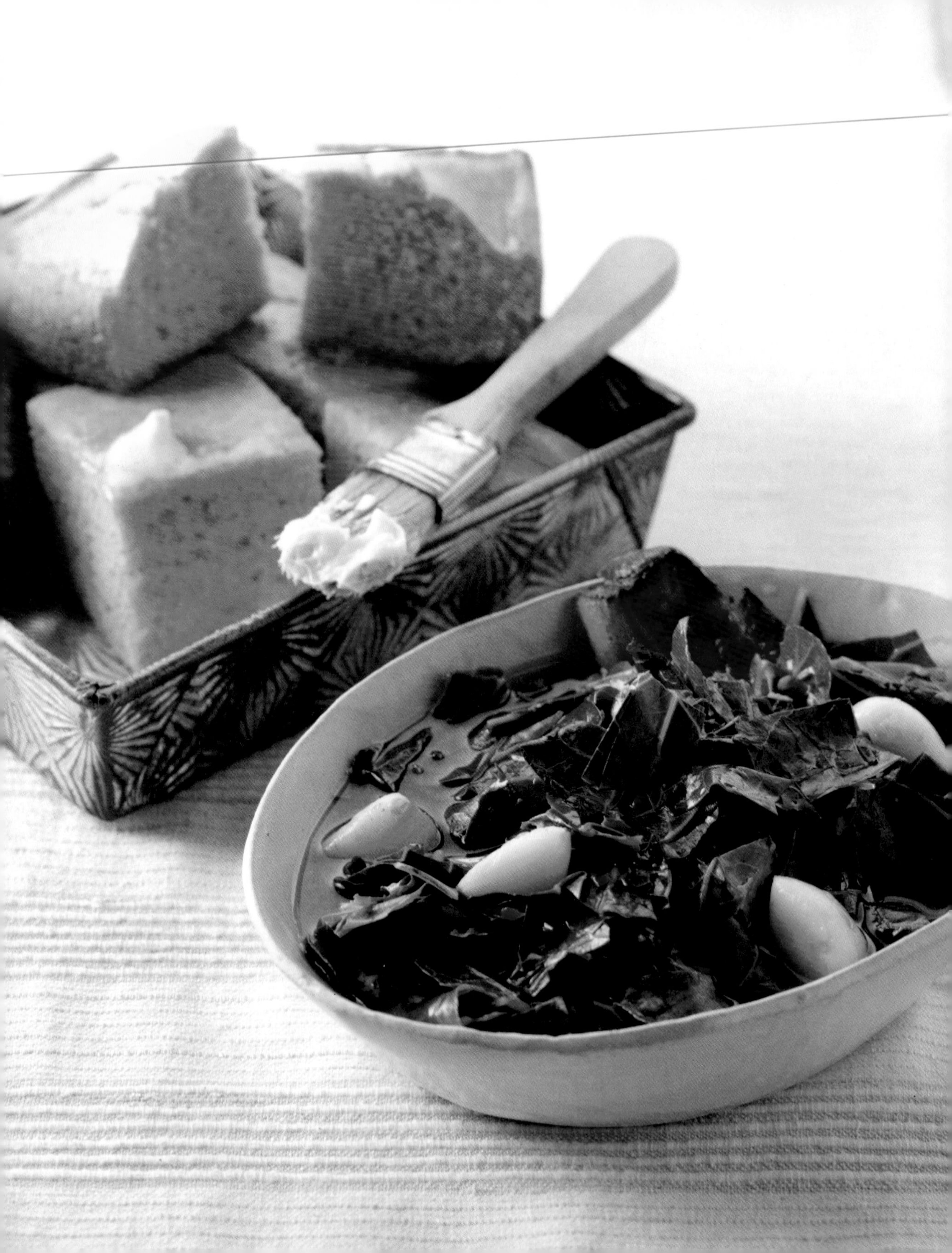

SPICY SOUTHERN COLLARD GREENS
with Sweet Maple Corn Bread

Recipe courtesy Jamika Pessoa

Yield: 6 to 8 servings ▌ Prep Time: 10 minutes ▌ Cook Time: about 1 hour 10 minutes ▌
Ease of Preparation: easy

2 tablespoons olive oil

1- to 2-pound smoked salt pork, thickly sliced, or turkey wings

1 onion, halved

1 quart chicken broth

1 teaspoon crushed red pepper

1 teaspoon salt

2 tablespoons white vinegar

½ teaspoon garlic powder

2 pounds collard greens, washed, stems removed, and roughly chopped

6 garlic cloves, peeled

Sweet Maple Corn Bread (recipe follows)

SWEET MAPLE CORN BREAD
Cooking spray

1 cup cornmeal

1 cup all-purpose flour

4 teaspoons baking powder

4 tablespoons maple syrup

2 teaspoons fine salt

¼ cup vegetable oil

2 eggs

1 cup milk

2 tablespoons butter, softened

Heat the olive oil in a large pot over medium-high heat. Add the pork pieces and brown on both sides, about 7 minutes. Add the onion, cut sides down, and brown, 5 to 6 minutes. Stir in the broth. Season with the vinegar, crushed pepper, salt, and garlic powder. Bring the mixture to a boil, then turn down the heat and let it simmer. Adjust the seasoning, if desired. Add the collard greens and garlic cloves, stir to combine, and cover. Cook until the greens are tender, 35 to 45 minutes. Remove the onion, garlic, and pork. Transfer the greens to a serving bowl. Serve with the corn bread.

SWEET MAPLE CORN BREAD

1. Preheat the oven to 375°F. Coat an 8 by 8-inch baking pan with cooking spray.

2. In a large bowl, whisk together all the ingredients except the butter and pour into the pan. Bake for 18 to 20 minutes, until lightly golden.

3. Remove the corn bread from the oven and brush with the butter. Serve immediately.

Questions of Integrity

Jeffrey and Michael (Halloween) both felt moved to make Mexican food. There was no connection, admitted Jeffrey, but Bob said it was okay to be so charmingly conned. Katie (Earth Day) talked about protein and anti-oxidants rather than food. Brett connected April Fool's Day with his mother ("He's a little wacky, right?" said Rosemary), and Eddie was about to give too much information about his first date with his girlfriend before Bob cut him off.

In evaluation, Giada said that she liked Teddy's food but that he had to make his presentation real. Bob wondered if Brett was sure he wanted to be on TV. Brett said he did. Bob said Melissa made delicious food but there was a lot of "mommy mayhem." In the background, Brett patted Teddy on the back. Giada asked Brett if he wanted to say something. "In the culinary world you do have to be able to produce your dish and put it out," said Brett. Melissa said it was great that Teddy and Brett had helped her plate.

To Brett, he and Teddy had saved Melissa, but Melissa said her plates wouldn't have been any different without help. Not wanting to "throw anyone under the bus," Teddy had nothing to say.

Bob pressed Melissa. "I don't think that sixty seconds of taking a spoon and putting it into a ramekin is part ownership of a dish." Melissa was shocked. "That's questioning my integrity, and that's just a whole different thing."

> "We're looking at character under pressure. It doesn't just make for good TV; character is essential if you are going to be a Food Network star. If you don't have the qualities of humor and kindness and grace under pressure, it's going to trip you up in the long run. You're not going to have a fan base.
>
> "In other shows, whether it's a dish or a dress, only the final product can send finalists home. The judges don't have to be concerned with how they got to make it. In our show, the person is not going to be disposable at the end of the series. It's really important how they got to where they are. If they have lied, cheated, or stolen, their character isn't one that people are going to embrace a year or two on."
>
> —Bob Tuschman

The gap between where Brett was and what Bob needed from him was too wide, and he was sent home. "I don't know if I brought the full Brett August," he said. "I tried."

Jamika's gamble completely paid off, and she won the challenge. She went into *Good Housekeeping* to cook for its "Healthy in a Hurry" feature. "Look out, world," said Jamika.

"Winning that challenge gave me a great boost of confidence. I proved that you must never underestimate the power of simplicity. Although this is a simple dish, it is also a very good dish. And it gave warning to my competitors to watch out for this chick!"
—Jamika Pessoa

CRAB CAKES with Basil Mayonnaise

Recipe courtesy Brett August

Yield: 4 servings, 8 (3½- to 4-ounce) cakes ▮ Cook Time: 20 minutes ▮ Prep Time: 20 minutes ▮ Inactive Prep Time: 30 minutes ▮ Ease of Preparation: easy

FOR THE CRAB CAKES
¼ cup finely diced white onion

1 stalk celery, finely diced

Vegetable oil

1 large egg

2 tablespoons Dijon mustard

1 teaspoon kosher salt

½ teaspoon freshly ground black pepper

1 pound lump crabmeat, picked over for shells

1 cup dry white bread crumbs

1 cup all-purpose flour, for dredging

2 tablespoons unsalted butter

2 teaspoons vegetable oil

FOR THE DRESSING
1 cup mayonnaise

2 tablespoons Dijon mustard

10 fresh basil leaves, thinly sliced

1. **FOR THE CRAB CAKES:** In a medium-size saucepan over medium-low heat, sauté the onion and celery with 1 tablespoon of the vegetable oil until translucent. Remove the pan from the heat and allow the mixture to cool. Lightly beat the egg in a medium-size bowl, then add the onion mixture, mustard, salt, and pepper. Fold in the crabmeat and bread crumbs. Form the mixture into 2- to 3-inch cakes, approximately ½ inch thick. Dredge the cakes in flour, and refrigerate for 30 minutes—this will allow them to hold their shape.

2. In a large sauté pan over medium high-heat, melt 1 tablespoon of the butter with 1 teaspoon of the oil until you achieve a nutty aroma. Sear the crab cakes in two batches for about 6 minutes total, flipping once halfway through, until they are golden brown.

3. **FOR THE DRESSING:** In a small bowl, mix the mayonnaise, mustard, and basil. Serve with the crab cakes.

"Love the crab cakes! I make a lot of different types; the crab cake is very versatile."
—Brett August

Tyler's Tips

For their next challenge, the finalists took a trip to Stew Leonard's supermarket, where Tyler Florence gave them sixty dollars each for a budget dinner party for twelve. And they had to stop shopping to give a thirty-second tip on camera about how to stretch their food dollar.

> "Melissa, the tips fall out of her mouth. She can't even help it because she is that woman, teaching you how to cook on a budget. She could be in a five million–dollar kitchen, she still just knows how to cut the budget. Like Sandra Lee, she is bringing you her life."
>
> —Susie Fogelson

Teddy was over-the-top, "cartoonish" even. Eddie seemed insincere. Michael said he typically spent a thousand dollars on a dinner party and couldn't give a coherent tip. Jamika suggested reusing a marinade, which is a big no-no from a food-safety perspective. Eddie's idea of adding fresh herbs to salads was not really money-saving at all. Tyler announced Jeffrey won the challenge.

MONEY-SAVING TIPS

1. Add bread crumbs to ground meat to stretch it. *(Teddy)*

2. Make crêpes with Nutella for dessert; have the leftovers for breakfast. *(Jeffrey)*

3. Put the white part of a green onion or scallion in water and the green will regenerate. *(Melissa)*

4. Squash and zucchini are very economical vegetables. *(Debbie)*

5. Cut back on meat and use more grains and beans. *(Katie)*

Dinner at Ina's

As the finalists drove to East Hampton, Debbie figured correctly that they were going to see Ina Garten. "It's just so warm and welcoming and intimidating at the same time," said Teddy as they arrived.

The task: Make a dinner party using what they bought earlier for sixty dollars. The twist: They were in teams of two. Each teammate cooked one course, and they collaborated on a third. Challenge winner Jeffrey picked Michael; the other pairings were random. "I don't know if I can trust him," said Debbie of teammate Teddy, referencing the previous elimination. When Eddie was teamed with Melissa, he said, he was not excited. "I'm afraid I'm going to have to pick up some slack."

Teddy and Debbie planned their menu: Vegetable Linguini with Asian Marinara was Debbie's, and they'd collaborate on a Pan-Asian Meat Loaf, leaving Teddy with dessert—Strawberry Shortcake Trifle. "I don't know why I take on the dessert," said Teddy.

Eddie planned to make Sweet Onion, Watermelon, and Feta Salad; Melissa, Lemon Thyme Chicken; and together, a Bananas Foster Nutella Quesadilla. Eddie was disconcerted by having a teammate, and Melissa complained that he talked to her like she was five.

Teddy described Debbie's sauce as fantastic, and there was chemistry there. But Teddy hadn't focused on dessert and when he did, he had about five minutes to make it. He didn't grill the shortcake and left out the pine nuts.

Melissa talked to the diners about her

"Clean the Pantry Week," when to save money she wouldn't grocery shop for a week. "Melissa glows in the dark," said Ina. "She has a presence and a light about her that I think is stunning." But Clarkson Potter publicist Kate Tyler said Melissa made her crazy with her "overeagerness." The chicken lacked flavor, and Ina's friend Barbara Liberman called Eddie's salad inedible. Debbie's calm presentation seemed to help Teddy. Their collaborative meat loaf was a hit. "This may be my second-favorite meat loaf after Ina's," said Bob.

Michael and Jeffrey presented their Roasted Tomato and Red Chili Soup; Michael, his Pesto-Rubbed Grilled Chicken on Crostini; and Jeffrey his crêpes. Jeffrey was confident and connected with the guests: "The great thing about chiles, you can use them to flavor lots of food. It doesn't have to be just salsa or Mexican." Bob said it looked like elegant dinner-party food.

> "The show was such a turning point in my life. Since then, I capture almost everything I cook into my recipe software so that I can remake things and share the recipes. Before the show I probably almost never made the same thing twice. It has been ten years since I was the chef/owner of my Sweet Heat restaurants, so I did not have a fixed repertoire. Although I am capturing the recipes for my cookbook, I still tend to make variations on most of them based on what's in the kitchen, my mood, and the people I'm cooking for."
>
> —Jeffrey Saad

Katie and Jamika compromised on an "international" style. Ina loved Jamika's Salmon with Seaweed and Pepper Slaw, but Katie again overplayed the healthy aspects of her food (Whole Wheat Pasta with Chicken Sausage and Broccolini).

In evaluation, Jamika and Katie's international viewpoint was deemed a cop-out.

Bobby thought Jeffrey and Michael's soup needed more chile. Bob asked for more of Jeffrey than his story about making crêpes. Michael's food was delicious, but he seemed lost. "You've got to get your shows rockin', and you have to be happy about it," Bobby said. When he looked at the tape of Eddie cooking with Melissa, he said, Eddie's eye rolling drove him nuts. "A little chivalry in the kitchen goes a long way," he said.

Bob liked Debbie's linguini. Susie said Teddy's dessert was "an abomination . . . just embarrassing." The meat loaf was "awesome," however. Teddy said, "I feel like that was my dish." Debbie said the meat loaf was collaborative, and again Teddy took credit even though at the dinner he'd said the dessert was his.

"This whole thing that's going on here is driving me crazy," said Bobby. "I don't like the spirit of it."

Teddy eventually agreed that he should have taken ownership of the dessert, and Debbie reaffirmed that they'd both worked on the meat loaf. "I'm having a really hard time with your honesty and integrity here," she told Teddy.

The winning team was Jeffrey and Michael. Waiting for the verdict, Teddy apologized for not being a gentleman. "I'm truly sorry," he said. But it was Eddie who was sent home.

what is AN ANAHEIM CHILE?

Jeffrey's red Anaheim chile is a sweet pepper with a good kick (the riper it becomes, the redder and sweeter it gets). For comparison, it is rated 2 or 3 on the Scoville scale (a scientific measure of a pepper's heat), with 100–1,500 units of heat. A jalapeño runs 2,500 and more units; a habañero, 9 for more than 100,000 units of pleasure and pain.

ROASTED TOMATO AND RED CHILE SOUP

Recipe courtesy Jeffrey Saad

Yield: 6 appetizer servings, ½ cup per serving ▌ Prep Time: 25 minutes ▌ Cook Time: 20 minutes ▌ Ease of Preparation: easy

FOR THE SOUP

2 tablespoons olive oil

1 yellow onion, sliced

2 red Anaheim chiles, 1 roasted

1 (16-ounce) can whole San Marzano tomatoes

3 garlic cloves, chopped

¼ cup chopped fresh cilantro leaves

2 teaspoons kosher salt

Juice of 1 lime (about 2 tablespoons)

Quesadilla Croutons (recipe follows)

Cilantro Sour Cream (recipe follows)

QUESADILLA CROUTONS

4 (7-inch) flour tortillas

1 cup shredded Jack/Cheddar cheese mix

1 teaspoon ground cumin

CILANTRO SOUR CREAM

½ cup sour cream

2 tablespoons chopped fresh cilantro leaves

½ teaspoon kosher salt

1 to 2 teaspoons freshly squeezed lime juice

1. In a medium-size pot, heat the oil over medium-high heat and add the onion. Cut 1 fresh chile in half lengthwise and remove the seeds and veins. Chop the chile and add to the onion. Sauté, stirring often, until golden brown, about 7 minutes. Add the tomatoes, garlic, cilantro, and salt and bring to a boil. Reduce the heat and simmer for 10 minutes.

2. Transfer the chile mixture to a blender or use a wand hand blender and purée until smooth.* Return to the pot. Seed and chop the roasted chile and add to the soup along with the lime juice. If the soup is too thick, add water.

3. Ladle the soup into bowls. Lay a Quesadilla Crouton in each bowl and top with a dollop of Cilantro Sour Cream.

* When blending hot liquids, remove the liquid from the heat and allow to cool for at least 5 minutes. Transfer to a blender or food processor; fill it no more than halfway. If using a blender, release one corner of the lid. This prevents the vacuum effect that creates heat explosions. Place a towel over the top of the machine, pulse a few times, then process on high speed until smooth.

QUESADILLA CROUTONS

1. Preheat a grill over medium-high heat.

2. Lay 2 tortillas on a work surface. Divide the cheese between the tortillas. Sprinkle with the cumin. Top each with one of the remaining tortillas. Grill the tortillas

until golden brown on the outside and the cheese starts to melt. Remove to a cutting board. Cut into ½-inch strips, then cut each strip on an angle to create 2 smaller strips.

Yield: 4 croutons ❙ Prep Time: 5 minutes ❙ Cook Time: 2 to 3 minutes ❙ Ease of Preparation: easy

CILANTRO SOUR CREAM: Combine all the ingredients in a bowl and stir.

Yield: about ½ cup ❙ Prep Time: 10 minutes

The Ultimate American Meal

Nothing is more American than a great burger. Bobby offered to put the finalists' best burger—one that most successfully represented an American region—on the menu at Bobby's Burger Palace, which he was opening in Connecticut. Finalists had twenty minutes to cook and thirty seconds to present.

The committee's least favorite burgers were Jamika's, which had sausage on it (they didn't like her overrehearsed presentation either), and Katie's undercooked pink-raw turkey burger. The top two were Melissa's Burlington Burger, inspired by her time at college in Vermont, with turkey chili, Vermont Cheddar, and spinach, and Michael's, but the winner was Michael's. "I want to make out with Bobby I'm so excited," he said.

> "Winning that challenge was so much fun, and I got to represent a New York City 'hood that I happen to love . . . a lot."
>
> —Michael Proietti

Michael chose to represent Mulberry Street, the heart of Little Italy in New York City. The Italian influence was in the mozzarella and the pancetta on each side of the burger. "I like that," Bobby said, and praised the classic ingredients, the tomato and basil. Bob enjoyed the fact that it was served on garlic bread—something he'd never thought of for a burger. And Michael presented with energy and charm, where in previous weeks he'd stumbled.

> "I came up with the Mulberry Street Burger on the spot. I was thinking in my head what I could do, and I looked at the pancetta and thought, 'That can work.' It's the same shape as a burger and it would just sit great on a burger and it'll get über crisp! Who doesn't love pancetta?
>
> "I do make the burger a lot, and I no longer put the mozzarella inside it because you can't get accurate doneness on it . . . so now the mozzarella goes on top. It just works better."
>
> —Michael Proietti

MULBERRY STREET BURGER

Recipe courtesy Michael Proietti

Yield: 4 servings ▌ Prep Time: 30 minutes ▌ Cook Time: 20 minutes ▌ Ease of
Preparation: easy

1½ pounds ground beef

8 slices fresh mozzarella
 cheese

½ teaspoon kosher salt

¼ teaspoon freshly ground black
 pepper

8 slices pancetta (3 ounces total)

1 tablespoon plus 1 teaspoon
 olive oil

¼ cup unsalted butter

1 garlic clove, finely chopped

2 large fresh basil leaves, finely
 chopped

¼ teaspoon crushed red pepper

4 hamburger buns

½ cup baby arugula (about
 ½ ounce)

Basil Ketchup (recipe follows)

8 slices tomato, from 1 small
 vine-ripened tomato
 (4 ounces)

BASIL KETCHUP

¼ bunch fresh basil leaves

½ cup ketchup

2 garlic cloves

½ teaspoon crushed red pepper

2 tablespoons water

recipe continued on next page

1. Preheat the oven to 350°F.

2. Divide the beef into four equal parts, about 6 ounces each. Divide each portion in half and shape into patties about the size of the bun (you should have 8 patties altogether). Place 2 mozzarella slices on one patty, then top with another patty. Pinch the edges of the patties to enclose the cheese, basically stuffing the burger with the mozzarella. Season with the salt and pepper and press a piece of pancetta onto the top and bottom of each burger.

3. Heat the 1 tablespoon olive oil in a medium-size ovenproof skillet over medium heat and brown each burger on both sides. Place the burgers in the oven to finish cooking.

4. Melt the butter in a small saucepan and add the garlic, basil, and crushed red pepper. Split the buns and brush both sides with the butter mixture. Toast under the broiler or in a toaster oven.

5. Toss the arugula and the remaining 1 teaspoon of the olive oil.

6. Spread some of the Basil Ketchup on the bun bottom and add a burger. Top with the tomato slices, arugula salad, and more ketchup. Cover with the bun tops and serve.

BASIL KETCHUP: In a small blender or food processor, mix all of the ingredients. Transfer to a small bowl and refrigerate until ready to use.

SPOTLIGHT ON

THESE INTREPID FINALISTS

Finalists were driven to the USS *Intrepid,* anchored on the Hudson River docks in Manhattan. Following a color guard, in walked Guy Fieri.

Finalists were asked to throw a homecoming party for soldiers returning from the Middle East, making an all-American home-cooked dish using seven ingredient baskets specific to a state. They had ninety minutes to prep and had to tell a story in their presentation. The winning dish would be featured on the cover of *USA Weekend.*

Teddy, with his New York basket, had Long Island duck, cream soda, and apples. He made a DLT—a BLT with duck instead of bacon. Jeffrey got Maine, with lobster, smoked sea salt, and blueberries. "I'm thinking this is impossible," said Jeffrey, when he had a sudden epiphany—potpies, with blueberries and chipotle chiles, which would bring his signature sweet heat. But the ship's tiny burners were a problem, so he had to scramble—and start praying. Presenting, Teddy talked about his grandfather serving in World War

Two, but he *ummed* and *ahhed* and used notes written on his hand.

Susie said that the "presentation bummed me out again." Bobby said Teddy's DLT was a good sandwich.

"Yeah, this is rockin' it," Guy agreed.

> "The DLT was an absolute hit back home. It stayed on the menu for six months [which is long at Granville's, Teddy's gastro-pub in Washington, D.C.], and we still run it as a 'throwback' special on Thursdays. One of my all-time favorites."
>
> —Teddy Folkman

Jeffrey found his own potpies horrifying. His presentation was flat; the pie was worse. Susie: "I think it's disgusting. I would never eat this unless I had to right now."

> "Was there anything I'd do differently at the *Intrepid*? Jump overboard from the get-go. . . . One of the many cool things about the show is that every episode had a life lesson in it. I made the mistake of being determined to stick to my idea of a potpie, which would tie into a great story. By the time I realized that those little electric burners were not going to let that happen, it was too late. I should have cracked those twenty lobsters open and broiled them in a chipotle-blueberry glaze (my assigned ingredients) and then made a salad. I truly thought it was over for me at that moment. I think they may have used my potpie to patch some holes in the ship!"
>
> —Jeffrey Saad

Melissa's New Mexico box had chiles, skirt steak, and mesquite honey. Her family didn't eat chiles, so she had to taste them raw to test the heat. She decided on a tostada with the skirt steak and a mango salsa to play off the honey and the heat. "I'm a little bit nervous about serving these flavor profiles to the king of this flavor profile, Bobby Flay," said Melissa.

In her presentation Melissa said her mom was a lieutenant commander in the Navy who died when Melissa was twenty. A single mom, raising two daughters in Tucson, she was Melissa's inspiration. This was a new side of Melissa, said Susie. For Bob it was "a delicious home-cooked meal." Bobby said, "I think it's delicious. It's nice and crispy, it's well cooked."

"I had never made this recipe before, but I took inspiration from my childhood. My mom used to make a marinated steak for our birthdays when I was younger. And I grew up in Tucson eating tostadas all the time as a kid. So I married the two ideas and the result was the Skirt Steak Tostada."

"Melissa started out talking about being a mother at home and about cooking for her family every night. I kept looking at her, thinking, Does she know what she's talking about? Finally I said, 'Melissa, this is a critical moment for you. I have a question. You talk about all these chicken dishes that you make. Fine, give me ten right now.' And she did. I said to myself, This is a woman people will tune into, people who are like her, who need to get things on the table. I knew she was smart and not afraid and that showed me she was the real deal."

—Bobby Flay

SKIRT STEAK TOSTADAS
with Black Beans and Mango Salsa

Recipe courtesy Melissa d'Arabian

Yield: 4 servings ▮ Prep Time: 25 minutes ▮ Cook Time: about 40 minutes ▮ Inactive Prep Time: 1 hour ▮ Ease of Preparation: intermediate

FOR THE STEAK
½ cup soy sauce

½ cup olive oil

Juice of 3 lemons

½ cup honey

1 cup finely chopped onion

1 habañero chile, seeded and chopped

Kosher salt

Freshly ground black pepper

1 (1¾-pound) piece skirt steak

FOR THE BEANS
1 (15.5-ounce) can black beans, drained

½ cup olive oil

½ cup red wine

1 jalapeño pepper, seeded and chopped

FOR THE TOSTADAS
Vegetable oil, for frying

4 corn tortillas

Mango Salsa (recipe follows)

Sour cream (optional)

Grated cheese of choice (optional)

MANGO SALSA
1 red onion, finely chopped

1 large ripe mango, finely chopped

¼ cup chopped fresh cilantro leaves

1 poblano chile, seeded and minced

¼ cup honey

Juice of 3 limes

Kosher salt

Freshly ground black pepper

1. **FOR THE STEAK:** In a large shallow bowl or baking dish, whisk together the soy sauce, olive oil, lemon juice, honey, onion, habañero, and salt and pepper to taste. Add the steak, cover, and refrigerate for at least 1 hour, preferably several.

2. **FOR THE BEANS:** In a saucepan over medium-low heat, combine all of the ingredients and let simmer for 20 minutes.

3. **FOR THE TOSTADAS:** Pour enough oil into a large pot so that it comes about 3 inches up the sides. Heat to about 350°F. Carefully slide a tortilla into the oil and fry until crisp, 1 to 2 minutes. Remove the tortilla and drain on a paper towel. Repeat with the remaining tortillas.

4. Preheat a grill pan or grill to medium-high. Remove the steak from the bowl and discard the marinade. Grill for about 5 minutes for medium-rare to medium, flipping halfway through. Transfer to a cutting board and let rest for about 5 minutes. Slice the meat into thin pieces on a diagonal.

5. ASSEMBLY: Place the fried tortillas on a large platter or individual plates. Spoon some of the black bean mixture into the middle of the tortillas. Lay the steak slices over the beans and top with the Mango Salsa. Garnish with the sour cream and cheese, if desired.

MANGO SALSA: Combine all of the ingredients and set aside for 10 to 20 minutes for the flavors to marry.

❚ Yield: about 2 cups

Occupational Hazards

With Georgia ingredients, Katie made Cornmeal-Crusted Catfish with Sweet Vidalia Onion Greens. Jamika had Wisconsin—Cheddar cheese, beer, and kielbasa. She wanted to add her ingredients to mashed potatoes, but the potatoes wouldn't boil. Katie talked movingly about her Army Ranger cousin who graduated from West Point and had done multiple tours of duty. Bobby rated Katie in the middle of the road.

Jamika knew that her dish was sloppy and the judges agreed. But they said her presentation was very good. Michael's Hawaii yielded kampachi, macadamia nuts, and pineapple. Assigned to California, Debbie had chicken breasts, zinfandel, and almonds. As they were cooking in the galley, Michael turned and whacked Debbie hard in the face with the corner of his baking sheet.

"The whack happened so fast that I didn't start feeling the pain till a few minutes later. It felt like someone literally took a long nail and screwed it right through my head! Add the not being able to see out of your right eye . . . yeah, it hurt a lot! But all I kept thinking about was the episode in *Iron Chef* when Bobby Flay got injured and kept going. I felt I had to live up to that. As Susie had said, the show must go on."

—Debbie Lee

what is KAMPACHI?

Michael's kampachi was a farmed version of the Hawaiian yellowtail, with a high fat content that makes it an excellent source of essential omega-3 fatty acids.

Under the circumstances, Debbie did a creditable job. Michael talked about getting macadamia nuts at home in the Bronx. Bobby liked the food: "It looks like Hawaii and it totally tastes like Hawaii."

In evaluation, the judges were shocked that Jamika and Jeffrey made the food they did because it fell so far below their standards. Teddy's DLT was delicious to Bobby, but Teddy on camera made him nervous, and Susie wanted to see the normal guy. The winner of the cover of *USA Weekend* was Melissa. "They underestimated me," she said. "There's a lot more to me than Melissa the stay-at-home mom."

Teddy left. "Nobody is grabbing it," said Bobby. "Grab the title."

> "I first made this dish at my first executive chef job in D.C. We had a great brunch crowd before I got there, and I needed something my first week to prove that I had some fun ideas. It was a huge hit but a pain in the ass because I only had a small griddle and didn't anticipate that many people ordering it.
>
> "As far as the pancakes go, we are serving them at the Capitol Lounge, a local watering hole in Southeast D.C. that I'm part of. The sausage made it to a bunch of different mussel concoctions at Granville Moore's, most recently with fennel, leeks, and a Dijon broth that we threw a bunch of savory into."
>
> —Teddy Folkman

KATIE'S FAVORITE USES FOR SWISS CHARD

1. Sautéed with garlic, olive oil, and dried cherries, to balance the bitterness.

2. Chiffonade in a salad.

3. Sautéed for pasta, along with white beans, shallots, and pancetta (topped with roasted shrimp. "Double yum").

BOURBON PANCAKES
with Sausage Patties

Recipe courtesy Teddy Folkman

Yield: 6 cups batter, about 25 pancakes and 10 to 12 sausage patties ▌ Prep Time: 20 minutes ▌ Cook Time: 20 minutes ▌ Inactive Prep Time: 12 hours ▌ Ease of Preparation: intermediate

FOR THE PANCAKES

3 cups all-purpose flour

2 tablespoons baking powder

½ teaspoon baking soda

2 teaspoons fine salt

2 tablespoons sugar

3 cups buttermilk

2 large eggs

8 tablespoons unsalted butter, melted

2 ounces bourbon

Clarified butter

FOR THE SAUSAGE PATTIES

¾ pound ground beef

½ pound ground pork

¼ cup diced pork fat

1 teaspoon cumin seeds, toasted

1 teaspoon coriander seeds, toasted

2 teaspoons fennel seeds, toasted

1 teaspoon ground red pepper

2 garlic cloves, minced

½ small shallot, minced

2 teaspoons kosher salt

Pinch of allspice

1. **FOR THE PANCAKES:** In a large bowl, whisk together the flour, baking powder, baking soda, salt, and sugar. In a medium bowl, combine the buttermilk, eggs, butter, and bourbon. Add the buttermilk mixture to the flour mixture and combine gently with a whisk until smooth. Don't overwork the batter. Let it rest for about 15 minutes.

2. Coat a griddle with the clarified butter and heat to medium-high. Drop the batter by ¼-cupfuls onto the griddle and cook until golden brown on both sides and cooked all the way through, 2 to 3 minutes per side. Serve with sausage patties.

FOR THE SAUSAGE PATTIES: Combine all the ingredients in a large bowl, cover, and refrigerate 8 to 12 hours. Form the meat mixture into 2½-ounce patties and cook the patties on a flattop or grill pan until golden brown on both sides and cooked through.

First Demos

For their midterms, finalists had to perform a cooking demo for Rachael Ray. In honor of her Yum-o organization, they turned a traditional dish into something kid-friendly. The ingredients: Brussels sprouts, squid, and tofu. Jeffrey had never cooked with tofu.

> "*Next Food Network Star* was my first date cooking with tofu. Since then I have had a solid relationship with the curd. Like everything, when used and cooked properly it adds value to a dish. I have been using it in some of my stir-fry dishes as well as soup. I've even marinated it in soy, hoisin, and chiles and grilled it."
>
> —Jeffrey Saad

Katie planned a Calamari Fruit Salad with Quinoa; Jamika cut her tofu small to hide it in a salad. Melissa said that the key is to attach a new ingredient to a texture kids know and give them a piece of the raw vegetable. You never know what they'll like. The experts were kids Kylie, Michael, and Angela . . . and Rachael Ray.

The kids liked almost all the food. The presentations were good, but Jamika forgot to cook and talk at the same time.

In the Main Challenge, finalists had to take kids' food and turn it into adult fare, live on the *Rachael Ray Show*. And they had to do it in pairs. Katie and Debbie were assigned chicken nuggets and mac and cheese; Michael and Melissa, tomato soup and grilled cheese; Jeffrey and Jamika, hot dogs and baked beans. Jeffrey and Jamika made an uneasy team, and neither was happy with the food. Katie decided to bake rather than fry her nuggets for health reasons.

The pairs had a hard time gelling in front of the audience. Melissa took over and talked very fast, while Michael seemed overcome by nerves. "Cook something, man!" Bobby told him. In the last ten seconds Michael started to have fun.

Debbie again said that she was Korean but didn't take her story further. When Katie took over, she didn't look up till the very end. And her chicken was dry. As Jeffrey performed a solo act, Jamika stood like a statue.

"**People talk about, 'Oh, you can make tofu taste like anything,' so for me, I'm like, 'Well, eat that then!'**"

—Jeffrey Saad

Miami Mayhem

For their next challenge, the final five finalists were off to Miami. But before they could board their plane from JFK, Ted Allen intercepted them and asked them to cook a meal for one of the restaurants in Terminal 5. The winner would go on the menu. Jeffrey got the Italian restaurant AeroNuova and made Bruschetta with a Poached Egg for his "Cooking Without Borders" POV. Jeffrey finally told the story of his life: He's Lebanese; his wife is Iranian, she was raised in Italy, and their lives are reflected in food. Bob loved the presentation and Jeffrey won the challenge.

At the Eden Roc hotel in Miami Beach, Ted Allen outlined the Main Challenge: Work as a team cooking for a cocktail party at the Nikki Beach nightclub. Each chef must create at least two hors d'oeuvres and the group would need to come up with a signature cocktail. Challenge winner Jeffrey made the assignments: In addition to their two dishes, Michael would work at the bar, Jeffrey handle the front of the house, and Debbie expedite in the kitchen.

They had two hours to prep, and no one had enough time. Before they left the kitchen area, Jeffrey showed Melissa how to make his dish, and Michael gave Debbie instructions for his Chili Lime Shrimp and his Margarita Salmon Skewer.

Jeffrey and Jamika were able to serve some of their food on the beach, but back at the cooking station, most of the food was labor-intensive: Debbie's Passionfruit Chicken on a Daikon Crisp and Korean Torta; Melissa's Salmon Shooter, Chicken Bite, and Roasted Vegetable Asada on a Tortilla; Jeffrey's Tostada with Crab and Cuban Bites; Jamika's Jerk Chicken Skewers and Shrimp with Pineapple Coleslaw; and Michael's Margarita Salmon Skewer. Melissa was making her dishes and Jeffrey's; Jamika, hers and Michael's, while Debbie did her own.

> **"The beach party was so crazy. Time was not on our side that day, but I still had a blast. That experience taught me two things: No matter what, always keep the party going, and never wear high heels when cooking on the beach."**
>
> **—Jamika Pessoa**

Michael had a great time serving at the bar even if his drink, a Serrano Chile Margarita, lacked bite. Jeffrey found tables of hungry people—every tray was attacked—and the kitchen had to hustle. Bobby Flay went back to see what was up. "Get that food out," he said. Michael came out from behind the bar and quickly served the committee, but the food was forgettable, if he wasn't. When Debbie eventually presented her food, hers were by far the best dishes.

> "No, I don't wish I'd spent less time at the bar. In fact I wish I was still there! I was having way too much fun. I spend a lot of time cooking in the kitchen for my career, so when I got the chance to be in front of people and out of the kitchen, I jumped at the opportunity."
>
> —Michael Proietti

> "It was really stressful. I am not someone who lives with regrets but if I were it would be that challenge. There were things I would have done differently and it made me definitely not want to be a caterer. Catering is much harder than you think."
>
> —Melissa d'Arabian

The committee criticized the service and a lot of the food. Bobby liked Debbie's two dishes the best. Debbie said that only she'd been in the kitchen at all times and she'd tried to get the food out. She thought the leader should make sure the food went out and that she could only do so much. "I was being selfless." Melissa said that she made five dishes; Jamika did four. Bob did the math and said that Debbie basically did two. Meanwhile, larger-than-life Michael was not the crowd favorite, and his salmon had no flavor.

In deliberations, Bob said Michael had a lot of personality, but Michael himself admitted that he couldn't perform in front of the camera. Bobby said he'd neglected his food. Susie said Debbie showed an unattractive side, but Ted said she'd made the best dishes. It was a tough decision, they admitted, and Michael, to his surprise, was sent home.

> "The judges do disagree. When we sent Michael home, I felt that was the wrong decision. I was angry that he was sent home at the time, and when I watched the episode, I was still mad. He was not my decision. I hate being overruled."
>
> —Bob Tuschman

> "Michael I think was the best chef of all, he was so creative and he was a great friend. There was one night when I couldn't sleep and was missing my family. At about two in the morning I went into Michael and Jeffrey's room and the lights were off and said, 'I just need a hug,' and he said, 'Come here,' and gave me the biggest hug. Ten minutes later I was at ease and I went to bed and got to sleep."
>
> —Melissa d'Arabian

"Miami was my favorite episode. That may sound weird considering it's the same episode I went home!" —Michael Proietti

Getting Grilled

In the first challenge of episode seven, Chef Michael Symon told the final four that they would be demo'ing for four minutes live on a local morning show. But the demos were rigged to fail. Debbie's catfish was replaced with chicken and her utensils sabotaged. Still, she sailed through and improvised well, even when she saw that the catfish wasn't catfish. "Flawless," said Bob.

Melissa (or Melinda or Melanie as the host called her) got a little frenetic. Jeffrey dealt with the technical snafus well, but Jamika closed down and struggled with the fake time cues and the camera being shoved in her face. Debbie won the challenge.

CRISPY CATFISH with Edamame Succotash

Recipes courtesy Debbie Lee

Yield: 4 servings ▮ Prep Time: 10 minutes ▮ Cook Time: about 15 minutes ▮ Ease of Preparation: easy

4 catfish fillets (approximately 6 ounces each)

¾ teaspoon kosher salt, divided

¼ teaspoon freshly ground white pepper

1 cup all-purpose flour

2 large eggs

1½ cups panko (Japanese bread crumbs)

1 teaspoon smoked paprika

1 teaspoon garlic powder

Canola or vegetable oil, for frying

Edamame Succotash (recipe follows)

1. Season both sides of the fillets with ½ teaspoon of the salt and the pepper. Set aside.

2. Place the flour in a shallow bowl or pie tin. In a separate shallow bowl or tin, beat the eggs. Combine the panko, paprika, and garlic powder in a third shallow bowl or tin and stir with a fork.

3. Pour enough of the oil into a large deep skillet to go ½ inch high and heat over medium-high heat. Dust each fillet with the flour, then dip into the eggs, then press in the panko mixture. Fry the fillets in the hot oil until golden, crispy, and cooked through, 3 to 4 minutes on each side.

4. Transfer the fish to a plate lined with paper towels and season with the remaining ¼ teaspoon salt. Make a bed of Edamame Succotash on a serving platter, top with the fillets, and serve.

EDAMAME SUCCOTASH

2 tablespoons toasted sesame oil

½ cup red onion, finely diced

1 teaspoon minced garlic

2 strips (1½ ounces) applewood-smoked bacon, finely chopped (⅓ cup)

1 cup frozen edamame (6 ounces), thawed

½ cup fresh corn kernels, from 1 small ear

¼ cup small-diced red bell pepper

½ teaspoon kosher salt

⅛ teaspoon freshly ground white pepper

EDAMAME SUCCOTASH: In a large skillet, heat the oil over medium heat. Sauté the onion and garlic until softened, about 2 minutes. Add the bacon and cook until it has rendered its fat and begins to crisp, about 5 minutes. Add the edamame, corn, and bell pepper and sauté for another 2 to 3 minutes. Season with the salt and pepper. Remove from the heat and serve hot.

Yield: 4 servings (2 cups) ▌ Prep Time: 10 minutes ▌ Cook Time: 12 minutes ▌ Ease of Preparation: easy

"My mom would make catfish once a week. When I got to be in my late twenties, I reinvented that old-school version from my childhood. I just recently made it with a pounded pork cutlet—what we call *tonkatsu*."

—Debbie Lee

Symon Says

At the Eden Roc, Michael Symon stood in front of four outdoor grills to introduce Michael LaDuke of Red Lobster, who again was offering a spot on his restaurant's Fresh Fish menu for the challenge winner. Finalists had to make a dish on the wood-fired grill paired with a crustacean or shellfish. Mini-challenge winner Debbie chose tilapia because she could cook it Korean-style; Melissa, arctic char for a citrus duo with orange and lime. Jamika took shrimp, mahimahi, peppers, and pineapple for a tropical theme. Jeffrey chose chiles, barramundi, scallops, and shrimp.

Time for a twist. On Bobby's instruction, Chef Symon took away all Jeffrey's chiles and gave him Asian sauces—a new border for Jeffrey to cross.

"For me, this was the opposite of my experience on the *Intrepid*. I was able to adapt and it was really rewarding. That was by far my favorite episode. We were pushed to the limit while baking under the ninety-degree sun in front of eight hundred–degree wood-burning grills! Michael Symon was an awesome addition to the episode."

—Jeffrey Saad

Michael then took Jamika's pineapple and gave her two big celery roots. She wasn't happy. He took all Melissa's citrus and give her habaneros. "I have never made fish without citrus," said Melissa. Then he took away Debbie's Asian ingredients and Bobby gave her olives, anchovies, and capers.

"It's hard to say what would have happened if they had sprung that kind of thing on us the first week! I definitely was feeling the loss of

my sesame oil. But it's all about coping and being able to modify at a moment's notice."
—Debbie Lee

Jeffrey used a wasabi broth to cook his fish *à la nage,* but he was worried about the array of strong flavors he used. Melissa grilled a passel of habañeros—did she know how strong they were? Jamika told Bob, "I think I'm just pissed right now." She didn't know what she was making until she had six minutes to go, when she grilled the celery root.

> "Jamika got mad at me. I have made that mistake on *Iron Chef.* A judge has tasted something and I thought it was perfect and they didn't like it and I've got into arguments with them. It tends not to go well for you in the long run."
> —Michael Symon

Debbie presented Tilapia with Fennel, Orange, and Crab Salad with an Anchovy Olive Vinaigrette. Bobby Flay asked, "Where are the capers?"

In the dressing, Debbie said. Then she said that she didn't have them. "My bad. I must have left them out."

The food lacked brininess. Bobby loved the habañero flavor of Melissa's scallops and char. Jeffrey too got good marks for his flavor. Bobby liked Jamika's grilled celery root and her grilled mahimahi, but she got aggravated by the challenge. You have to have fun, Bob said.

In evaluation, Bobby said that Jeffrey cooked with style, finesse, creativity. But what would he do on the network? His POV was "Cooking Without Borders," but he always gravitated to the same ingredients. Bob said his Zen calm could be vanilla and that part of being a star was unpredictability.

"Jeffrey: What was he going to do? This is why I kept worrying about him. Even at the eleventh hour, I was asking, 'What am I going to do with you?' "

—Susie Fogelson

Jamika's food lacked flavor, according to Chef Symon, and she shut down, got flustered and snippy. Bob said Melissa was calm and in control and her food was amazing. But Chef Symon wondered how she would prove that she was an expert. Melissa got fired up, talking about her credibility with moms. Bobby liked seeing her get passionate.

The winner of the Red Lobster Challenge was Jeffrey's Fish à la Nage. The next person sent home was Jamika.

"I was a huge fan of Jamika's. She was an excellent, inventive cook. She is beautiful and charming in person but wasn't able to translate that to the camera consistently. You're not just doing ten episodes of *Star.* We're looking for someone who is going to do hundreds of episodes of a series and appear as a guest in situations where they have no control. Consistency is one of the key points, which is why a single bad performance really can send you home."

—Bob Tuschman

what is *À LA NAGE?*

A *nage* is a vegetable broth (or *court-bouillon*) in which fish or lobster can be poached and is served as part of the finished dish. The lobster or salmon is then *à la nage,* which in French means "swimming."

The Thousand-dollar Dinner

The finalists arrived at Emeril's Miami Beach restaurant where they were greeted by the man himself, Emeril Lagasse. Emeril talked about one of the original food stars, someone whose culinary passion inspired millions, his friend Julia Child. Emeril described the movie *Julie and Julia*, which weaved together Julia's story with that of blogger Julie Powell, who was inspired to cook her way through Julia Child's classic, *Mastering the Art of French Cooking.*

In the Main Challenge, Emeril wanted to see all passion on a plate presented in the spirit of the movie in a three-course dinner for twenty members of the culinary elite. "A very, very tough crowd," he said. They had one thousand dollars each to shop with and would have to demo some portion of their meal live.

After watching the movie, finalists planned their menus: Melissa: Potato Torte with Ratatouille; Herb Chicken with Mushroom Port Sauce and Orzo; Cheese Trio with Salad and Chocolate Orange Pochette. Debbie: Chile-Rubbed Barbecued Shrimp with Corn Salad; Korean Short Ribs (*Kalbechim*) with Crispy Grit Cakes; Asian Pear Eggrolls with Rum and Butterscotch. Jeffrey: Seared Scallops with Green Chile Chutney; Seafood Risotto; Chocolate Mousse with Biscotti. Shopping for all that, Jeffrey spent just $317.14. Am I a savvy shopper, he wondered, or am I screwed?

MELISSA'S RATATOUILLE TIP

Melissa learned to cook ratatouille from her mother-in-law from Nice. The trick: Cook the vegetables in this order: Eggplant, Zucchini, Peppers, Onions, Tomatoes, or "E-Z-Pot."

"Should I have spent more of my thousand dollars? Hell, yeah! Although execution and balance are vitally important in cooking, a few chunks of saffron-laced lobster wouldn't have hurt anything!"

—Jeffrey Saad

In the cavernous dining room, the three read the place cards of the guests: François Payard, Marcus Samuelsson, Rick Bayless, John Besh, Emeril, Bobby Flay, Masaharu Morimoto, Tyler Florence, Anne Burrell, Gina and Patrick Neely, Alex Guarnaschelli—a tough crowd indeed.

"Rick Bayless, John Besh, Marcus Samuelsson, François Payard: This is the very tip-top of the food world. It was fascinating to hear how they reacted."

—Bob Tuschman

Thankfully, the chefs had help: sous-chefs Katie (for Jeffrey); Michael (for Debbie); and Jamika (for Melissa). Jeffrey took a huge risk making risotto—Katie presciently wondered if it was going to sit too long. Melissa's orzo was much too salty, and the torte didn't brown, so she decided to serve the torte with the chicken so it could cook longer and plate the ratatouille with the orzo first.

"I want this job because it matches who I am," Melissa told the guests. Her mom had been a single college student raising two girls. They had a mother-daughter holiday tea every year that they spent months cooking for. That's where she learned how to cook for people and bring them joy. When she was in college, her mom committed suicide and Melissa was left to cook on her own. That's when she became good at getting a meal on the table. She went to business school and had ten successful years working. Her mind was

fed but her soul was undernourished. Julia Child said, "Don't be afraid." "I'm standing in front of you not afraid, because I may fail but I'm failing at the right thing," Melissa said.

Bobby Flay said Melissa seemed completely different—"unbelievably thoughtful and poetic." I'm not a harried housewife, she said. That's not who I am.

Patrick Neely and Rick Bayless liked the ratatouille's textures and flavors. Melissa demo'ed the brick chicken, which Rick loved; François Payard said his was overcooked. The pastry pochette was "bangin,' " said Sunny Anderson, and Marcus Samuelsson concurred.

> "The Potato Torte was one of the judges' favorite things, We had a budget of $1000 and one of their favorite dishes was one that cost me pennies per person. I love that— that's exactly what *Ten Dollar Dinners* is about. No one is saying, 'That's good, for cheap food.' It should be good even when you are serving a $1000 dinner."
> —Melissa d'Arabian

Debbie talked about her folks immigrating sixty years earlier, and all her mom could make was fried chicken, greens, and corn bread. Debbie met her grandmother, learned to make Korean food, and melded the two cuisines together: "Seoul to Soul." Tyler Florence said the shrimp was southwestern. The short ribs were tough, said Payard, but Rick Bayless liked them a lot. Debbie demo'ed her eggroll, and Patrick Neely was captivated. Marcus loved the sauce on the roll but "the dough is raw."

The drama of the challenge lay in Jeffrey's risotto. Jeffrey undercooked his risotto deliberately because he knew it would sit. He talked to the diners about going to Fisherman's Wharf and eating a scallop raw, the first time he got really excited about food. He demo'ed cooking scallops, how they must be dry to get a sear. It was "as flawless as communicating gets," said Tyler Florence.

Then the risotto. "All I see is a sea of unhappy faces," said Jeffrey.

It's like a soup, Payard said. "I think the risotto is the worst risotto I ever have in my life." "This is a disrespect to Italy," said Marcus Samuelsson. Bobby couldn't believe that Jeffrey had spent so little money. The dessert was delicious, said Alex Guarnaschelli, offering a small mercy.

The room was divided on who they liked; it was down to the judges. In evaluation, Melissa's pastry for dessert was the best thing the guests ate all day. But her demo was a little flat. Bob said that there were gems here and there but so much verbiage that she would need heavy editing. Jeffrey's demo was flawless, but the food was hit-and-miss and the risotto failed. Jeffrey had charisma and authority, he said, but "Are you a star?" Bobby saw Debbie as comfortable and confident, but he wanted more flavor. It was incredibly hard to decide, but the result was that Debbie was leaving.

JEFFREY SAAD'S CHILE KITCHEN

"There are never fewer than five or six types of chiles in my kitchen. I have two big jars of dried chiles. One with guajillo and one with ancho. I also have a small bag of chile morita with a spicy, dried raisin–like heat. Also flakes of chiles de árbol by the stove for adding when needed. I keep a bag of fresh jalapeños, serranos, and orange habaneros in the freezer at all times. I grate them on a Microplane to give a fresh chile kick to a sauce or salsa or to drop into a bottle of silver tequila."

FINALE

The two hopefuls left standing and facing each other were Melissa and Jeffrey. Cameras went to each of the finalist's hometowns. At home in Los Angeles, Jeffrey introduced his wife, Nadia, and his kids. Martial arts had helped keep him focused. Up until seven years earlier, he had run restaurants, and now he worked in real estate. Jeffrey talked about his family's love of travel and how they were enriched by other cultures.

"Jeffrey and I connected because we're both family people. We both felt very strongly about how we were receiving support from our spouses and our families and the sacrifices they had made for us to be there."

—Melissa d'Arabian

Melissa was shown at home with her four girls in Keller, Texas. Melissa talked about aspects of her life. After her mom died, she had lived in her sorority house; women had been a huge part of her life. As a volunteer on the city economic development board, she gave back. But she wanted to go to work at the Food Network.

Back in New York, Alton Brown directed the finalists' pilots to be shown to a live audience. He reinterpreted Jeffrey's "Cooking Without Borders" POV as "Ingredient Smuggler"—bringing spices back from other countries and using them in American cuisine. "He's consistent," said Alton. "He's likable; he's going to knock it out of the park." Alton suggested "Kitchen Survival Guide" to Melissa. "She is utterly authentic," he said.

After several takes, Alton calmed Melissa down by telling her to be herself. She nailed the last take. "There's a little movie star tucked away in there," said Alton.

Flexible Four-Step Chicken for Family and Company

For the pilot, Melissa used her own technique: four-step chicken. The ingredients can be interchanged in any step to give you a whole new dish. The steps:

1. Dredge and sauté the chicken.

2. Cook up the herbs and vegetables.

3. Add the liquids.

4. Finish the sauce.

"I've been making some version of four-step chicken my entire adult life! It's really just some sautéed chicken with a pan sauce—easy and inexpensive to make. Plus, you can swap out ingredients depending on your tastes and what your pantry holds."

RUSTIC LEMON ONION CHICKEN

Recipe courtesy Melissa d'Arabian

Yield: 4 to 6 servings ▪ Prep Time: 30 minutes ▪ Cook Time: 30 minutes ▪ Ease of Preparation: easy

3 skinless and boneless chicken breast halves, butterflied, cut all the way through

1 teaspoon dried thyme

Kosher salt

Freshly ground black pepper

4 tablespoons olive oil

¼ cup all-purpose flour

1 medium red onion, thinly sliced

Leaves of 1 small bunch fresh thyme, chopped (about 2 teaspoons)

¼ cup white wine (optional)

1 cup chicken broth

Juice of 2 lemons (about ¼ cup)

1 to 2 tablespoons unsalted butter

Spinach Bed (recipe follows)

SPINACH BED

1 (10-ounce) bag prewashed spinach

1 tablespoon unsalted butter

Juice of ½ lemon

Kosher salt

Freshly ground black pepper

1. Season the chicken with the dried thyme and salt and pepper. Heat a large sauté pan over medium heat and add the oil. Dredge the chicken in the flour and sauté until cooked through. Set on a plate, tent with foil, and let it rest.

2. In the same sauté pan, cook the onion and fresh thyme over medium heat until aromatic.

3. Combine the wine, the broth, and the lemon juice. Add to the pan, turn the heat up to high, and deglaze the pan until the liquid begins to reduce.

4. Remove the pan from the heat and whisk in the butter. Season the sauce with salt and pepper to taste.

5. Place the Spinach Bed on a serving platter and top with the chicken. Spoon the sauce over the chicken and serve.

SPINACH BED: In a microwave-safe dish, cook the spinach with a few tablespoons of water on high for 5 to 6 minutes, or until hot. Drain and toss with the butter, lemon juice, and salt and pepper to taste.

what is HARISSA?

In his pilot, Jeffrey talked about finding harissa in Paris. A staple of North Africa and the Middle East, harissa is a paste typically made of cayenne, coriander, cumin, oil, and garlic and is used with couscous dishes, soups, and stews.

Down to the Wire

Jeffrey made a Harissa Steak Sandwich with Sun-Dried Tomato and Mint Mayonnaise. On the first take, "he smiled exactly no times," said Alton. Then Jeffrey called tomatoes "onions." But on another take, he had more feeling, proving to Alton that he was up to the task.

The pilots were shown to a live audience, the committee, and the Season Five finalists. The judges were impressed by both pilots. Bob said that Melissa was truly a confident star; Susie, that there was so much information; Bobby, that he was "totally stealing" Melissa's idea of making potato gratin in muffin tins.

"Terrific job," said Bobby about Jeffrey's performance. Bob said watching Jeffrey made him hungry.

"Wow," said Susie. "Flawless."

Bob said that the final deliberation was officially the most difficult one. In front of network president Brooke Johnson, Bobby declared the winner: Melissa.

"The first episode, Susie and Bobby and I walked into a room and the finalists were lined up waiting to greet us. I was watching Melissa and Debbie and Jeffrey and Jamika, and I said, 'I bet these will be our final four because they were just radiant in the room.' I hadn't heard them speak yet."

—Bob Tuschman

SEASON FIVE	ELIMINATIONS
EPISODE ONE "Sweet Sixteen" First Elimination	★ **JEN ISHAM:** "I thought I'd make it all the way to the end. . . . It's bittersweet. I'm going home to my husband, Gabe. He's my best friend and my whole world."
EPISODE TWO "Holidays with Giada" Second Elimination	★ **BRETT AUGUST:** "I probably brought too much Brett August! Looking back, I realize I should have been smoother."
EPISODE THREE "Dinner at Ina's" Third Elimination	★ **EDDIE GILBERT:** "I think the only time I was myself was during the *Esquire* challenge, and since I won that challenge, I think given more time, I could have learned to get better. I don't know if I would have done anything differently. Since we don't have a DeLorean to take me back in time, I guess we'll never know."
EPISODE FOUR "The Ultimate American Meal" Fourth Elimination	★ **TEDDY FOLKMAN:** "Without practice or guidance it was impossible to get my personality to come across on camera. We never got a chance to see ourselves. When I did, I was shocked and a little embarrassed. When it's a live or group situation, no problem, I can relax."
EPISODE FIVE "Rachael Ray" Fifth Elimination	★ **KATIE CAVUTO BOYLE:** "I'm happy with my decision to spotlight healthy food on the show. I think it's important to nourish our bodies well and to know that you can do so without sacrificing bold flavor. I want to inspire people to get back into the kitchen and create meals that focus on clean, fresh, flavorful ingredients."
EPISODE SIX "Miami 'Up All Night' " Sixth Elimination	★ **MICHAEL PROIETTI:** "I'm always making the best out of any situation. If you can't have a good time, well, what's the point? If you're gonna do something, you may as well have a smile while doing it! . . . I know I deserved to be there, and I know entertaining and cooking is what I'm great at!"
EPISODE SEVEN "Beachside Wood Grilling Challenge" Seventh Elimination	★ **JAMIKA PESSOA:** "With so many big personalities in the house, it's tough to let yours shine. I think my personality stood out because I was true to myself and my food. No matter what was going on around me, I managed to keep my composure while looking fabulous at the same time."
EPISODE EIGHT "VIP Party in Miami" Eighth Elimination	★ **DEBBIE LEE:** "As each week went by, I was able to get acclimated and just go with the notion that I was going to be myself. That's probably the best advice I could give anyone who goes on the show."
"Finale" Runner-up	★ **JEFFREY SAAD:** "When I get focused on something, I am in the zone! *Calm* is not a word that anyone has ever used to describe me. But I wanted to win that show so badly I think my focus took over to a point where I did not show enough of my highs and lows as I normally do."

MELISSA D'ARABIAN

Melissa's show *Ten Dollar Dinners* premiered on Food Network on August 9, 2009.

Melissa d'Arabian: A Q&A

You were badly underestimated for a lot of the competition.

When you first look at the other finalists it's human nature to size people up and wonder "Where do I fit into this?" "How many weeks of safety do I have?" There are always people you know aren't going to win, I watch enough reality TV to know that. I don't blame anybody for saying of me at first glance, "She's my week of safety."

So you didn't feel like you fit in?

I look around and see these nine amazing chefs. The first day they were discussing what different chefs were doing in different restaurants. There was a lot of chef talk and I'm sitting there thinking the last meal I had out was at PF Chang's. I live in suburban America; I have four babies; I change a million diapers.

But you beat all of them!

In week one, I came out on top with my food. Instead of saying, "We've underestimated her," they said, "there must have been a mistake." The way forward for me was to think I am not perfect but I am enough. Focus on what you are good at and celebrate that full force.

How did you turn it around?

The way some of the guys treated me was upsetting and very difficult, but competitions like this can be very tough and they bring out weird things in people. Winning for me was about asking, "What am I better at than anybody else here?" I played a game I could win. It's very easy to get sucked into playing someone else's game, and the minute you do that you're in second place. If I play the game of who has the better knife skills, I won't win. I said to myself, "I'm the only one here with an MBA so I understand about marketing, strategy, and planning. I'm going to make it easy for the judges to know how to market me. I'm the only one here who gets dinner on the table with four screaming babies quickly and affordably. I can do that better than anyone here." I chose to play a game I could win.

So the show was a means to an end for you?

I saw it as a job interview to get my own show. While some people might have been focusing on getting on *Next Food Network Star*, I was thinking about how this would shape the next ten years of my life.

You had a vision of where you wanted to go?

I was always very clear about what I brought to the table and what my show would be like. I was also very clear on how it would fit into my life plan and how this might help other people. I didn't apply as a lark; I don't throw stuff at the wall to see what sticks. I'm a far more purposeful liver than that. Whether it made sense to the judges and whether it would be compelling from a marketing perspective was up to them to decide.

Where does *Ten Dollar Dinners* fit into the plan?

I knew I wanted to have a show that in some small way will help someone not feel alone. At a very basic level that is what *Ten Dollar Dinners* is about, not about how to eat cheaply. I've been a full-time career woman putting in eighty hours a week in an office getting a dinner party on the table in a Thursday night. I've been a graduate student with absolutely no money finding a way to cook delicious meals. I've been a stay-at-home mom of four little kids and have had to get dinner on the table. I'm clear on how I want to impact people.

The financial executive is a side of Melissa we didn't see much on the show.

There was more focus on the show on the stay-at-home mom than the businesswoman. I had an interesting and intense career in finance and consulting for years before meeting my husband while I was working for Disney in Paris. I was in my mid-thirties, so we had four kids in two years and that's when I became a stay-at-home mom. I think the other finalists had this picture of a minivan-driving mom, which I am but that's just one piece of my experience. So when they found out I was a consultant it was like, "You used to *work*?"

You're a student of the spreadsheet, I understand.

I am a linear thinker and a planner. A few years ago it was the twenty-fifth anniversary of the spreadsheet and there was a book on its twenty-five most innovative uses. The publisher found out that when I got married, I had put together a wedding guest predictor model on Excel with coefficients for different guests and it was featured in this book. I am analytical to a fault.

Tell us about the speech you made where you talked about your mom.

I had been spending many hours over the weeks with these three judges. It felt like I was sharing with friends because it's a very intimate relationship. They're thinking of bringing you into their team. It's not as though I had talked about my mom on the first day I showed up. It doesn't define me but it is a big part of who I am and has a lot to do with the decisions I make as a woman who is raising four more women. It's not a cocktail party topic, but when we are getting into these deep discussions of our life philosophies there's no discussion of that with me that doesn't include my mom.

They expect a lot of you, personally.

I love connecting with my fans and I'm happy to share with them. When someone comes up to me and says, "I have twins too," we'll look at each others' pictures and I enjoy that side of it very much. But my personal life is not an open book—I do have boundaries.

That authenticity is important.

On television people can tell when they are being BSed. It's too close; it's not theater. It's closer than real life. In real life you can't see people's nose hairs. On TV you do. The tiniest thing comes across.

You talked about Julia Child in the speech too.

She is an inspiration. I love her embracing when things don't go right, saying it's okay and never apologizing for her food. I love her spirit and love for food and the fact that she just went and did this later in life. It was lovely watching *Julie and Julia.* It was a perfect tee up for me and got me in the space.

You must have been excited about the reaction to your pastry.

That recipe was something I had in my hip pocket. My pastry recipe is very versatile. I can put jam in it, I can put chocolate in it, I can fill it with pumpkin purée—there are so many ways I can go with it. François Payard saying he loved that pastry—I can sit there and watch that piece over and over again. That was one of the highlights of my life.

So you had a specific dessert strategy?

Someone always gets stuck with dessert and they say, "I'm going to make a hot fudge sundae because I don't know how to make dessert" and I'm thinking, "Duh you're on a cooking competition! Have a dessert or two in your repertoire." I made sure I had a couple I knew how to make without a recipe. With baking you have to be precise. I had to be able to make sure I could make my apple tarts and my pochettes. The judges would later say to me, "You're such a good dessert maker." I really saw this as being smart about the competition.

Clearly the wrong woman was under-estimated here . . .

One of my girlfriends told me after I won, "You were the surprise winner to everybody except those who know you." Those who know me know I am very focused and know what my strengths and weaknesses are.

How did you find the judging process?

I love that the judges were so forthright because then you know when they are saying nice things, they mean it. I do not want to hear false praise from anyone. The judges should be tough; these are the best chefs in the world. If they hadn't been tough I would have been disappointed. A lot of people hated the evaluations. I didn't like the fact that someone was going home but I loved them. I had these people who are the best in the business spending hours just talking about us, about our food and how we can make it better. It was like a tuition-free university and there are only ten students. And then nine and then eight. It was one of my favorite things I have ever done. Minus the stress of someone going home at the end of it.

How hard is it to mix the job and your home life?

The biggest challenge of the last couple of years has been becoming a working parent. I love what I'm doing. The secret to job satisfaction is very simple for me—have a personal life mission—know what you want to do before you die—and pick a job that helps with the personal life mission, not just your professional goals. That's especially important for a working parent. If I get up in the morning and get on a plane and say good-bye to my kids and if my professional world is detracting from my personal life goals, it becomes very anguishing and difficult to continue pursuing my life professionally. My family is a higher priority than my job will ever be. That doesn't mean my job isn't important and that there aren't difficult moments. There have been tough calls I've had to make on both the personal and professional fronts. You're constantly faced with that decision as a working parent. When you are clear with your life mission it makes those choices easier.

You're happy with the balance you've struck?

Happiness is an inside job. I love everything about my job and life, but if all the outside stuff went away I have to be happy with that. If not, then I am getting my happiness from the wrong place.

How far ahead does your plan extend?

Every New Year's over dinner my husband and I look at our personal, family, and professional goals and make sure they are in line. It's not a sterile, dry, process: "You know what I'd love to do." It's a great touchstone and strategic planning is a powerful tool. We don't have a binder with a ten-year plan in it, but in my perfect world I would.

You'd been a fan of Bobby Flay before the show began?

Eight months before *Star*, I bought his book *Grill It* and waited five hours in line at Williams-Sonoma with my daughter for him to sign it. I asked him to sign all four kids' names and he had a big smile on his face and said, "Let's take a picture." He'd been signing books for hours and I'm sure he was exhausted yet he was personable and engaged. That's the kind of person I want to be. If your fans like you less after having met you, then that's a problem.

Season SIX

S eason Six opened with more finalists than ever: twelve finalists and in a new location—Los Angeles. The same goal was in sight even if it was many grueling weeks away: the chance to host a Food Network series plus a feature in *Food Network Magazine* and a slot at The Food Network New York City Food and Wine Festival. The finalists arrived at the dramatic multilevel home in the Hollywood Hills that replaced the Greenwich Village carriage house.

THE FINALISTS

1. Doreen Fang. Doreen, a caterer, started cooking at a young age because her mom always made Chinese food and she got sick of it. "Food is everything to me. . . . I know I can do this," said Doreen. "I will be the next Food Network star."

2. Aarti Sequeira. Aarti a food blogger, was born in India and grew up in Dubai. "It's just crazy that I'm here," she said. "I really love to cook, but I never thought about it as a career."

3. Paul Young. Paul had seven years' experience as a waiter, bartender, and chef and had attended Second City improv school in Chicago as well as culinary school. "I know I can take on anyone in this competition." His first POV was "Cooking It Old-School." Then it was "Cooking on a Blue-Collar Dollar."

4. Herb Mesa. A personal trainer, chef, and stay-at-home dad, Herb had struggled with his weight all his life. His dream show would feature food and fitness: "Herb the Energy Chef."

5. Brianna Jenkins. Brianna said she could be sassy and a diva but very serious too: she went to culinary school in Paris. "I feel like I'm a star," she said. "This is my dream."

6. Tom Pizzica. Tom described himself as being "on sabbatical." He had been the executive chef at a hotel in Maryland but was currently unemployed. Tom's show idea: "The Big Chef."

7. Alexis Hernandez. Although he lived on a small farm, Alexis said he wasn't a farmer. He had researched food his whole adult life and was a food writer.

8. Dzintra Dzenis. A Cordon Bleu graduate and culinary instructor, Dzintra, who'd been cooking since the age of five, described herself as fun, vivacious, and quirky.

9. Brad Sorenson. Brad got his first job in a kitchen when he was seventeen and opened his first restaurant at twenty-two. "People underestimate my cooking ability because of my age, but I can cook alongside anybody." Brad wanted to call his cooking-techniques show "Pro."

10. Serena Palumbo. Of Italian descent, Serena had no culinary education other than strong women in her life who taught her how to cook her Mediterranean home-style food. She'd been a ballerina and an attorney; now her eye was on this prize.

11. Darrell A. Smith. "Das" was a culinary instructor who said he was aiming at the guy who can't cook. "I'm a great cook," Das said. "I have a great personality. . . . Nobody's standing in my way."

12. Aria Kagan. A private chef, Aria said that being away from her three-year-old son, Luca, was the hardest part of doing this. She wanted to show him, "if you want something, go for it." Aria's POV: "Family-Style Dinners."

The First Challenge L.A. Doubleheader:

The finalists headed for the new Food Star Kitchens, where they met Bobby Flay who introduced the other members of the Selection Committee. Bob Tuschman said one of these twelve would have a fast track to stardom; Susie Fogelson asked, "Who is my next powerhouse brand?" This season, the finalists would have a dedicated mentor: Giada De Laurentiis. Giada said she was proof that the network could make you a star—seven years earlier, Bob had read about her and asked her to put her face and recipes in front of the camera.

The challenge was to create a dish that outlined their Point of View and them—"you on a plate"—using chicken and potatoes.

Tom tried to make gnocchi in forty-five minutes but had to go to Plan B, a hash and roasted chicken dish. Das made chicken roulade, which was "him" because it was colorful and easy on the eye. But Das and Aarti were worried that their chicken wasn't cooked through.

After cooking, the finalists were put on the spot. They presented the dishes in their first Camera Challenge.

A few finalists presented and cooked well, and the top two were Aria and Herb ("Cilantro is like who I am—you either like it or you don't."). Many cooked well but didn't present well, or vice versa: Doreen, Dzintra, Serena, Brianna, Brad, Alex, and Aarti (Bob gave her a 10 for presenting, a 0 for food). A few, such as Paul, did neither. Bob liked Tom's shaggy-dog look, but did he want to be there? Das apologized for his embarrassing raw chicken. He and Tom were the bottom two.

Giada De Laurentiis: A Q&A

Did you find the mentoring fun to do?

It's always nice to help people attain their dreams . . . Only one person wins, but it's nice to help the others along the way.

Was that a more intense involvement for you with the finalists?

It was more of a one-on-one involvement mentoring them, being able to sit down with them in their house and actually chat—about feelings, about the competition, and about what I thought they could work on. Some listened, some didn't.

Can you empathize with what the finalists are going through?

Yes! I can't even imagine how they do it! It is incredibly difficult and stressful, and must be extremely hard on their families. It's like an intense ten-week therapy session and you never get a break from the therapy! We can all empathize, I think.

And you've done *Iron Chef* so you know what that's like!

Iron Chef is probably the hardest thing I have done on TV. It takes incredible focus and energy, preparation, and skill. Plus you have to talk to the camera, and look like you are having fun . . . and of course, you want to win! I am still scarred by the fact that I didn't win!

How do you think you'd have done if you'd competed on *Next Food Network Star*?

Oh, I would not have made it. You really have to drop everything and then think extremely strategically. It's hard.

Do you think the challenges are a fair test of what someone will face on TV?

Those challenges are really set up to see how creative you are. To be a chef and on the Food Network you need to be able to be creative. Like on *Iron Chef* you do not know what ingredients are coming your way, and you need to be able to adapt to whatever is given to you.

You've created a great many recipes for your shows—is it difficult to remain creative in the kitchen?

Yes. You get writer's block. That's why I think the challenges that are set up for *Next Food Network Star* are so important, because they really do prepare you for this job.

Can you ever forget about the camera being there?

Yes. But it takes practice, practice, practice. I tell them to practice talking to themselves in the mirror!

Do you think it's possible to learn how to look natural on TV or do you just have "it"?

You can learn to be comfortable in front of the camera but it can take years, so on *Next Food Network Star* we are looking for someone who has at least that glimmer of having it, knowing it will come with time once you are in front of the camera more.

Do you ever get nervous being on TV?

Yes, I always get nervous for the first shot of the day, then as the day goes on, it gets easier and easier.

What's the hardest part of being on TV?

I think the hardest thing about being on TV is thinking on your feet. You can learn everything else but being spontaneous and being organic at the same time takes a lot of energy and is harder than you think.

Was it difficult to be part of the decision-making process?

It's agonizing, because you never want to send anyone home. Especially when you get down to the last six finalists—they are all good, and at that point you are just nit-picking, they are all talented and deserving of a show at that stage.

In Season Three you saw Nikki cooking in heels and told her, "I cook in flip-flops . . ." It's important to be comfortable in the kitchen.

I just don't think it's very realistic to cook in heels. Part of having a show on Food Network is to be real, and it's dangerous in a kitchen to be in heels!

"I made this for the first time on the show. I wanted to make something that shows how I like to eat: good comfort food—meat and potatoes—but with a modern twist, integrating flavors and plating options from around the world—in this case Italy, Indonesia, and France—to make sure cooking and eating is never boring.

"I've made a variation of this dish using roasted duck breast, duck-fat fried potatoes, and thick slices of winter pears sautéed in a little bit of apple cider vinegar, honey, Thai chiles, and cinnamon sticks."

—Dzintra Dzenis

CHICKEN AND POTATO NAPOLEON
with Spicy Tomato Sambal Sauce

Recipe courtesy Dzintra Dzenis

Yield: 4 servings ▮ Prep Time: 25 minutes ▮ Cook Time: 1 hour ▮ Inactive Prep Time: 10 minutes ▮ Ease of Preparation: easy

FOR THE SAUCE
1 tablespoon olive oil

1 small onion, diced

3 garlic cloves, chopped

1 (15-ounce) can crushed tomatoes

2 vine-ripened tomatoes (10 ounces), seeded and diced

2 tablespoons chili garlic paste, such as sambal oelek

1 tablespoon sugar

2 teaspoons kosher salt

1 sprig fresh rosemary

2 tablespoons chopped fresh parsley leaves, plus 4 sprigs for garnish

FOR THE CHICKEN
2 tablespoons olive oil

2 boneless chicken breast halves, with skin on (about 1¼ pounds total)

½ teaspoon kosher salt

1. Preheat the oven to 375°F.

2. **FOR THE SAUCE:** In a medium-size skillet, heat the olive oil over medium heat. Sauté the onion and garlic until softened. Stir in the canned tomatoes, fresh tomatoes, chili garlic paste, sugar, salt, and rosemary. Cook the sauce until it thickens, about 10 minutes. Remove the rosemary sprig and stir in the chopped parsley. Set aside and keep warm.

3. **FOR THE CHICKEN:** In a large ovenproof sauté pan, heat the olive oil over high heat. Season the chicken breasts with the salt and pepper and place them in the skillet, skin side down. Cook for 3 minutes on each side. Transfer the pan to the oven and bake the chicken until it is cooked through and has reached an internal temperature of 170°F., 20 to 25 minutes. Transfer from the oven to a cutting board and allow to rest, covered, for 5 to 10 minutes.

4. **FOR THE NAPOLEON:** Slice the potatoes ¼-inch thick. Heat both of the oils in a large skillet over medium-high heat. Add the potato slices in batches and fry until

¼ teaspoon freshly ground black
　pepper

FOR THE NAPOLEON
4 large Yukon gold potatoes
　(about 1¼ pounds total)

¼ cup olive oil

¼ cup grapeseed oil

Sea salt

crispy on the outside and tender on the inside, turning once, 8 to 10 minutes. Lay the potatoes on paper towels to drain and sprinkle them with the sea salt to taste.

5. **ASSEMBLY:** Arrange the potato slices in a circle on each plate. Top with the tomato sauce, leaving a small border. Slice the chicken breasts and arrange the slices on top of the potato and tomato layers. Garnish each serving with a sprig of the fresh parsley.

Star Challenge

At Paramount Studios, for Part One of their two-part Star Challenge, finalists made fifteen-second promotional videos with Giada and movie director Andy Fickman. Were they putting across their real self? Was Brianna the party girl she presented? What was "Dining with Doreen"? Why was Paul yelling? Was Brad really a robot? Why was Das waving his arms around? What happened to Herb's energy?

> "I love being in front of the camera and don't usually have a difficult time, but I think the desire to do well, mixed with having tons of people watching you and a big celebrity like Giada, made it more nerve-wracking."
>
> —Doreen Fang

Giada outlined Part Two—to cater a six-course lunch for the "ultimate celebrity chef." She wasn't saying who. There were two teams, and each team member was responsible for one course of the California cuisine–inspired food. Promo winners Herb and Aria were captains. For the Gray Team, Aria gave Dzintra dessert; Brianna, seafood; Tom, meat; Aarti, soup; and Paul, salad. For the Black Team, Herb assigned Brad seafood; Serena, meat; Das, salad; Doreen, soup; and Alexis, dessert. Herb and Aria had the appetizers.

"It's a strange reward for winning a challenge to get to be team leader. It was all about the team's success, not just my own. I hardly knew everyone's name at that point, let alone their cooking abilities. I knew I had to make sure that everyone had the tools and the confidence to win. With that, I had faith that we all could put out some amazing food!"

—Aria Kagan

"I've been in charge before. I actually had a 'real job' once as I managed the catering for large hotels with an average staff of 130 and managed the $3.5 million food and beverage operation. I was good at what I did, but then gave all that up to be a stay-at-home dad. It was the best career choice of my life. It gave me a career in both fitness and food."

—Herb Mesa

Brad's Black Team, planned Pan-Seared Salmon with Asparagus, but at the store Herb and Das bought only one frozen fillet full of pin bones, and Brad was upset. The store had no veal or zucchini, so Serena's Veal Scaloppini with Zucchini Escabeche became Chicken Breasts with Sunburst Squash.

Dzintra, unhappy with being assigned dessert, planned to make a complex Lemon Sabayon with a Macadamia Nut Biscuit. As she prepped, she noticed a problem with her eye. The medic said she had to go to the E.R.

"Have you ever been in the nightmare where you're heading for *the* interview? Then out of the blue, your feet get stuck in cement blocks and no matter how hard you try, you just can't move. Yeah, the eye incident was pretty darn awful. . . . I think it put me at a disadvantage the rest of the way."

—Dzintra Dzenis

Brianna said *she* would only go to the hospital if she lost an arm.

With time running down, Aria and Tom tried to make Dzintra's dessert. Aria dealt with the sabayon; Tom had fourteen minutes to double-bake the biscuits and he gave it a 35-percent chance of success.

The finalists arrived at Cut restaurant in Beverly Hills. The mystery lunch guest was revealed as Wolfgang Puck, described by Bobby as the first true celebrity chef. "Good luck," Wolfgang said. "And don't mess up my kitchen."

> **"Wolfgang is old school. I've known him forever and he is the nicest guy, He has the same attitude I do. If you want the job, do the right thing. If you can't cook, don't be here. He suffers no fools."**
>
> —Bobby Flay

The Gray Team was up first. Dzintra arrived and said she'd scratched a cornea and couldn't be in a kitchen for twenty-four hours, leaving Aria and Tom to work on her dish as well as their own. Aria presented first and showed her promo.

Wolfgang Puck liked the focaccia but said it should be brown. Bob said it was exactly Aria on a plate: "warm and generous."

"I like her so much that I'd basically buy anything she's saying," said Susie.

> **"This is my total go-to dish! I switch around the cheese—Brie is also really yummy baked with the olives and garlic."**
>
> —Aria Kagan

what is SABAYON?

Sabayon is the tricky-to-make Italian dessert also known as zabaglione. Egg yolks are mixed with wine and sugar and very gently heated while they're whisked into a light foam. Too much heat and you get scrambled eggs.

SANTA BARBARA OLIVE FOCACCIA
with Baked Goat Cheese

Recipe courtesy Aria Kagan

Yield: 6 servings ▮ Prep Time: 20 minutes ▮ Cook Time: 1 hour 10 minutes ▮ Inactive Prep Time: 35 minutes ▮ Ease of Preparation: intermediate

FOR THE FOCACCIA

1¼ cups warm water

1 envelope active dry yeast

2 cups plus 2 tablespoons all-purpose flour, plus more for kneading

2 cups plus 3 tablespoons bread flour

4 teaspoons kosher salt

1 tablespoon honey

1 tablespoon olive oil, plus a little extra for baking

½ cup green olives, such as picholine, pitted and chopped

FOR THE BAKED GOAT CHEESE

¾ cup olive oil

12 garlic cloves

12 ounces goat cheese

12 niçoise olives, pitted and halved

1 tablespoon chopped chives, for garnish

1. **FOR THE FOCACCIA:** In a small bowl, stir together the warm water and yeast until the yeast dissolves. Set aside for 5 minutes.

2. In a stand mixer fitted with a paddle attachment, blend the flours and salt. With the mixer running on low, pour in the yeast mixture. Mix for 1 minute, then add the honey and olive oil. Once the dough comes together, mix in the green olives until they are just incorporated.

3. Turn the dough out onto a lightly floured surface and knead by hand until smooth and elastic, 2 to 3 minutes. Place the dough on an oiled 13 by 9-inch baking sheet, cover lightly with plastic wrap, and let rise in a warm place for 30 minutes.

4. **FOR THE GOAT CHEESE:** While the dough is rising, heat the olive oil and garlic cloves in a small skillet over low heat and simmer until the garlic is golden and tender, 15 to 20 minutes.

5. Preheat the oven to 375°F.

6. Divide the goat cheese among six small ovenproof bowls or ramekins. Divide the garlic and olive oil, then the niçoise olives, among the bowls. Set the ramekins aside.

7. When the dough has risen, press it down with your fingertips until it fills the baking sheet and brush with some of the olive oil. Bake 45 to 50 minutes, until it is golden brown and hollow-sounding when tapped.

During the last 10 to 15 minutes of baking, put the goat cheese bowls into the oven and bake until the cheese is warm and lightly browned. Remove from the oven.

8. Slice the focaccia into thick wedges while warm and serve 2 slices with each bowl of warm goat cheese. Garnish the baked cheese with the chives.

A Food Pioneer

The presence of Wolfgang Puck made finalists nervous. Paul overdressed his salad. Tom's pork was dry, but his silly promo was likable. Aarti's mum's dal was delicious. "We'll get you a job here," said Wolfgang, which helped her self-confidence.

"She's very exciting to me," said Susie of Aarti. Dzintra looked at her dish and said it wasn't close to her conception.

> "I am a huge Wolfgang Puck fan. He was a pioneer in the food world who took American cooking places it had never gone before. As a personality, he is so funny, so engaging, so adventurous, and so brutally honest that he's always fascinating to watch. His advice in both camera performance and food was on the mark and equally colorful and true."
>
> —Bob Tuschman

As for the Black Team, Serena had never been in a professional kitchen and the first was Wolfgang Puck's. Serena was proud of how she performed. Alexis was concerned about using a commercial fryer, as he normally made his beignets in a small pan. "I'll see if it works."

Herb introduced his team and his Ceviche with Plantain Spiders. As it ran, he said his food-and-fitness promo was "horrible."

Wolfgang Puck: How many push-ups can you do?

Herb Mesa: How many would you like me to do?

Wolfgang Puck: Show me.

Doreen apologized for not finishing garnishing her potato soup. Chef Puck said, "Never let the dish go out if it's not finished. . . . Do it right or don't do it." Bob said that star power is confidence and being apologetic is the exact opposite of confidence. Brad's salmon was Chef Puck's favorite dish.

"This is my kind of food," said Giada.

> **"When Chef Puck made that comment about the food, I felt all the nervousness leave me. It was a huge burst of confidence for me. I made the best of the situation and cooked the food to the best of my ability."**
>
> **—Brad Sorenson**

Wolfgang Puck [of Serena]: Can the Food Network live with two Italian princesses?

Giada De Laurentiis: The more, the merrier.

Alexis said his beignets looked horrible, but he had to plate them anyway. With enough time to cook, it's a great recipe. Wolfgang went after him: "The dough is completely raw inside. My wife would divorce me if I would give her that to eat. . . . This is not acceptable."

> **"I was deeply disappointed in Wolfgang's reaction to my dish. He was merely giving honest feedback. It didn't change the fondness I have for him as a professional. I knew that my donuts were a little raw, but I thought it best to serve something than serve nothing, since my fellow finalist Dzintra did not make a dish. I made the error of not returning them to the fryer, like I had originally intended, but followed my team's suggestion to finish them off in the oven.**
> **"I wouldn't suggest that people avoid making desserts in a competition. What I would suggest is to pay close attention to how you are executing the dessert and make sure you're dotting your i's and crossing your t's."**
>
> **—Alexis Hernandez**

In evaluation the question was what to do with Dzintra. Her first chicken dish was liked, and she wanted so badly to stay. Bobby liked Aria's dish a lot, and Susie said that she had all the right stuff. Paul had to bring the funny. Aria's team was the better one, and the challenge winner was Aria. Dzintra was dangling by a thread, but she got a second chance.

The Black Team had issues: Herb's camera presence, Doreen's defeatism and lack of POV, Serena's inauthenticity, Alexis's beignets and joylessness, Brad's timidity, Das's overconfidence. It was Alexis who was asked to leave.

"This is a dish I made with my sister when she moved into her first apartment. A little work is required, but the result is fantastic."

—Alexis Hernandez

BEIGNETS
with Rosemary Caramel and Local Honey

Recipe courtesy Alexis Hernandez

Yield: 6 servings, about 24 beignets ▌ Prep Time: 15 minutes ▌ Cook Time: 30 minutes
▌ Inactive Prep Time: 5 minutes ▌ Ease of Preparation: intermediate

FOR THE CARAMEL
½ cup water

2 (6-inch) sprigs fresh rosemary

¾ cup plus 2 tablespoons granulated sugar

1 tablespoon light corn syrup

½ cup heavy cream

FOR THE BEIGNETS
½ cup water

½ cup milk

4 tablespoons unsalted butter

1 tablespoon plus ¾ teaspoon granulated sugar

⅛ teaspoon salt

1 cup all-purpose flour, sifted

1 teaspoon vanilla extract

4 large eggs

Canola oil, for frying

Confectioners' sugar, for serving

¼ cup local honey, or any good-quality honey

1. **FOR THE CARAMEL:** In a small pot, bring the water and rosemary to a simmer over medium heat. Simmer until the liquid has reduced by half, 6 to 8 minutes. Strain the liquid and reserve it. Discard the rosemary and pour the liquid (you should have about ¼ cup) back into the pot. Add the sugar and corn syrup and bring to a boil over high heat. Reduce the heat to medium and simmer until the syrup turns a deep amber color. Carefully add the heavy cream (it will bubble vigorously) and cook, stirring, until smooth. Set the caramel aside to cool slightly. Serve warm or at room temperature. Store any extra in the refrigerator for future use.

2. **FOR THE BEIGNETS:** In a medium-size pot, bring the water, milk, butter, sugar, and salt to a boil over medium heat. Add the flour and stir vigorously with a spoon, cooking until the dough becomes a solid mass and begins to pull away from the sides of the pot, 3 to 5 minutes. Turn off the heat and stir in the vanilla extract. Add the eggs, one at a time, incorporating each before adding the next. Work quickly or the eggs will curdle.

The dough should be flexible and soft but firm enough to hold its shape. Cover with plastic and set aside for 5 minutes.

3. When you're ready to make the pastries, pour enough oil into a deep skillet or deep-fryer so that it's two-thirds full and heat it to 300–325°F. Using a small ice cream scoop or spoon, drop about 2 teaspoons of the dough into the hot oil. Do this with the remaining dough to fry the beignets, in batches, being sure not to crowd them. Cook, turning occasionally, until golden brown, about 7 minutes. Remove from the oil and place on a cooling rack.

4. Arrange the beignets on a serving platter and dust with the confectioners' sugar. Serve in small bowls with the rosemary caramel and local honey.

Cooking and Talking

For episode two's Camera Challenge, Giada asked the finalists to do something *Star* finalists often struggle with, at least at first: Cook and talk at the same time. She had a vegetable lasagna recipe broken down into eleven steps, and each had to present one step in one minute.

The familiar problems from other seasons arose: Aarti dried up; Tom couldn't stretch for time; Serena talked a mile a minute; Dzintra tried too hard; Brianna was nervous; Das didn't finish his step; Brad said "nice" a lot.

Sweet to Savory

For the Star Challenge, Duff Goldman told finalists to create a savory party bite inspired by a sweet chosen for them by slightly freaky animatronic fortune-teller Zoltar. Their dish would feed one hundred at a party at the Santa Monica Pier carnival.

Aarti drew funnel cake, something she'd never eaten; Paul, caramel corn; Doreen, a root beer float; Dzintra, cotton candy—in her opinion, the hardest task.

Serena decided to turn her chocolate-covered waffle ice cream into crunchy Cheese Croquettes with Marinara Sauce. Aarti opted for a Scallion Ricotta Pancake with Tandoori Barbecued Chicken. Aria had to replicate a banana split and used meatballs and garlic toast. Brad built a smoker to smoke pork with the shells from his circus peanuts. Paul's caramel corn garnished his Asian Chicken Wrap. Aarti wasn't just worried for herself—she was concerned that Doreen wouldn't have time to get her pork tender enough for pulled pork.

"In retrospect I think I would have done something a lot smaller, something you could just pop into your mouth, maybe topped with an infused caramel sauce."

—Paul Young

When they got to the pier, Aria realized that she was fifty meatballs short (she'd left a pan in the oven) and scrambled to make another batch.

It was time to serve. Some guests felt that Paul ("Hello, ladies!") came on a little strong. Das's Lemon Pepper Chicken Wings, and Das, were a hit.

> "Das was talking about impressing the ladies and we got to the tasting and I said, 'Guys, there is nothing sexy about eating a chicken wing.' Wings, you're watching football. When you're on a date, here's Duff's love advice: don't order wings."
>
> —Duff Goldman

> "I guess those Lemon Pepper Chicken Wings were my famous TV recipe because everywhere I go, people always ask me to make them. I'm teaching an adult cooking class, and one of the first things we're making are the wings."
>
> —Darrell "Das" Smith

The judges enjoyed Herb's Smoked Salmon Mousse Roulade, his take on a lollipop, but not Paul's use of caramel corn as a garnish. Guests liked Aarti and her food, but she was scared of the committee and almost said she didn't think she was capable of anything. But Duff said, "Whatever she's making, I want some." Dzintra couldn't plate and talk, and Bobby was confused by her dish.

Duff had to remind Serena to breathe. "She is like a Maserati going four hundred miles an hour," said Bob. Her marinara sauce was, Duff said, "kind of awesome."

"I believe there is an objective component—Italians speak rather fast—and a subjective component to this; being in front of culinary experts is definitely intimidating, along with the fact that I was aware of all the viewers. I live my life at a very fast pace, and my job requires fast thinking. I realize I often came across as a very confident and self-assured person, but I have my weakness and uncertainties as well. Speaking fast was probably the reaction to that."

—Serena Palumbo

Once more, Doreen couldn't articulate her Point of View clearly, and the pork wasn't tender. Bobby said that Brad burned the peanut shells, which made his pork taste acrid.

In evaluation, Brianna was told that she was aloof to the pier guests. Neither Paul nor Tom's demeanor was universally liked. Dzintra needed to get out of her own way.

"If your attitude toward the audience is 'Take it or leave it,' trust me, they will leave it."

—Bob Tuschman (to Tom)

"I said to Tom the first day, 'Do you want to be here?' He seemed tired, like we were putting him out. You're trying to get a TV show, show us how ambitious you are. I have no patience for that. He woke up after that. Maybe I misread how he really was but that was my feeling."

—Bobby Flay

"I knew I belonged in that competition—it just took the judges a little while to understand my personality type. Their doubts actually just stoked the fires of my competitive side."

—Tom Pizzica

Duff Goldman: A Q&A

That was a strong group of finalists . . .

I met all the finalists and talked to everyone and before I tasted their food, I thought, "Aarti's going to win this thing." I think a lot of people felt that.

At that point, she didn't.

I wanted to grab her and say, "Listen to me. You have already won this. You have it so wrapped up! All you have to do is show up and not make a fool of yourself." Susie Fogelson would say, "Stop apologizing for who you are! Don't apologize for your food, your food's awesome. You're so beautiful and warm, I want to eat your food, I want to hang out with you." I don't think she had the verve. She does now. She is such a joy.

Now it looks like TV comes very naturally to you.

I'm very comfortable being me. If I don't have actual lines to say and points to make, I'm a hundred percent golden. I'll get really excited talking about food. When it comes to saying lines, I turn into Mr. Game Show Host. I have an old-school hip-hop background. I was a graffiti artist and a dumb jock in high school and college. I have different ways of speaking than people who were trained to speak on TV. People like to watch me on TV because I am different from what's out there even if on *Ace of Cakes* we all mumble all the time.

How was *Iron Chef* for you?

Michael Symon and I had so much fun. We lost but we walked out and we were high-fiving and freaking out. It was like that big rush after a busy Saturday night and the last ticket is out and you get a beer and say holy #*%! that was crazy!

You enjoy your work, obviously.

My shop is a fun place to be and people feel comfortable. I've worked at French Laundry and for Todd English and at some pretty serious places where it's very regimented. There wasn't a lot of screaming but not a lot of goofing around either and I definitely encourage a lot of goofing around on and off screen. We do take what we do super-seriously but it doesn't mean you have to be super-serious while you're doing it. If you don't enjoy it, what's the point?

At the Movies

The Camera Challenge, introduced by Guy Fieri, was to make a dish inspired by one of the classic movie genres finalists pulled out of a box of popcorn.

In many cases, the food had at best a tangential relationship to the theme, and the presentations were nervy. Brianna had Comedy and made Tempura Shrimp and Scallops because shopping for seafood made her giggle. Bob loved the dish, but it wasn't comedy. Aarti's Turkey Meat Loaf with a little bit of blood represented Horror perfectly. Dzintra's Adventure had udon to represent a car chase. Das's taco (for Foreign) was nothing special. For Drama, Paul's Strip Steak with White Truffle Oil had a too-sweet sauce, and Paul didn't find balance in his presentation.

> "My heart did sink a little when I saw that I had Drama. I feel as if though I executed the dish well, and in my eyes the plate held plenty of drama, I think I may have been better off with a different movie genre."
>
> —Paul Young

Paul and Das struggled the most. Aarti won again.

Grammy Award Celebration

All dressed up, finalists had somewhere to go—the Highlands club on Hollywood Boulevard, where Guy made them walk the red carpet flanked by fans, paparazzi, and reporters. How would they handle the spotlight?

For the cooking part of the Star Challenge, Guy announced that it was party time, for 150 people for the MGD 64 after party for Grammy winner Colbie Caillat. The finalists were divided into teams of two, with each finalist assigned a special ingredient. Each one had to prepare a dish with the ingredient, and each team had to collaborate on a dish using both special ingredients. As they paired off, Paul looked unhappy to be teamed with Serena. "She's a home cook, and I come from a professional-kitchen background," he said.

> "I studied ballet for fifteen years, so teamwork was somehow embedded in my DNA from a young age. On top of that, being a corporate attorney requires a great deal of teamwork, so I can say that my other skills came in handy when it came to meeting halfway with people with whom I had a complicated relationship."
>
> —Serena Palumbo

Das and Tom were given red cabbage and a bunch of bananas; Herb and Brianna got beer and fennel; Dzintra and Aria, mushrooms and blueberries; Aarti and Brad, Taleggio cheese and dark chocolate; Serena and Paul, peanut butter and parsnips.

"Herb and I are 'Team Sexy,'" said Brianna. "I mean look at us." Brianna worked on Pork with Fennel Chutney and Herb made Beer-Marinated Flank Steak. Together they created Bruschetta with Beer Fondue and Fennel Ragù. While Aria prepared a Blueberry Napoleon, Dzintra made Beef with Mushroom Gravy, and they combined their ingredients in a vinaigrette for a salad. There was no communication.

Paul's shrimp dish was paired with Serena's Mozzarella en Carozza—an Italian grilled cheese with peanut sauce instead of béchamel. Their joint dish: Tenderloin with Parsnip Slaw and Spicy Peanut Sauce. Thinking Serena needed his help, Paul offered to make the slaw. As he tried to open a bottle of soy sauce with a knife, he broke the top and ruined the slaw.

Serena was injured when she walked behind Brianna and Brianna accidentally stepped on her foot. "I'm not really feeling bad about the situation because she didn't inform me she was behind me," said Brianna. Serena kept going.

> **"I was in real pain. I carried through the challenge because I did not want to let Paul down and I was afraid the reaction would be similar to that given to Dzintra's eye injury. My nerves held me up throughout the challenge, but when that—and the adrenaline—was over, I realized I was really in horrific pain."**
>
> **—Serena Palumbo**

At the party, Herb and Brianna's food was popular. Colbie Caillat said of Herb's steak, "It has this light refreshing taste to it." Brad and Aarti presented passionately and warmly, but their collaborative beef was leathery. During her presentation, Dzintra shushed Aria. Guy found her tenderloin tasteless.

When Das and Tom drew red cabbage and bananas, Das wondered, "What in the hell are we going to do with red cabbage and bananas?" Tom made a Banana Avocado Mousse, and together they worked on Banana Tempura with Caribbean Jerk Cabbage. Das prepared Pancetta-Fried Cabbage.

Colbie said that Tom and Das were "cute" but the jerk spice in their joint dish was too much. Bob agreed. "That's inedible. How you can get that many unpleasant flavors into that one little bite is beyond me," he said.

"I could just dive into a bowl of this cabbage," said Susie.

> **"I have indeed made that salmon dish again, and I also make that dish with halibut. Both are really tasty."**
>
> **—Darrell "Das" Smith**

PAN-SEARED SALMON
with Pancetta-Fried Cabbage and Thyme Beurre Blanc

Recipe courtesy Darrell "Das" Smith

Yield: 4 servings ▌ Prep Time: 10 minutes ▌ Cook Time: 40 minutes ▌ Ease of Preparation: intermediate

FOR THE SALMON AND CABBAGE

4 (6-ounce) wild-caught salmon fillets

Kosher salt

Freshly ground black pepper

Canola oil, for sautéing

4 ounces diced pancetta

½ small head red cabbage, thinly sliced (about 5 cups)

2 tablespoons white wine vinegar

FOR THE BEURRE BLANC

1½ cups white wine

1 shallot, diced

1 garlic clove, crushed

1 sprig fresh rosemary

1 sprig fresh thyme

1½ sticks (6 ounces) unsalted butter

1. **FOR THE SALMON AND CABBAGE:** Preheat the oven to 350°F. Season the fillets with salt and pepper. Coat the bottom of a large ovenproof sauté pan with oil and heat over medium-high heat. When the oil is hot, pan-sear the seasoned fish, skin side down, until browned, 3 to 4 minutes. Transfer the sauté pan to the oven and bake the fish for 10 minutes.

2. In a large skillet over medium-high heat, cook the pancetta until crisp, stirring frequently, 12 to 15 minutes. Add the cabbage and toss it with the pancetta until it softens. Stir in the vinegar and season with salt and pepper to taste. Continue to cook, tossing, until the cabbage is crisp and tender, 6 to 8 minutes. Adjust the seasoning.

3. **FOR THE BEURRE BLANC:** In a saucepan, combine the white wine, diced shallot, crushed garlic, rosemary, and thyme. Cook until reduced by three-quarters, then strain into another saucepan. Gradually whisk in the butter until the sauce is smooth.

4. Serve the salmon over the cabbage and drizzle the beurre blanc over the top.

A Brave Face

Serena put on a "smiley face" when they presented, but her foot was killing her. Paul introduced his Parsnip Purée with Shrimp, and he and Serena stepped on each other's toes presenting their joint dish. Colbie said they made her feel very uncomfortable. The sandwich seemed stale, and the collaborative dish, ironically, was the best.

Serena went off to the hospital but was back, with nothing broken, in time for evaluation. Susie told Das that his cabbage was "awesome"—buttery and chewy from the pancetta. But the combined dish: "Daring, yes; good, no." On "Team Sexy," Herb was lovable and warm. Bob said that Brianna was "an expert chef" but could be chilly. Brianna said she'd struggled to have friends. That was her challenge to overcome, said Guy.

Bob called Paul and Serena "Team Chaos." Paul said Serena was "doing a home-cook thing," and Susie chided him: "Your behavior to me is really condescending toward Serena."

Guy said Food Network has both classically trained and home-trained cooks. "This is anybody's game to lose, okay?" Still, neither of their dishes worked.

Bob told Dzintra that she'd cut Aria off and talked over her. "That's not how I meant it at all," said Dzintra. Aria's dessert was popular; Dzintra's meat was forgettable.

The challenge winners were Team Sexy—Herb and Brianna. At the bottom were Dzintra, Aria, Paul, and Serena. Dzintra was sent home.

SHRIMP
with Parsnip Smash and Pickled Veggies

Recipe courtesy Paul Young

Yield: 2 to 4 servings ▮ Prep Time: 30 minutes ▮ Cook Time: 50 minutes ▮ Inactive Prep Time: 1 hour ▮ Ease of Preparation: intermediate

FOR THE VEGGIES

¼ cup white wine vinegar

½ teaspoon sugar

Generous pinch of salt

1 English cucumber, or slicing cucumber, seeds removed, cut into julienne

1 red bell pepper, stemmed, seeded, and cut into julienne

1 tablespoon lemon zest

FOR THE SHRIMP AND PARSNIPS

½ cup white wine vinegar

½ cup sugar

1 (2-inch) piece fresh ginger, peeled and thinly sliced

Juice of 1 lemon (2 tablespoons)

4 parsnips (about 1 pound), peeled and chopped

2 small Yukon gold potatoes (about 12 ounces), peeled and diced

4 cups chicken stock

¼ cup heavy cream

1½ sticks (6 ounces) unsalted butter

Kosher salt

2 tablespoons olive oil

12 large (16/20) shrimp, peeled and deveined

2 garlic cloves, minced

1. FOR THE VEGGIES: Whisk together the vinegar, sugar, and salt. Put the cucumber, red pepper, and lemon zest in a medium-size mixing bowl. Pour the vinegar mixture over the vegetables and toss gently to coat. Chill for 1 hour, then take out and let stand before serving.

2. FOR THE SHRIMP AND PARSNIPS: In a small saucepan, bring the vinegar, sugar, ginger, and lemon juice to a simmer over medium heat and cook until big bubbles start to form and it becomes a light golden brown syrup. Allow the liquid to reduce until it thickens. Remove the pot from the heat and smash the ginger with a fork.

3. In a large pot, combine the parsnips, potatoes, and stock and bring to a boil. Cook until the parsnips and potatoes are fork-tender, 15 to 20 minutes. Drain and mash with the heavy cream, butter, and ginger syrup. Season with the salt to taste.

4. Heat a large sauté pan over medium-high heat and add the olive oil. Season the shrimp with the salt and sauté for about 3 minutes, or until cooked through, adding the garlic during the last minute.

5. ASSEMBLY: On a warmed serving platter, make a bed of the parsnip smash. Top with the shrimp, then top the shrimp with the pickled vegetables and some of the reserved pickling liquid.

Hot Hot Heat!

In the Food Network kitchens: Bobby, Giada, and a table full of peppers. Bobby said he had made his career working with peppers. "In the best hands they can really enhance a dish," he said. "In the wrong hands they can really ruin somebody's day." The finalists had to choose a pepper and make a dish. The winner would make it onto the specials list at all three of Bobby's Mesa Grills.

Brianna grabbed the Fresno chile; Serena took Anaheim peppers, which she'd never seen before. Brianna made a Chile Chicken Skewer. She was feeling good—she had the energy and the attitude. "You can't stop me now." Brad used his Thai chiles to make Chicken and Shrimp Satay with Coconut Peanut Sauce.

Das's tuna was uninspired. Herb wasn't feeling it with his presentation, and his spring roll wasn't popular. Herb and Das were at the bottom. Of Brad, Bobby said, "My mouth is lit up. ...I think he uses chile pepper with finesse." Brianna's on-camera description was the best anyone had seen her, and she won the challenge.

"I was so delighted to win the chile challenge. It was the perfect boost of confidence at just the right time. I do cook with chiles a lot and coincidently I chose a chile pepper to best describe me during the audition process."
—Brianna Jenkins

Chef Challenge

For the Star Challenge, Bobby introduced three chefs: Bobby Flay's own mentor, Jonathan Waxman of Barbuto in New York; Susan Feniger, owner of restaurants Ciudad and Street in Los Angeles; and Eric Greenspan, owner of the Foundry on Melrose, also in Los Angeles. The chefs laid out the challenge: Reinvent the best dish the guest chef had ever eaten. The nine finalists were split into threes; for each chef, a threesome would compete head to head to head.

Chef Waxman told Tom, Aarti, and Herb that his favorite dish was lamb and potatoes, cowboy-style. For Serena, Brad, and Brianna, Chef Feniger selected fried chicken with iceberg lettuce and blue cheese dressing, which she remembered eating with her mother. Chef Greenspan recalled to Paul, Aria, and Das his father grilling a big, juicy steak to go with mac and cheese.

After shopping, the finalists had an hour to cook at Ciudad.

Brianna made Fried Chicken and Waffle Steak, which her father had taught her to cook. Serena's interpretation was *cotoletta*—Italian breaded chicken cutlets with Gorgonzola sauce. Brad planned to flash-fry his Blue-Corn-Crusted Fried Chicken at the end, but it was undercooked so he deep-fried it.

Brianna talked about her dad teaching her to make her dish when she was reunited with him after a separation. He'd started out homeless and now had a PhD. "So he's really shown me that I can do anything," she said.

Serena's chicken was the least favorite. Brad's was good, but is he the "pro" touted in his POV?

"Brad really struggled with his Point of View. There was a cut that didn't make it into the show. Bobby got a bottle of Kentucky bourbon because we were so mad at Brad for floundering. He pulled out the bourbon in evaluation, poured a glass for Brad, and said, 'Drink that. Taste that. Now tell me.' Bobby thought there was a good ole' southern boy there. It didn't work, but he was so unplugged with Brad and wanted to get him back to some roots."

—Susie Fogelson

Chef Feniger said Brianna's chicken was her childhood memory.

For Das, it was go hard or go home, so with his New York Strip Prime he made Tri-Berry Relish and Two-Cheese Mac and Cheese.

Paul's way of standing out was not to make steak or mac and cheese at all but rather Pork Tenderloin with Mascarpone Tarragon Spätzle. To the judges, Aria's fajitas and mac and cheese weren't complementary. Paul talked about his family not having much money when he was a kid, which Bob said was a new POV. Das's berries were not a hit.

> **"I wasn't confident at all that the pork wouldn't backfire on me. I was nervous about it, but I was inspired in a different way, and I felt at that time on the show that I needed to make a statement. I didn't sleep the night before. I cooked it out of worry."**
> **—Paul Young**

> **"I wanted to show that berries could be savory. You win some, you lose some. I wouldn't change anything—that dish is so my style of cooking with its bold flavors."**
> **—Darrell "Das" Smith**

For his rack of lamb, Herb made two sauces—a balsamic vinegar reduction and a shallot red wine sauce. But he burned his vinegar. Aarti said that the distinctive flavor of her kebabs came from pomegranate molasses that she made herself. Tom talked about memories he had of eating a peanut butter and jelly sandwich on the beach and thought it was called a sandwich because it was full of sand. "Honest food is the best food," he said. Aarti said that her mom made these kebabs—a little sweet and a little tangy.

> **"I was really proud that I managed to make the kebabs, the potatoes, and the raita. Bobby was on me about the raita, and I didn't think I'd finish on time. I can still hear him saying, 'I want that raita! You have to make it!' By that point in the competition, I was starting to get my legs. Still, when I think back to that challenge, it feels like a bit of an out-of-body experience. Something else was guiding me through that week!"**
> **—Aarti Sequeira**

Herb talked movingly of the first date he had with his wife, Linda, which was the first time anyone said he was special. Chef Waxman said Aarti's dish "was everything I wanted to see because it was different. It's an accomplished dish."

Aria won her group by default because Paul's risk didn't pay off and Das's berries were a mystery. The fried-chicken contest was won by Brad. He did a fantastic job, Bobby said. Serena's breaded chicken didn't work; Brianna's chicken was "ridiculous," said Bobby, but the waffle wasn't. Tom's lamb was underseasoned, but his presentation was most improved. Bob called Aarti's food a knockout.

Herb admitted to self-doubt: "I don't know if it's the right choice." He said he was still the little fat kid. He didn't have the memories with his dad.

Susie said, "You have to deliver joy."

"Those old demons are hard to shake sometimes," said Herb.

Bobby told him, "You are a success. Lift your head up and make it happen."

Of the bottom three, Serena, Das, and Herb, Das was the one sent packing.

GROUND LAMB KOFTA KEBABS

with Pomegranate Glaze, Bengali-Spiced Potatoes, and Persian Cucumber Raita

Recipe courtesy Aarti Sequeira

Yield: 4 servings ▌ Prep Time: 30 minutes ▌ Cook Time: 45 minutes ▌ Ease of Preparation: easy

---

FOR THE RAITA

2 Persian cucumbers, or 1 English cucumber, sliced ¼-inch thick (about 1¼ cups)

1 cup Greek yogurt

Leaves from 6 sprigs fresh mint, minced (about ¼ cup)

1 garlic clove, minced

Kosher salt

Freshly ground black pepper

FOR THE KEBABS

2 cups fresh parsley leaves, from ½ bunch

4 sprigs mint leaves, picked (about 1 cup)

1 shallot, roughly chopped

Zest and juice of 1 Meyer lemon, divided

2 garlic cloves

1 pound ground lamb

1 teaspoon baking soda

1 teaspoon kosher salt

½ teaspoon freshly ground black pepper

1. **FOR THE RAITA:** Mix all the ingredients in a large bowl. Season with plenty of salt and pepper to taste. Cover the mixture and chill while you prepare the kebabs.

2. **FOR THE KEBABS, PART ONE:** In a food processor, combine the parsley, mint, shallot, lemon zest, and garlic. Pulse until finely minced. Transfer to a large bowl and add the ground lamb, baking soda, salt, and pepper. Knead until it turns sticky, looks like a piece of knitted fabric, and holds its shape. Chill while you make the potatoes.

3. **FOR THE POTATOES:** Fill a large pot with cool water and place over high heat. Add the potatoes and a hefty dose of salt. Bring the water to a boil, then lower the heat and simmer for about 20 minutes, until tender. Drain the potatoes and push them through a ricer.

4. Heat the canola oil in a large sauté pan over medium-high heat. Once it shimmers, add the panch puran. Cook until the spices give off their fragrance and begin to pop, about 30 seconds. Add the onion and sauté until tender and lightly browned, about 6 minutes. Reduce the heat to medium. Add the potatoes, flatten with a spatula, and cook for about 5 minutes, stirring and flattening a few times, until the bottom gets a little crispy. Season with salt and pepper to taste, and keep warm until ready to serve.

Olive oil, for greasing

2 tablespoons pomegranate molasses

1 teaspoon stone-ground mustard

FOR THE POTATOES

1 pound new potatoes

Kosher salt

2 tablespoons canola oil

2 tablespoons panch puran spice blend (or a combination of fennel seed and cumin seed)

1 medium red onion, thinly sliced

Freshly ground black pepper

Special equipment: 12 (10-inch) bamboo skewers, soaked in water

5. FOR THE KEBABS, PART TWO: Take the meat out of the refrigerator. Divide into 12 small, equal-sized portions, and roll each portion into a cylinder. Thread a skewer through the cylinders lengthwise, and form the meat halfway down the skewer, keeping a long cylinder shape. Place the kebabs on an oiled baking sheet. Drizzle the meat with a little more of the oil.

6. Combine the pomegranate molasses, lemon juice, and mustard in a small bowl and set aside.

7. Light a grill or heat a grill pan over medium-high heat.

8. Place the kebabs on the grill, turning every 2 to 3 minutes, generously brushing with the glaze. The kebabs should be cooked and browned in about 6 minutes.

9. Serve with the potatoes and raita on the side.

Midterms

The Camera Challenge re-created the food-product test—"you in a jar." Could any of these finalists deliver a brand?

Serena had always wanted to bottle her own pasta sauce—"Serena's Trattoria Amatriciana Sauce." "If there's one thing I know how to do, it's a tomato sauce," Serena said. "I'm Italian, after all."

Rather than making an on-camera demo, the finalists would have the products tested before a live audience at the Grove in L.A. Giada stopped by the house to give advice on how to connect with an audience. Afterward, Brianna made dinner for the house and kicked Serena out of the kitchen.

"We just don't get along," said Brianna.

At the Grove, a stage was set up and the audience of one hundred had ballots for choosing a favorite among the three-minute presentations. Serena was unfocused and her sauce had no flavor. Paul and Aarti didn't finish their demos, but Paul's tomato sauce and Aarti's tandoori paste were good. Herb made a stir-fry to showcase his Energy Chef Oil Blend, a mix of coconut oil and extra-virgin olive oil. His product was a bit weak, said Susie, but Herb was electric.

"I went out there and was just myself. I had nothing to hide. And if I wasn't myself I knew that people would see right through me, so I just put it all out there. I find that most people like me . . . more than they don't! I wanted this more than anything in the world, I wanted to be the Jack LaLanne or the Richard Simmons of our generation without the funny pant suit or the sequin tops."

—Herb Mesa

A very nervous Brianna called her Oh Berry Chocolate Sauce "Oh Baby." Her voice quivered. And she finished thirty-five seconds early and tried to walk off. Giada said it was a "great product" but that Brianna had made steps back. "So irritated," said Bobby.

To the judges, Aria's Family-Style Apple Pear Chutney was undercooked. Tom's Big Chef's Bold Citrus Marmalade was spicy and flavorful and his demo made the crowd buzz, but his marmalade was bitter. As soon as Brad started his demo, his smile went off. His Three-Onion Cherry Marmalade had limited use but was special.

The bottom two in the audience votes were Serena and Brianna; the top two, Aarti and Tom, who got what he called his "elusive W."

> "The Big Chef concept was in front of my face for thirty-two years, it just took me a little soul searching and a little prodding from the judges to bring it out. Once I found it, I finally accepted where I stand as a cook and as a personality. The relief I felt was pretty crazy; not only had I found a cooking philosophy for the show but I finally was comfortable with my cooking philosophy in life. It was game on from there."
>
> —Tom Pizzica

Paula Deen: A Q&A

When you're judging, if you don't like something you're going to say so . . .

As much as I don't ever like to say anything to hurt somebody, it's just not in my nature to keep quiet. I find it very hard not to be brutally honest when it comes to food and my palate. I am guilty: If it sucks, I say it sucks. I don't like it when people skirt around the truth with me.

Is working in a restaurant good practice for a *Next Food Network Star* challenge?

In the restaurant business you have to be a real quick thinker. I've had to do so much on the fly. And by doing that I have created some things that are our favorites now at the restaurants. One day I said to my baker, "You have got to hurry, we have no desserts!" She was making Brown Sugar Chewies and she pumped the oven up high and she burned 'em. I just took a knife and cut all the burned parts off and made Chocolate Trifle out of it. It was incredible and we still make that. So you have to be able to think quickly on your feet. When you have an irate customer saying it's taking too long, you gotta figure out how to beat that clock and come up with a good product.

Did it take you a while to become comfortable on camera?

I was a little nervous that first time but I am definitely a survivor. I'll do whatever it takes to survive. You know what you have to do and you just do it. It's that simple. Do it or die, sister. I wasn't going to let nerves affect my performance. I moved into my survival mode.

You've done *Iron Chef America*—how was that for you?

They kept inviting me to do *Iron Chef* and I said, "Listen, I have lived that life in my restaurant. There was only one of me on the line preparing for a whole dining room of people." I said, "I have put that part of my life behind and I'm not interested in doing that style of cooking and being under that kind of pressure." But I did agree to go on for a lighter version, a Christmas special making cookies and candy. And we had a ball—Cat and I beat those boys. [Tyler Florence and Robert Irvine]

What's your best advice for these finalists?

You have got to take risks but you have to take calculated risks, not stupid risks. Nothing ventured, nothing gained.

And they have to develop a good Point of View . . .

It's great if you can have a hook but it can't be a setup. My hook is I'm southern and I have this weird accent that no one had ever seen or heard before on Food Network. Guy has a look that was his hook. These were not planned hooks. They were natural and they have to make sense, otherwise it looks forced.

Is it difficult coming up with new recipes?

When you are in the kitchen on a daily basis trying to feed the public and your mind is constantly in that groove, it's not that hard, especially when you have a kitchen full of people helping you think. So in the kitchen atmosphere it's not that hard. My rule is the old K.I.S.S. method: Keep It Simple Stupid.

What's the best food town in America?

Savannah, Georgia, of course. And a real food town is New Orleans. *That's* a food town.

Are shrimp and grits a signature dish of Savannah?

When you get to the coast—the Lowcountry—the fruits of the sea are very predominant. I was born and spent my first forty years in Albany, Georgia, which is in the southwest corner of the state and all we have there are ponds—no salt water. The food is so different from southwest Georgia to southeast. When I came to Savannah, I found people didn't want rice and brown gravy; they wanted red rice and they wanted fried shrimp and oysters and there we had catfish. But I would say fried chicken is the dish of Savannah.

Is cooking grits a test of a good chef?

It's not that difficult if you know a couple of tricks. I always use a quick-cooking grit, never an instant grit. We cook 'em for about 45 minutes. You have to salt your water and when you are putting in your grits you need a whisk because you have to get every one of those kernels good and wet, otherwise you will have lumps. It's simple but you have to do it right.

Your fans feel like they really know you.

They do know me because I pretty much tell it all. My TV show is like my real life. I bring my family in and I don't hide anything and I expose us all. So they do know me—we just haven't been properly introduced."

That's where the line between public and private is blurred . . .

My husband is on my show with me and when I do live shows he is always right by my side. He is one of the funniest people I have ever met. He is so hilarious but when he gets in front of that camera with me he starts editing himself. He is so afraid he is going to say something that is going to hurt me or make me look bad. So he edits himself and I have begged him to quit doing that, that's what the edit-room floor is for, Michael. I said take a risk. Run that risk and let people see the real you. If they see you they are going to adore you. Some people just have a hard time doing that.

Do you edit yourself?

Not too much. If I say something that should not be said, the edit room will get it. It's a little different on a live stage. Then I have to edit myself a little bit.

Whenever you appear, people's faces light up . . .

I've tried to figure it out. I could feel something happening out there as I became more and more known . . . I noticed there was some kind of rapport going on between me and the crowd and I think I have finally figured it out. I asked my husband if he knew what was happening and he said, "Paula, you know, bottom line is, you can't fool people. Those people know you're real. They know that what they see is what they are going to get."

What I think it is, I think I remind people of someone else who has loved them very much in their life, whether it's a grandmother, a mother, a favorite aunt . . . That's a great gift to me that these people have given me. And as far as I am concerned it doesn't get any better than that.

SPOTLIGHT ON

LUNCH TRUCKS WITH PAULA

Straight from the live demo, finalists were faced with four lunch trucks. And Paula Deen.

The lunch-truck challenge resonated with Paula because she'd gotten her start selling brown-bag lunches. In teams of two, based on the Grove challenge, the finalists would be serving lunch on Venice Beach. The top two, Tom and Aarti, were paired, as were the bottom two, Serena and Brianna, recent adversaries in the home kitchen. Brianna was worried. "The last thing I want is for there to be some type of drama." Tom and Aarti got to pick the other teams and strategically paired Brad and Aria to keep friends Brad and Paul apart.

Serena and Brianna planned their menu: Jerk Chicken, Beef Empanadas, Lamb Gyros, and Porketta Paninis. They had to name their lunch operation (Two Chix and a Truck). Tom and Aarti went for comfort food with Indian flavor: BLCs (Bacon, Lettuce, and Cucumber), Lamb Tacos, Curried Funnel Cakes, and the name Dick Bombay's. Brad and Aria, both from Wisconsin, decided that their All-American Cheesehead Grill would feature Wedge Salad with Blue Cheese, Beef and Buffalo Sliders, Hot Dogs, and Strawberry Milk Shakes.

When they shopped, Tom rejected frozen lamb and picked up tri-tip. Brianna bought the frozen meat. In a different store, Serena looked in vain for sriracha sauce—something they don't have in Italy—so she called Brianna. Brianna was not feeling confident.

At the beach, the truck galleys were a tight squeeze.

Each team had issues: Tom smoked out the truck. Paul bought a giardiniera mix rather than making his own relish. Aria and Brad didn't buy fresh strawberries for their shakes, and Brad didn't start cooking until the last minute. Brianna's lamb was still frozen, so she defrosted it in the oven. Suddenly, time was up, the crowd arrived, and Aria and Brad weren't ready. "Holy cow," said Aria, "where did you all come from?"

Working with Serena gave Brianna a new respect for her. Together, they brought it. "Empanadas are the quintessential street food," said Brianna. "You have your veggies, you have your meat, in one little bite."

"I love making empanadas! One of my favorite street foods of all time! I started making these tasty treats after returning from a trip from Uruguay in 2002 where they deliver these puppies like pizza!

"After winning the food-truck challenge Serena and I were ecstatic, I really felt I was getting some recognition for my cooking chops but this was a crucial moment in the competition for a lot of us, do or die."

—Brianna Jenkins

For Paul and Herb's Wraps truck, Herb planned healthy Cuban Wraps, Paul, Chicago-style Cheesy Beef Wraps with Spicy Sweet Potato Wedges, and Breakfast Egg Wraps.

Herb said that he and Paul were "killing it"—two big personalities not holding back. Herb came out of the truck to serve the committee; Paul admitted to Bobby that he'd bought the giardiniera. Bobby liked the Cuban Wrap a lot and thought the Breakfast Egg burrito was good. Paula said the guys were "cute as a bug's ear." Susie, however, said Paul was still figuring out the right vibe.

"My favorite challenge of all was the food trucks. I love it when they have to brand themselves and when they have to work together and they have to come up with concepts. I loved it."

—Susie Fogelson

Brad's burger was completely overcooked, said Bobby. And given their generous budget, the judges didn't understand why they skimped on the strawberries.

Paula Deen: My grandson could have made that [hot dog].

Bob Tuschman: And your grandson is how old?

Paula Deen: Three and a half.

"That challenge was so much fun. I was surprised by one of the trucks because they didn't challenge themselves at all. A hot dog is a hot dog. I can make a fabulous hot dog but you got to do a lot more than put a dog on a bun."

—Paula Deen

what is SRIRACHA SAUCE?

Sriracha is an Asian-style chile sauce named after a town in Thailand. The most famous version, sold in bottles adorned with a rooster, was created in the United States by David Tran, who immigrated to this country from Vietnam.

Together, Brad and Aria were a good team, Susie said, but Aria was becoming one-dimensional.

The committee loved the BLC. To Susie, Tom's funnel cake was "phenomenal," but Aarti's taco was way too hot for Paula. She said they made everyone welcome. Bob asked, Where was Aarti's confidence but Tom had come to life? Brianna and Serena sold the committee on their round-the-world flavors and girl power. Bobby said the empanadas were "very well flavored, and I love the chimichurri on the outside." Every other dish went down well. Serena was adorable and Brianna had some star power, said Bobby. According to Paula, "That truck looked good on them."

> **"I had a blast with my 'sister' Brianna. We are more similar than meets the eye: both strong-willed only children with very strong mother figures. We bonded a lot in the challenge, and to date we are good friends."**
>
> —Serena Palumbo

In evaluation, Bobby called the Lamb Gyro the best dish. Susie said girl power was radiating from the truck. Serena's midterm assessment from Bob was that she had a star's personality but could take it a bit too far. Brianna had wowed Bob with her food but hadn't conquered her nerves. Bob said this week was a game changer for Tom. He'd risen. Aarti had to grab her chance. "You're an adult," said Bobby. "Bring it on."

> **"Aarti was a front-runner from the beginning. She was very articulate, had a great voice, was very pretty, and had a point of view that was different from most people, but I have to say it took a long time for me to get used to the idea that we were going to give her a show because she was such a procrastinator. I told her, I'm not feeling sorry for you because you're so concerned about the time. Roll your sleeves up and go do the job. Or leave."**
>
> —Bobby Flay

> **"The food truck was awesome and Aarti and I killed it. We actually got robbed of the win that day. Once Bobby called it my mayo I ran with it just to get a fun little rise out of Aarti and plus, we both know whose food truck it was anyway!**
>
> **"Aarti and I get along because she is a great person, first of all, but also because we went through the same steps to get to where we are. We came up together on the same minor league team but now we play for different major league ball clubs at different positions. We'll always be close but at the same time want to win a World Series for our team."**
>
> —Tom Pizzica

Paul and Herb's breakfast wrap was good; the Cuban Wrap was *very* good. But could Herb harness his energy and manage his highs and lows? Bobby asked Paul about his new "Blue Collar" Point of View, but Paul got defensive. Bob asked somewhat skeptically if his POV was really him. "I don't know who you are."

The Cheeseheads kept people waiting, and the food wasn't executed well. A salad on a lunch truck wasn't a good idea, and fresh strawberries would have made the shake twenty times better. Brad had to figure out his camera issue while Aria had plateaued. Susie said early in the competition she glowed on camera but now she was forgettable. You need to fight, Susie told her.

The winning truck was the Two Chix, Brianna and Serena. The bottom three were Aria, Brad, and Paul. Going home was Paul.

"At some point, you're going to blink and you're going to be gone."

—Bobby Flay

BRIANNA'S EMPANADAS

with Serena's Chimichurri Sauce

Recipe courtesy of Brianna Jenkins and Serena Palumbo

Yield: 10 to 12 servings, 24 empanadas ▮ Prep Time: 45 minutes ▮ Cook Time: 30 minutes ▮ Ease of Preparation: intermediate

1 tablespoon olive oil

1 pound ground beef

1 large onion, chopped

6 garlic cloves, chopped

2 teaspoons ground chipotle

1 teaspoon ground cumin

1 teaspoon ground coriander

¾ teaspoon salt

Freshly ground black pepper

2 (4-ounce) cans mild chopped green chiles

2 hard-boiled eggs, chopped

24 empanada wrappers

Canola oil, for frying

Chimichurri Sauce (recipe follows)

CHIMICHURRI SAUCE

2 tablespoons lemon zest

¼ cup freshly squeezed lemon juice, or more, as needed

1 cup fresh cilantro leaves, roughly chopped

¾ cup fresh parsley leaves, roughly chopped

¾ cup fresh mint leaves, roughly chopped

6 garlic cloves

Kosher salt

1. Heat a large skillet over medium-high heat and add the olive oil. Stir in the ground beef, breaking it up with a wooden spoon. Cook, stirring occasionally, until browned. Remove the beef from the pan and reserve. Drain all but 1 tablespoon of the fat from the pan. Return the pan to the heat and add the onion, sautéing until softened, about 8 minutes. Stir in the garlic, chipotle, cumin, and coriander and cook until fragrant, about 3 minutes. Put the ground beef back into the pan and stir. Season the mixture with salt and pepper to taste. Turn off the heat and let cool for 5 minutes. Stir in the green chiles and chopped eggs.

2. Fill a small bowl with water.

3. Lay out a few of the empanada wrappers. Spoon about 3 tablespoons of the beef filling into the center of a wrapper. Dip your finger lightly into the water and run it along the edges of the wrapper. Fold the wrapper over the beef, to make a half-moon shape, and pinch it shut. Repeat until all of the filling is used up.

4. Heat a deep sauté pan over high heat and pour in the canola oil until it reaches halfway up the sides. Heat the oil to 350°F. Fry the empanadas until golden brown, 1 to 2 minutes on each side. Remove from the pan and drain on paper towels. Serve them with the Chimichurri Sauce for dipping.

¼ teaspoon crushed red pepper, or more to taste

½ cup light olive oil, or more, as needed

CHIMICHURRI SAUCE: In a food processor or blender, combine all the ingredients until everything is finely chopped and well combined. If the sauce is too thick, add more oil and lemon juice. It should be just thin enough to pour.

Recipe courtesy Serena Palumbo

Yield: About 2 cups ▮ Prep Time: 10 minutes ▮ Ease of Preparation: easy

Tips and Techniques

The Camera Challenge asked: Are the finalists experts? They had to create a "party bite" for a specific celebration using ingredients in a picnic basket and provide a tip on entertaining. The prize: presenting their tips on Food Network's sister channel, the Cooking Channel.

Brad got the bachelorette party, something he'd never attended, reasonably enough. He turned his strawberries, vodka, and kalamata olives into Crostini with Goat Cheese Strawberry Spread and Olive and Fig Salad with Orange Vodka Dressing. Brianna wasn't thrilled to get a five-year-old's birthday and made Chorizo Taquitos and Mustard Cheddar Queso. "What kid's going to eat that?" said Tom.

Presenting, Brad relaxed and smiled. Aarti suggested that viewers make her bite the night before, but she stopped before her minute was up.

Herb's food wasn't good, he gave no tip, and he had no energy. Brianna's angle was that her friend's son was coming over. "Let the kids get dirty while the ladies have a glass of champagne." Giada said she didn't know a lot of five-year-olds who'd eat that food. Aria was more serious, but Bobby and Giada didn't like her finger sandwiches. Serena scrambled for words, but her crostini was delicious.

"You can't let 'em see you sweat," said Giada.

Herb and Brianna were at the bottom; Tom and Brad won the day.

Tom had the ladies' luncheon; his ingredients: almonds, cheese, and English breakfast tea. "When your guests arrive it gives them a little conversation starter," said Tom. "You also may be wondering, 'Tom, why did you do a croque monsieur? Why didn't you do a croque madame?' But I can tell you what, this monsieur is rich, soft, and very ladylike."

"I came up with that dish the moment Giada said 'Go.' I had no idea what to do with English Tea and Gouda so I let my inner Big Chef take over and I was happy with the results. I was actually surprised it came out that well. I'm more likely to make the Croque Monsieur because I'm a traditionalist when it comes to eating classic French sandwiches. No, I have never made those little treats again. I should say, not yet . . ."
—Tom Pizzica

Bob said that despite Tom's shaggy, slacker look, he radiated expertise. "That was the most I've ever liked him," said Bobby. Giada said she could taste the almonds, which gave it a little crunch. And yes, "the ladies like it."

ALMOND-CRUSTED CROQUE MONSIEUR
with English Tea Béchamel Sauce

Recipe courtesy Tom Pizzica

Yield: 12 sandwiches ▌ Prep Time: 20 minutes ▌ Cook Time: 55 minutes ▌ Ease of Preparation: easy

1 quart whole milk, divided

1 bag English breakfast tea

2 tablespoons chopped fresh tarragon

5 tablespoons unsalted butter, divided

2 tablespoons canola oil

3 eggs

1¼ teaspoons kosher salt, divided

1⅛ teaspoons freshly ground black pepper, divided

1 cup blanched, sliced almonds

1 (12-ounce) baguette, ends trimmed, sliced on the diagonal into 12 (¾-inch) pieces

12 thin slices deli ham (8 ounces)

2 cups shredded Swiss or sharp Cheddar cheese (6½ ounces)

½ cup chopped yellow onion

2 tablespoons all-purpose flour

2 tablespoons grated Parmesan cheese

¼ cup chopped fresh parsley leaves

1. Preheat the oven to 400°F.

2. Reserve ¼ cup of the milk and pour the rest into a medium saucepan. Add the tea bag and tarragon and bring to a simmer over medium-low heat, stirring occasionally. Cook for 10 minutes. Set aside.

3. Heat a large skillet over medium-high heat and add 2 tablespoons of the butter and the oil. Whisk together the eggs, the reserved ¼ cup milk, 1 teaspoon of the salt, and 1 teaspoon of the pepper. Place the sliced almonds in a separate bowl. Dip the bread slices into the egg batter, then press into the almonds. Cook the bread slices in the skillet until a nice deep brown color, about 2 minutes per side. Transfer to a baking sheet and top each piece evenly with the ham and cheese. Bake until the cheese melts and starts to brown, about 10 minutes.

4. While the monsieurs are baking, heat a medium-size saucepan over medium-high heat. Add the remaining 3 tablespoons of the butter and sauté the onion until it is light brown and tender, about 3 minutes. Add the flour and mix until smooth and lightly toasted, 1 minute. Strain the tea milk into the pot, discarding the bag, and whisk vigorously. Cook the béchamel sauce, whisking constantly, until thickened, about 10 minutes. Whisk in the Parmesan and parsley and season with the remaining ¼ teaspoon salt and ⅛ teaspoon pepper. Turn off the heat. Remove the monsieurs from the oven and slather them with the béchamel sauce. Plate and serve.

SPOTLIGHT ON

CHEZ FRANK

At the Food Network Kitchens, a table of American Classic dishes such as Beef Stroganoff and Chicken Cordon Bleu was laid out. Ted Allen presented the Star Challenge. Finalists had to reinvent a classic fifties' or sixties' dish and serve it in Palm Springs at the former home of Frank Sinatra. Attending would be editor-in-chief of *Food Network Magazine* Maile Carpenter (pictured above) and *Esquire* editor-at-large Cal Fussman.

Brad picked Chicken Cordon Bleu; Tom, Lobster Thermidor. Brad gave Pigs in a Blanket to Aria and Beef Stroganoff to Herb. Tom gave Tuna Noodle Casserole to Brianna and Deviled Eggs to Aarti, leaving Pineapple Upside-Down Cake for Serena.

"I fell in love with Ol' Blue Eyes in my early teens, thanks to my grandfather. The whole mystique of the Rat Pack and how cool they were made the experience amazing. As we walked in, there was the piano-shaped pool that I had read about in books on Sinatra."

Just thinking of the people who had swum in that pool was enough to make you starstruck. Imagine that, starstruck by a swimming pool. It was an amazing experience that I am very thankful for. Maybe the results of the show would have been different if every week we did a challenge at the house of a sixties' icon."

—Brad Sorenson

"I didn't love that so much because it was freezing. Ted was delirious and I'm not a big Sinatra fan. They were saying, 'What's your favorite song?' and I said, 'Give me one.' I was impressed with the people who knew Sinatra and used it, like Brad. I loved that presentation. I would have failed miserably at that."

—Susie Fogelson

What's Old Is New

Up first was Aria, who reinterpreted Pigs in a Blanket into Buttermilk-Battered Shrimp. "You threw the pig right out the window," said Bobby. Ted said it was a very strange choice; Bobby, that pork belly would have been awesome. Susie liked the dish and Aria's energy.

Tom made Lobster and Fried Fennel Napoleon, but his lobster stuck to the grill. His presentation rambled and the dish wasn't focused either.

Aarti's Devil-ish Egg Curry Over Red Rice Pilaf was a lot to cook. She didn't feel the glamour, and Bob said that they didn't want to hear her talk about budget considerations in this venue. What's more, there wasn't much curry flavor and the dish was dry.

Brianna wasn't confident about her Crab and Brie Casserole, and she burned her bread crumbs and mushrooms. Bobby said there was a luciousness to the dish but her presentation was negative.

Herb's "Healthy" Stroganoff included four types of mushrooms, but no one liked the dish. He had to move away from "Energy Chef."

> "This was a low point. I was knackered [tired out]. I was a little intimidated by that place. And taking classic American retro dishes and classing them up was hard. I've been here a while but I've never had a connection to deviled eggs. We don't eat them in India. So I psyched myself out."
>
> —Aarti Sequeira

Next, it was Serena's turn, in her case reinventing the Pineapple Upside-Down Cake.

> "Every year for my father's birthday my mother and I would cook millefoglie, my father's favorite dessert. Even after my father passed away, we keep preparing it religiously each January 31st. We usually presented the cake to him in the morning so we'd have it for breakfast. It was so big we would have leftovers for a week! My dad would be thrilled to know the recipe is being published."
>
> —Serena Palumbo

PINEAPPLE MILLEFOGLIE with Maraschino Cherry Sauce

Recipe courtesy Serena Palumbo

Yield: 6 servings ▪ Prep Time: 45 minutes ▪ Cook Time: 1 hour ▪ Inactive Prep Time: 3 hours ▪ Ease of Preparation: intermediate

FOR THE CUSTARD
2 cups milk

1 vanilla bean, halved lengthwise, seeds scraped

4 egg yolks

¼ cup granulated sugar

3 tablespoons all-purpose flour

FOR THE MILLEFOGLIE
1 (17.3-ounce) box puff pastry, thawed

FOR THE SAUCE
1 (12-ounce) bag frozen black cherries, thawed

1 cup pineapple juice

¼ cup maraschino cherry juice, from a jar of maraschino cherries

FOR THE PINEAPPLE
6 slices fresh pineapple (about 1 pound), from 1 small peeled and cored pineapple

½ cup confectioners' sugar

FOR THE CHANTILLY CREAM
1 cup heavy cream

¼ cup confectioners' sugar

¼ teaspoon vanilla extract

6 maraschino cherries, for garnish

1. Preheat the oven to 400°F.

2. **FOR THE CUSTARD:** In a medium saucepan, warm the milk with the vanilla bean and seeds over low heat. Whisk the egg yolks with the sugar, then the flour, in a medium bowl. Remove the vanilla bean and whisk the warm milk into the egg mixture. Pour the mixture back into the pot and cook over medium heat, whisking constantly, until the cream is thick, about 8 minutes. Transfer the custard to a bowl, lay plastic wrap directly on the surface of the custard, and cool in the refrigerator for about 3 hours. Transfer it to a large pastry bag fitted with a wide, round tip.

3. **FOR THE MILLEFOGLIE:** Cut the puff pastry into 18 (3-inch) rings using a ring mold or a sharp paring knife. Place the rounds on parchment-lined baking sheets and bake until golden brown, 10 to 15 minutes. Set aside to cool.

4. **FOR THE SAUCE:** Combine the cherries, pineapple juice, and cherry juice in a small saucepan. Bring the liquid to a simmer over medium heat. Simmer until the cherries are softened, about 5 minutes. Carefully transfer the mixture to a blender or food processor and purée until smooth. Strain the purée and set aside to cool. Store any extra sauce in the refrigerator up to 2 weeks.

5. **FOR THE PINEAPPLE:** Dust the pineapple slices with confectioners' sugar and place on a baking sheet. Bake until softened and lightly browned at the edges, about 30 minutes. Let cool.

6. **FOR THE CHANTILLY CREAM:** Whip the cream, sugar, and vanilla until fluffy and stiff peaks form. Chill until ready to use.

7. **ASSEMBLY:** Place a pastry round on an individual serving plate. Pipe the custard over it in circles and place a slice of the caramelized pineapple on top. Cover with a pastry round and pipe some of the whipped cream on top. Top with one more pastry round and drizzle with the sauce. Garnish with a cherry on top.

Brad's Way

Before the challenge, Brad was feeling "Rat Packy"—good. "If I execute my game plan properly, it's going to go over really well." His risotto he declared "fantastic"; the chicken, "amazing."

On the estate, the song "My Way" popped into his head. Chicken Cordon Bleu Brad's Way meant a lot of bacon, a lot of creaminess, a lot of fun. Brad said he'd had doubts, but now he had a new lease on life.

Maile instantly liked him. Ted said the dish was beautiful. For Susie, however, he was this close to going home.

Cal Fussman didn't know about that, but "wherever he's going, I'm going with him." Bob said he had effortless style. "He was magic."

CRISPY BACON-WRAPPED CHICKEN
with Three-Cheese Creamy Risotto and Arugula Fennel Salad

Recipe courtesy Brad Sorenson

Yield: 4 servings ▮ Prep Time: 45 minutes ▮ Cook Time: 1 hour 15 minutes ▮ Ease of Preparation: intermediate

FOR THE CHICKEN
4 skinless and boneless chicken breast halves (1 pound total), preferably organic, trimmed and squared off a bit

Kosher salt

Freshly ground black pepper

1. Preheat the oven to 375°F.

2. **FOR THE CHICKEN:** Season the chicken lightly with salt and pepper. On a cutting board, lay 4 slices of bacon crosswise and slightly overlapping. Place a chicken breast on top, perpendicular to the bacon. Bring the bacon slices up and around the chicken to wrap the

16 slices bacon, *not* thick cut, from 16-ounce package

2 tablespoons olive oil

FOR THE SALAD
2 tablespoons freshly squeezed Meyer lemon juice

1 tablespoon extra-virgin olive oil

Kosher salt

Freshly ground black pepper

2 cups baby arugula, trimmed and washed

1 small bulb fennel, thinly sliced (1½ cups)

Three-Cheese Creamy Risotto (recipe follows)

FOR THE THREE-CHEESE CREAMY RISOTTO
1 tablespoon olive oil

2 slices pancetta, diced ¼ inch thick (1 cup)

3 garlic cloves, minced (1 tablespoon)

1 shallot, finely chopped (4 teaspoons)

1⅓ cups arborio rice

½ cup white wine

4 cups chicken stock, heated

¼ cup grated Parmesan cheese

2 tablespoons mascarpone

1 ounce goat cheese

¼ cup fresh basil leaves, thinly sliced

1 tablespoon butter

Kosher salt

Freshly ground black pepper

entire breast. Repeat with the remaining chicken breasts and bacon.

3. In a large ovenproof skillet, heat the olive oil over medium heat. When the oil is hot, add the bacon-wrapped chicken and cook until the bacon on both sides of the chicken is crispy, about 8 minutes per side. Transfer the pan to the oven and bake until the chicken is cooked through, 15 to 18 minutes.

4. FOR THE SALAD: Whisk together the lemon juice and olive oil and season with salt and pepper to taste. Toss with the arugula and fennel until well coated.

5. FOR THE THREE-CHEESE CREAMY RISOTTO: Heat a large wide pot over medium heat and add the olive oil and pancetta. Sauté until the pancetta begins to crisp, then add the garlic and shallot, cooking until browned. Add the rice, stir well to coat, and cook for 1 minute.

6. Stir in the wine and continue to cook the rice, stirring, until the wine is almost completely absorbed. Add enough of the stock to just cover and stir again until the stock is absorbed, about 25 minutes. Continue to gradually add the stock, stirring well after each addition, until the rice is cooked through but still has a bite. You might have some stock left over.

7. When the rice is cooked, stir in the cheeses and basil. Remove the pot from the heat and stir in the butter. Season with salt and pepper to taste. The risotto should be smooth, creamy, rich, and delicious.

8. To serve, scoop some of the risotto into the center of each dinner plate (make sure it has some height). Cut the chicken on the diagonal and place one portion on top of each plate of risotto. Top with the arugula salad.

Try Not to Lose

In evaluation, the committee wondered whether Serena could be an expert, a consistent master of Italian cooking. Herb was frustrating Bobby. But a light had gone off in Bobby's head regarding Herb—why didn't he do Latin cuisine? "That's when you smile," Susie told him. Tom's dish was good, but he rambled. Brianna was sabotaging herself. Why couldn't she express herself?

Bob called Brad commanding. Bobby told Brad that his "Pro" POV was tough unless you're Alain Ducasse or Thomas Keller. "Take advantage of who you are. Whoever that is, I want it on a plate." Aria was off the mark; Aarti misstepped. Aarti's food wasn't well received, and she talked about saving money. You can't just try not to lose, Aarti said of herself. If you're trying to win, said Bobby, it's hard for me to get you to join my team.

The bottom three were Aarti, Herb, and Brianna. Brianna's was the name called for dismissal.

> **"The camera side of the competition was unfortunately my downfall. I really didn't prepare for this. While I'm used to teaching classes and giving demos, it's quite different when you're standing in front of some of your idols. My nervousness was unexpected and when there are no options to do over, it leaves little room for flubs."**
>
> **—Brianna Jenkins**

Cereal Challenge

Having been in the bottom three, Aarti felt pressure to win a challenge. She got the chance with a Kellogg's cereal test presented by Season Five winner Melissa d'Arabian: The six finalists had to make dinner using breakfast, in twenty minutes.

Herb produced Cereal-Encrusted French Toast with Latin Sausage Patties. This was the debut of Herb's new POV: "Cooking *con Sabor.*" When he presented, he had a new light in his eyes. Bob said that Herb had found himself.

Aarti made Quinoa and All-Bran Pilaf. It was crunchy and had a nutty flavor; Melissa said it was delicious. Serena sang "O Sole Mio," but Bob said she wasn't real. Tom and Brad took steps back—Tom was sloppy, Brad's presentation was unconvincing, although his Rice Krispies–Encrusted Tuna was very good.

what is QUINOA?

Quinoa has been grown in the Andes for thousands of years. It's high in protein and also a ready source of calcium and iron and makes a healthy addition to soups or stews or served like rice. Although it resembles a grain, quinoa is actually the seed of the goose-foot plant.

"Herb had a hard time switching his POV. Energy Chef is so much who he is. Every morning he would come down to the girls' area. 'Girls, have you had breakfast?' And he'd run upstairs and make us egg white omelets over whole wheat pancakes with a little syrup and fresh fruit. It was great."

—Aarti Sequeira

Secret Supper Club

For the Star Challenge, finalists had to cook for an "underground supper club" of what Bobby called "superfoodies" at SmogShoppe. As one team, finalists had to make dinner for forty ultra-serious gourmands—and they had only one hour to prep.

Team leader Aarti's idea was "Our L.A."—a culinary tour of Los Angeles. Herb's Latin offering was a flan. In the store, he passed up the chance to buy pans to cook it, but he kicked himself when he saw that the kitchen's pans were only an inch and a half deep. Aria made Spiced Carrot Soup to represent Santa Monica; Serena, Pasta Alla Norma, an old-school dish of fried eggplants, tomato sauce, and ricotta, for Beverly Hills. Aarti's Little India dish was Green Chicken Curry.

Serena was intimidated and rushed her presentation; Bob worried that her range was very narrow. For Thai Town, Tom made Seared Black Cod in Asian Broth. It was very ambitious and he himself thought it was a mushy mess, with too much soy sauce. "Garbage," he called it. The critics agreed. "God-awful," said one.

For Downtown, Brad made Spice-Rubbed Lamb Chops over White Bean Ragù, but he left it late to cook the lamb and had to scramble to get it cooked. Brad's food won kudos, but his presentation was clearly flat. When Aarti served her curry, Bobby said, "Finally we got some flavor," and her story was arresting. Herb had been expediting and serving other peoples' food, but he overcooked his flan. His personality came through, but as Bobby said, "Once flan is overcooked, for me there's no reason to eat it."

In evaluation, Bobby rated Aarti's curry fantastic. Aria was placed in the middle of the pack in food and presentation. Susie told her she had to be a good teammate. Susie wondered what Brad's Point of View really was. Now Herb's POV was good, but his food lagged behind the conception. Next time, said Susie, buy the pans. And Serena wasn't making the progress the committee needed.

It wasn't a good week for Tom. His dish, "It was just soy sauce, period," Bobby said.

The top two were Aarti and Brad, the winner, Aarti. Serena was going home.

"The crowd wasn't tough at all. I know what it's like to manage a dining room and deal with people that know food. I shortchanged myself thinking I could make a flan in an hour, when it really takes me a good three and a half hours to make a really perfect flan. What was I thinking?"

—Herb Mesa

Least Favorite Ingredients, Part Two

At the Food Network Kitchens, Giada asked the top five to create a signature dish that reflected their Point of View. Only Brad had no POV. All of a sudden before they started Giada told them to stop. There was a twist: They had to add their least favorite ingredient.

Aria's anchovies were brought in by her son, Luca, and her mom, and Aria lost herself. Aarti's husband brought her okra; Tom's fiancée, Rachel, brought white pepper; Brad's brother Alex brought ranch dressing; and Herb's family, canned peas.

Aria made Mashed Potato Pizza with Caramelized Onions, hiding the anchovies among the onions. Brad made Bacon and Spinach Risotto with Ranch Dressing and presented his POV, "Culinary Quest"—inviting people to join him on his adventures through the culinary world. Aria told a good story about her dad making pizza. Herb was scattered. Tom put the white pepper in Couscous Cakes to go with poached salmon. He was focused and on point and Rambling Man was put to rest. Aarti was entertaining but her fried rice fell short. Aria won the challenge.

Cooking for Eva

Giada announced that the final four would be going to New York. "It's the play-offs, baby," said Tom. "It's the play-offs!" Before that, there was a Star Challenge. Out came Todd English, who started the restaurant Beso ("Kiss") with Eva Longoria. The contest: Create a dish inspired by an emotion. Aria drew Melancholy; Brad, Surprise; Herb, Joy; Aarti, Fear; and Tom, Jealousy. Aria, as winner of the previous challenge, could swap out, and she took Herb's Joy—literally.

One more thing: The finalists would be serving Eva. For Melancholy, Herb decided to make a dish that incorporated all the flavor he remembered from childhood: Braised Short Ribs with Seared Scallops and Mofongo Cakes. Aria made Sunday dinner, in honor of her family's weekly time together. Brad opted for Grilled Steak over Mushrooms and Sea Bass over Creamed Leeks, a surprise pairing of two dishes that he loved. Aarti said that when she was scared she thought of her mom, so she would make her mother's Lamb Pulao.

Tom said, "What in God's name am I going to do with Jealousy on a plate?" Since everyone was going to tell a personal story, he said he would tell the tale of two tunas: Tuna Tartare with Gala Apples and Seared Tuna with Tomato Purée.

At Beso, Brad didn't get his steaks on in time, and they were too rare. His presentation was flat—he didn't make the connection to Surprise. Eva Longoria defused his discomfort.

Eva Longoria: When did you lose your virginity?

Brad Sorenson: Actually, I haven't.

Bob said that Brad wasn't confident or charismatic as he'd been at the Sinatra home, and Bobby called his food a misfire.

Tom told a long shaggy-dog story that posited how his tuna duo made it onto the plate. Bobby Flay liked his use of the chiles de árbol; Todd English liked the herbed brown butter on the tartare. Eva praised Tom's "fantastic execution," and Bobby loved his dish. "I loved Tom today," said Giada.

"A lot of what happened to me during the competition was simple inspiration. I can only relate it to writing songs, which I did when I was younger. The best songs were always the ones that came to you in a flash and you wrote in five minutes. I felt like all the judges had awoken a sleeping giant. I had struggled with my passion for cooking prior to getting on the show and during the show a new passion for cooking had emerged and I was so happy I got it back that things just flowed."

—Tom Pizzica

Aarti overcooked her rice, and her nerves took over. She said she thought about her mom, but to Susie it was a weak presentation.

Herb knew he had to put it out there. He talked about being a short, fat kid from Elizabeth, New Jersey. Other kids ate mac and cheese, while he ate tripe and oxtail. That made him sad, but you

couldn't have happiness without some sadness. He turned his mom's oxtail into short ribs. Eva said he had star quality, and Bobby said it was his best dish.

Aria's Potato Gratin wasn't cooked. She talked about rebuilding her family with Sunday dinner but forgot to mention Joy. "Maybe she should have kept Melancholy," said Todd English.

Giada left the final five before elimination. Herb and Tom were the top two. Bobby affirmed that Latin roots was the best place for Herb. Susie called Tom's presentation "nothing short of genius." Tom was the winner.

That left a bottom three. Not only did Aria fail to mention Joy, but she hadn't tasted her potatoes. Bobby said they were crunchy, which isn't a good word for a potato unless it's a potato chip.

Brad's food was a little clunky to Bobby. Bob said he was stiff at first, then his charm and smile appeared. Could he bring that to the lens? Bobby liked Aarti's raita but not the lamb. Susie said she was apologetic, and that's high-maintenance. "What you don't get . . . is a bunch of shrinks telling you you are worth it before you go on," said Susie.

"If you want it, you have to act like it." The bottom three were sent out and the judges debated three potential stars with different problems. Aarti had gone backward; Brad's charm disappeared on camera; Aria's food was very up and down.

With Susie visibly upset about the result, Aria was saved and Brad was sent home.

"We have said it was the hardest decision before, and we weren't being disingenuous. Paul and Jag were hard. Debbie and Jeffrey . . . but Brad was the hardest. Now we can't say it anymore. We're busted."

—Bob Tuschman

Allez Cuisine!

Assembled in New York, Aarti, Aria, Herb, and Tom had no idea what was in store. What could be big enough for the final four? *Iron Chef,* of course.

— "It was a dream come true to do that challenge. I felt at home in this element and it was by far the coolest challenge in the competition and made it worth it to make it so far. I can definitely see myself doing this again. Watch out, Bobby Flay!"

—Herb Mesa

"I smell fear."

—Alton Brown

It was the fiery furnace that is *Iron Chef America*: two hour-long battles, three dishes judged by Iron Chefs Cat Cora, Bobby Flay, Masaharu Morimoto, and Michael Symon. "We expect the unexpected," said Bobby. The commentary would be half the score. Iron Chefs always have a sous-chef. Challenge winner Tom picked Brianna; the others drew: Herb got Paul, Aarti got Brad, and Aria got Serena. Herb said, "This is the Super Bowl for foodies." The first secret ingredient: shrimp.

Aarti planned her White Gazpacho, but there were no cucumbers. A tomato gazpacho would lack the surprise element. She stared at the produce table . . . Meanwhile, Tom reported to Alton, that's not extra-virgin olive oil; it's sherry vinegar.

Aria was a little more vague—is that cilantro in there? Alton asked of a pan of Herb's. Alton had to come over to check for himself.

Aarti seemed to be in outer space as she figured out what to do with her Gazpacho. "Adapt or die!" said Alton. Could she cook quickly enough?

"She's not going to finish," said Bobby.

Aarti's other dishes were Stuffed Shrimp and Prawn Garam Masala. Tom asked her what garam masala was—it means "hot masala," masala being a mix of spice and vegetables—then reported in. Herb made Enchiladas de Camarones with Brown Rice, a shrimp soup he'd never made before, and Mousse-Stuffed Colossal Shrimp. Herb was all action, loving every minute; Aarti was more serene. Alton prompted Aria for her reports. "Aria, where does paprika come from?"

Tom answered: It's dried ground pepper.

COCONUT TOMATO GAZPACHO
with Coriander-and-Mint-Pickled Shrimp

Recipe courtesy Aarti Sequeira

Yield: 4 to 6 servings (7 cups) ▌ Prep Time: 10 minutes ▌ Cook Time: 5 minutes ▌
Inactive Prep Time: 1 hour ▌ Ease of Preparation: easy

FOR THE SHRIMP

2 cups sherry vinegar

½ cup water

2 tablespoons coriander seeds

1 tablespoon black peppercorns

½ teaspoon whole cloves

½ teaspoon crushed red pepper

½ pound shelled colossal shrimp, tails intact (6 pieces)

5 sprigs fresh mint

5 sprigs fresh cilantro

FOR THE GAZPACHO

5 large vine-ripened tomatoes, chopped, plus 1 large vine-ripened tomato, whole

1 small red onion, chopped

1 (1-inch) piece fresh ginger, peeled and minced

1 cup coconut milk

Kosher salt

Freshly ground black pepper

2 tablespoons finely chopped fresh cilantro leaves

1. **FOR THE SHRIMP:** In a large saucepan, bring the vinegar, water, coriander seeds, peppercorns, cloves, and crushed pepper to a boil over medium-high heat. Add the shrimp, mint, and cilantro, turn off the heat, cover the pan, and let sit for 30 minutes. Drain the shrimp and set aside.

2. **FOR THE GAZPACHO:** Combine the chopped tomatoes, red onion, ginger, and coconut milk in a blender and purée until smooth. Season with salt and pepper to taste. Core the whole tomato and add to the mixture. Pulse five times, or until the tomato is coarsely chopped. Transfer the soup to the refrigerator to chill for at least 30 minutes.

3. Serve the soup in small chilled bowls with a shrimp on top. Garnish with the cilantro.

In tasting, Michael Symon liked Herb's enchilada a lot. "It's soulful," he said. Chef Morimoto and Cat Cora liked Herb's energy. His soup had great, complex flavors, but there was something gritty in there. His stuffed shrimp was tough.

Everyone loved Aarti's gazpacho. The coconut milk had made Cat nervous, but it worked. Bobby wanted twelve of her giant shrimp. "Outrageously delicious," said Chef Symon. When he ate the prawns, Bobby said, "I'd like to open an Indian restaurant with you tomorrow."

"Can I put some in on that?" said Chef Cora. "Damn, girl!"

"I think this is the third season I've done *Next Food Network Star,* and this is the best food I've had in those three years," said Michael Symon.

> "Aarti blew it out of the water. I loved every single thing she made. I was very impressed. It was restaurant quality and I didn't expect that from anyone at that stage. She knows she can pull it off in the time limit and she's not trying something she's never tried before and gone off into left field. She pulled it off beautifully."
>
> —Cat Cora

Finally, Aarti had decided to use coconut milk in her gazpacho, something she'd never tried.

> Every summer I make a white gazpacho with cucumber, mint, and yogurt, because in all honesty, I'm not a big fan of traditional gazpacho. Actually, that day in the kitchen stadium was the very first time I'd made a tomato gazpacho in my life! I think coconut milk is a godsend. It's luscious, silky, and creamy, and since I have issues with lactose, it's a great substitute for cream."
>
> —Aarti Sequeira

Battle Bacon

Aria and Tom staged Battle Bacon. "I want to give these guys a meal they will never forget," said Tom. "We're doing breakfast" said Aria, zeroing in on her "Family-Style" POV.

> "Every challenge had its level of intimidation! The *Iron Chef* Challenge was intimidating because I really look up to those chefs, especially Michael Symon. I just wanted to serve them really good food and I tried my hardest to put out really delicious food in the time that was given. Food is totally subjective. You never know who is going to love it and who is going to hate it!"
>
> —Aria Kagan

Aria worked on French Toast Tacos, a Cheddar Cheese Omelet with Roasted Potatoes and Bacon, and Waldorf Salad with Fennel. Aarti was less comfortable commentating than Herb was. "I think that's sliced smoked bacon," she said, and Alton said, "Tell me what you know."

Tom got creative and asked himself, "Can I make a crab cake out of pure bacon?" Dish Number One: Bacon Cake. Then a Bacon Steak, and finally an over-the-top Savory French Toast. How would it stand out? Chorizo and clams. It was *Iron Chef*. "If anyone's going to appreciate clams on French Toast, it's these people," said Tom.

"Is he off his rocker, or is he really genius? We'll see," said Cat Cora.

Meanwhile, Aria struggled to plate. Her family-style food was good but lacked what Cat called "*Iron Chef* finesse." And as Michael Symon said, "You didn't make bacon the star."

Big Chef Tom's Bacon Cake was very dense but different and interesting. He hadn't tried his Bacon Steak; it was so leathery and tough that no one could cut into it. Chef Symon said that he respected people who go for it, but Susie said the Bacon Steak was a big mistake. And Tom's French toast was an oily mess.

> "Did you hear the sound of my knife going 'eek eek'? That was the funniest."
>
> —Susie Fogelson

> "The bacon steak works, I just didn't execute it properly. All of those dishes have since worked out (yes, even French toast and clams!). I just got caught up in the time limit and also the difficulty. I mean, we had to make bacon the star of the plate, the other group got shrimp! Come on, who had the more difficult challenge?"
>
> —Tom Pizzica

> "Tom rolled the dice. Sometimes you have to. But you also have to accept that craps is always an option. As a tactic that kind of gamble can pay big, but it's a two-edged sword."
>
> —Alton Brown

Aarti was up first in evaluation. The Iron Chefs loved her dishes. But Susie said her commentating was tentative. "I felt it was a weak attempt," said Susie. Herb's personality popped, but his food was inconsistent. Aria was so focused on her Point of View that she missed the challenge; she had enthusiasm but not expertise in commentating. Tom's commentary was terrific, but Bobby said his food was three swings and misses; the spirit was great, but not the result.

"I lied when I said it [the bacon steak] was the worst thing I have ever eaten, because it was inedible. You actually could not eat it."

—Bob Tuschman

"I loved Tom's creativity but you can't take a big chunk of bacon and grill it and have it be tender. That's never going to happen. Unless you are going to braise it like you would pork belly and that's what pork belly is—basically braised bacon. I knew when he brought it to table it wouldn't be tender. We've all made those kinds of mistakes when we were learning. You just don't do it on television and you don't serve it to Iron Chefs. That's something to do at home and practice on people who love you unconditionally."

—Cat Cora

The winners of the head-to-heads were Aarti and, because of his commentary, Tom. The judges said that Aria had a radiance and ease in front of the camera but her food hadn't evolved. Herb was unpredictable, Susie said. But he had a Point of View, confidence, energy, drive . . . He was moving on, and Aria would be leaving.

Michael Symon: A Q&A

You gave Tom a lot of credit for being bold . . .

At the end of the day they have to make food that tastes good. But in a challenge like that, even though Tom may have missed on some things it was impressive that all the cards are on the table and he's taking big risks where a lot of people get in a shell and would rather not take a chance. He swung for the fences and that said a lot about his personality.

The bacon cake was his best dish?

The bacon cake was good, it wasn't great. Aria's food tasted better but she could have taken much bigger chances. I've been doing Food Network on and off since 1998 and the one thing I've learned is that to be successful you can't be guarded. So I wasn't judging exactly on how the food tasted because they can tweak the recipes. We wanted to see who was willing to take a chance, who was willing to let their guard down. You need to get out of your comfort zone and you need to be comfortable doing it.

Iron Chefs have such high standards that you are going to be the toughest judges.

That's very fair. On *Iron Chef* you're not getting judged on personality, on flair, on talking to the camera. You're judged on food. Period. On *Star,* yes we're judging these people on food but there's a lot more that goes into being a Food Network personality than just being able to cook. The best cooks on Food Network are without a doubt the Iron Chefs but that doesn't mean we are the best hosts.

Can you forget when the camera is on?

I think I'm at my best when it doesn't matter if the camera is there or not. When you're in that groove the camera is not there anymore. You need to play to the camera so you really know it's there but when you're very conscious of it, it doesn't feel natural. On *Iron Chef* I couldn't tell you where one camera is in that whole stadium unless I trip over a cord. I'm very aware of Alton and his dialogue throughout and giving times but not the cameras. By the way, I don't know that I've met a person on Food Network who's better at what he does than Alton.

Finale: Rachael Ray Directs!

In the final Star Challenge, Aarti, Herb, and Tom had an expert to direct their last pilot: Rachael Ray. The pieces would be shown to the Selection Committee and a focus group of Food Network viewers. Rachael conceptualized the pilots: Aarti injecting Indian flavors into American food; Herb emphasizing the flavor; Tom getting Big in the kitchen.

Herb was frazzled until he taped pictures of his family onto the camera. Then he didn't even see a camera. "When he smiles, I mean forget-aboutit," Rachael said. "You just want to watch him."

As Aarti demo'ed her Indian Pizza, everything ran too fast for her at first. But then she gathered herself and presented excellently.

Aarti was so comfortable on camera, Rachael said.

Tom had brought Rambling Man out of retirement. "All I can think is Susie in my head going, 'Tom, shut up.'"

"Calm down," said Rachael. "Relax." And Tom got on a roll and cooked his Roast Chicken.

After the focus group watched the pilots, Aarti, Herb, and Tom stood in front of the new Food Network Wall of Fame and the committee.

Herb had developed into a seasoned pro, and the focus group loved him. Susie said, "You are a star." Bob told Aarti that she had natural star power, and the Big Chef that he had big heart, big humor, big personality. You make cooking fun. "Whatever 'Big Chef' means, I'm buying it," said Susie.

In deliberations, Bob said Herb might have the most star potential, Susie that Aarti had it going on from the get-go. Bobby said that Tom took more risks than anyone else.

With network president Brooke Johnson on hand, Bobby revealed the *Next Food Network Star*: Aarti.

"It doesn't matter where you are . . . just hold on, just keep going, because something huge could happen."

—Aarti Sequeira

SEASON SIX	ELIMINATIONS
EPISODE ONE (DOUBLE) "Welcome to Los Angeles" First Elimination	★ **ALEXIS HERNANDEZ:** "You have to be yourself. If you are quiet, then be quiet. If you are loud, then be loud. If you are opinionated, then be opinionated. . . . What was difficult for me was displaying and reminding the Selection Committee the reason they selected me to be a finalist on the show, in a compelling manner."
EPISODE TWO "Sweet to Savory Carnival" Second Elimination	★ **DOREEN FANG:** "I actually had a Point of View coming into the show, but I think the judges were looking for something different, so I had to change it, so it seemed like I didn't have a Point of View. . . . Just let your personality shine. Because that's why they picked you in the first place."
EPISODE THREE "Grammy Award Celebration" Third Elimination	★ **DZINTRA DZENIS:** "I have many layers, so it would take more camera time, with different types of circumstances, for my personality to truly come across. I still am so thankful for the many fans who keep telling me how I was 'definitely memorable,' 'with an eclectic and zany cooking style,' and 'oh so funny.' Hopefully, I'll have other opportunities to get folks fired up about cooking à la Dzintra."
EPISODE FOUR "Spicy Competition" Fourth Elimination	★ **DARRELL "DAS" SMITH:** "It was really hard to get my energy/personality to come across on camera because that first episode when I didn't do so well, I was an emotional mess. . . . I always felt like I had to catch up. No more mistakes, so I put a lot of pressure on myself."
EPISODE FIVE "Lunch Trucks with Paula" Fifth Elimination	★ **PAUL YOUNG:** "At first it didn't seem so tough to come up with a Point of View for the show. However, when the judges don't seem to respond to your idea, then it seems impossible to come up with a new one! Make sure you're doing your thing from the start. Be authentic and genuine. The minute you're not, they see right through you and you lose their interest."
EPISODE SIX "Retro Palm Springs" Sixth Elimination	★ **BRIANNA JENKINS:** "I was surprised to be voted off. I felt I had the potential to go further and get better on camera because, let's face it, my food had already won. I just needed time to master the camera, but time is not something you have in a competition like this."
EPISODE SEVEN "Secret Supper Club" Seventh Elimination	★ **SERENA PALUMBO:** "Life is about balance. I have a desk job that I love because it allows me to use the discipline and organization I've pursued all my life. Being a great chef is about execution but also inspiration, which can come from many places. The more I exercise my disciplined self, the more my creativity increases. After a full weekend testing a recipe, I might have the epiphany on how to improve it while I'm at work, drafting some complicated finance contract!"
EPISODE EIGHT "Cooking for Eva" Eighth Elimination	★ **BRAD SORENSON:** "I felt like at that point I was one of the stronger competitors and may have had a shot to win the whole thing. Seeing how hard it was for the judges to send me home did give me the sense that I had made an impact on them. That was a consolation. But I was disappointed I didn't get an opportunity to continue and try to win the whole thing."
EPISODE NINE "*Iron Chef* Battle" Ninth Elimination	★ **ARIA KAGAN:** "I just walked out in front of the camera during the first challenge and told myself to just relax and be me. As the time went on and the judges critiqued my performance, I became really uncomfortable and so much more aware of how I was standing and what I was saying. I never really got my groove back."
EPISODE TEN "Rachael Ray Directs" Runners-up	★ **HERB MESA:** "Making it to the end of *Next Food Network Star* was the best thing to ever happen to me. I haven't stopped. I'm all over the place. I'm doing charity events, guest judging at food competitions, corporate team building. I've even done an event with Dr. Oz. I know God has always had big plans for me. Now I'm ready."
	★ **TOM PIZZICA:** "I set out to be a TV personality and that's exactly what I became. I didn't necessarily go into it thinking I was going to win. I went in just hoping to do enough to get recognized for my talents and that's what happened. Without the show, however, I would never have honed the skills necessary to make it on TV. It was TV boot camp and that's how I looked at it the whole time." Tom's show *Outrageous Food* previewed on Food Network on November 5, 2010.

WINNER ★ WINNER

AARTI SEQUEIRA

Aarti's show *Aarti Party* premiered on Food Network on August 22, 2010.

Aarti Sequeira: A Q&A

Why did you enter the competition?

A lot of people told me to. I really didn't think I stood a chance. I thought I might get on the show but I thought what the heck am I going to do then? I knew I wanted to be a cooking show host and Food Network is the best place to do it. I had to try. I really didn't expect to be selected the first time I tried.

I knew if I thought about it too much I would freak myself out. When it came to making the video, we made it on the last possible day. My husband was shooting our YouTube show in the kitchen and when we finished he said, "Okay let's shoot your video right now." "Now?" "Yeah, just make something up." So I didn't have time to think about it.

Did it help you that you had your "Aarti Party" POV already thought out?

I was all over the map (literally!) at the beginning of the show. I think I pitched something like a little bit India, a little bit Middle East, a little bit California . . . You should have seen Giada's face when I said that! But my cooking never changed. That's the thing about your POV; it should be inherent to who you are, not something you put on. It's always so much simpler than you think it is.

And I didn't feel like I had a zipped-up POV because I was clear I didn't want to be the Indian food expert on Food Network. Because I'm not. But I didn't have a good sense of how to market what I was doing. I'm thankful they left me alone for a while and I feel it percolated.

Are you surprised other finalists seem to struggle to come up with a POV?

I was a bit surprised. Perhaps because I come from a news background, I intrinsically understood the value of "pitching." You must have an angle. Without a POV, Bob and Susie don't have a lot of patience for you.

You'd worked in TV before. Did that give you some sense of what this might entail?

I went to a good journalism school and was a producer at CNN so I was very opinionated about what makes someone good in front of the camera. I wanted to be a journalist. It was going to be me and Christiane Amanpour arm-in-arm dodging missiles, but I think I was too cheery for CNN.

So you had a head start on the competition?

God gave me a talent to be in front of the camera and I worked at it. I'd done the You Tube show every week for nine months and that's incredible practice. I was improving in ways I wasn't even aware of. If you look at the first one, it's night and day from the last. For the others, the cooking came naturally and that was the thing I questioned all the time. They were trying so hard on the camera front and for me that was my moment to chill out.

Where did your lack of confidence come from?

I'm Indian and we were brought up to get A pluses in everything. If you brought home a

report card with a 98 percent the question was, "What happened to the other 2 percent?" So it was really uncomfortable for me to be on this public stage presenting something that I didn't think was an A plus. I'm always worried about the 2 percent. I'm working on it but it will still drive me nuts.

How did you build your confidence as the show went on?

My fellow finalists were brilliant morale boosters. We'd spend the nights nursing a beer and talking about our strengths and weaknesses. I know it was a competition but there was a rare sense of camaraderie among us. The only thing that kept me going was my faith in God; I had little to no faith in myself.

At what point of the competition did you think, I can actually win this?

"I didn't think I could win this thing until after the *Iron Chef* challenge. Until then I knew that you were only as good as the challenge you just won. If I couldn't keep the wins going, then I would fall to the middle, which is a dangerous place to be. After *Iron Chef* and the amazing compliments the judges gave me about my food, I thought, "Okay" all I have to do now is my pilot and I know how to do that.

What was the hardest challenge?

Iron Chef. That's the kind of thing I never imagined I'd be doing. The only experience I had was cooking for myself and my friends in my little kitchen in L.A., not cooking for Chef Symon and Chef Morimoto! I nearly peed myself when I saw Morimoto standing there. These guys are culinary giants. How was I going to make anything impressive enough for them?

But you were so serene at *Iron Chef*...

That was a really surreal, out-of-body experience. The challenge before was at Beso and I was running around like a chicken with its head cut off. It meant the food didn't turn out well and I couldn't present very well. So I said no matter what they throw at me next, I've got to keep calm. I was going to trust my ability, no matter what. But at *Iron Chef* I was not happy standing there figuring out what to use. That happens to me at the supermarket now. My husband says, "Will you just make a decision?"

Bobby Flay's not there in the supermarket saying, "What are you doing?"

I was touched that he was nervous for me. We're very different types of people. He'll make a decision and go with it and I want to make the best decision ever so I never have to look back at it and question it.

And your favorite challenge?

The food trucks, even though my buddy Tom got the credit for the sandwich and it was my mayo . . .

Who was the toughest judge?

Susie killed me. Bobby said if your food isn't good you're going home so I felt I didn't need to have unpacked. But he always liked the food. Susie almost wants you to do well more than you do. When you don't perform like she expects she gets frustrated. I just didn't want

to let her down. She's very good at keeping a poker face and I never thought she liked me. When I saw the show I thought, "She kind of does." Now we're friends and I love hanging out with her.

Did you watch the show before you were on?

Maybe two episodes. Because I knew I wanted to be on a show like this I'd get heart palpitations watching. It helped because I didn't know what to expect and I hadn't had years of studying Bob and Susie and Bobby figuring out what they liked. I could just be who I am. I watched every minute of our series but mostly through my fingers.

Did you have any desserts up your sleeve?

That is not my strong point. With baking you have to be precise and I have a terrible memory for quantities and proportions. And I was a fat kid growing up so we didn't eat a lot of dessert. Now I have my own show I make more desserts. I'm so glad I never got a dessert on the show, like the Pineapple Upside-Down Cake Serena had.

What would have happened if they had said, "You can't use any Indian spices?"

I would have been okay. I don't always cook with spices. I went to a semi-professional cooking school that is very French and go to farmers' markets all the time. I would have freaked out for ten minutes but I would have worked it out. If we had swapped I would have felt very sorry for whoever got my spices.

What spices should every well-stocked kitchen have on hand to make basic Indian dishes?

Ground turmeric (try to get it from a trusted source, look for the organic version too). Sometimes you'll find turmeric has no aroma at all; that's when you know you've been hoodwinked. Ground paprika (my substitute for Indian red chile powder, which is both hard to find and spicy!), coriander seeds, cumin seeds, brown mustard seeds, garam masala, and green cardamom pods. No curry powder, please!

How has your life changed since you won?

In many ways it's the same. We're still living in the same apartment and driving the same car and I still wash my own dishes but days are filled with cooking and coming up with recipes. It's slowly dawning on me that people may know I am this person on TV so I still get a rush when people say, "Do you mind if we take a photo?" Why do you think I would mind?

Some of it does take getting used to. I was at the gym one day on the treadmill and I was a hot mess and this guy walks up. "Oh my god, my girlfriend will never believe this!" He takes his phone, calls a number, and thrusts the phone at me, "Will you talk to her?" I jump off the treadmill and say hi.

But thank goodness because before we weren't sure if we could make rent every month and just to know we can make rent is a blessing. My youngest sister is in India and she never got to go to college and to know I can help her makes you feel like less of a loser. Now when I wake up in the morning I know why I am here.

Season SEVEN

F*ood Network Star* returned to Los Angeles, and Bob, Susie, and Bobby, aided by the roster of Food Network stars, began a new search for a great cook with a surpassing personality to add to the team. Who among the new finalists would be the next Aarti Sequeira, Melissa d'Arabian, Aaron McCargo, Jr., Amy Finley, or Guy Fieri? Was there another Hearty Boys team? Would there be a tight contest? And recently the judges had seen that more than one standout star could emerge from a single season.

THE FINALISTS

1. Alicia Sanchez. Alicia received a diploma in Pastry and Baking Arts from the Institute of Culinary Education and loves to put her own twists on everyday dishes. After moving to New York from Kansas City, Alicia opened a bakery specializing in customized cakes and cupcakes. This upbeat New Yorker combines her expertise and passion while teaching young adults how to cook as the chef instructor at Manhattan's Grand Street Settlement.

2. Chris Nirschel. Chris matches his vivacious personality to his culinary style, bringing bold and intriguing flavors to the kitchen with no recipes at all. He found his passion and focus in life when he attended French Culinary Institute and most recently served as the sous chef at a New York restaurant. Now this culinary bad boy creates exciting flavor profiles with confidence to boot.

3. Howie Drummond. A local radio show host, Howie worked in the restaurant business for seven years striving to become a chef before he won a radio contest that changed his life. Although his career path changed, his love for food did not. Howie, who also hosted a local TV cooking show for three years in Denver, believes that food at its best brings family and friends together with love and entertainment.

4. Jeff Mauro. A private chef at the Chicago corporate headquarters for a large mortgage company, Jeff graduated from California's Hollywood Kitchen Academy and has worked in the food industry since high school in various roles including line cook, caterer, and chef instructor. After pursuing a career as an entertainer and comedian in Los Angeles, Jeff returned to Chicago to spend time doing what he loves: cooking. Jeff's down-to-earth personality coupled with his comic relief make a great combo in the kitchen.

5. Juba Kali. Juba thrives on bringing creativity to recipes, combining tastes and elements from a variety of cultures. An energetic new father, he focuses on the science of food, drawing from his culinary background and his role as research chef at a popular spice company for inspiration. Juba received a bachelor of science degree in nutritional studies from Johnson & Wales University and combines his two passions—science and food—to create culinary masterpieces.

6. Justin Balmes. A graduate of the Art Institute of Atlanta with a degree in culinary arts, Justin has worked on almost every level in the kitchen including line cook, sous chef, and executive chef. When he's not concocting organic recipes with local ingredients, this adventure seeker takes it outside for competitive cycling. In his current position as farmer's market specialist at a large organic retailer, Justin is the jack-of-all-trades as a fishmonger, a butcher, and an instructor.

7. Justin Davis. Justin brings experience from all levels of the restaurant business, including host, waiter, bartender, and line cook. The stay-at-home

dad and current food blogger draws from cookbooks for inspiration, but rarely follows a recipe to a tee. His no-nonsense attitude is reflected in his culinary style, as he values rustic cooking and favors bringing the farm to the table with few steps in between.

8. **Jyll Everman.** Jill attended the Epicurean School of Culinary Arts and has worked in several high-end restaurants in various roles including server, dining room manager, and line worker. Jyll revels in comfort food and can turn any true classic into a scrumptious appetizer. She relays her "can-do" attitude to the students in the monthly classes she teaches, inspiring others to achieve their culinary dreams.

9. **Katy Clark.** A food and fitness life coach, Katy previously owned and operated Silver Spoon Café, a western-inspired café in Kunming, China. Now this mother of three runs food and fitness company Fit Chef Katy, encompassing the Dessert Lady Catering Company and children's cooking division Look! I Can Cook. Inspired by the recipes of the women in her family and her experience in restaurants over the years, Katy loves to add her special touch to make every dish her own.

10. **Mary Beth Albright.** A former attorney, Mary Beth decided to follow her passion for food and began seeking out a culinary career of her own. After studying ingredients in professional areas and as a home cook, she now shares her expertise with others as a food writer and local expert for print and broadcast media outlets. She also works with children through her U.S. House of Representatives preschool cooking and gardening program.

11. **Orchid Paulmeier.** A first-generation American of Filipino descent, Orchid started her culinary career as an ice cream scooper in high school, and only went up from there. She's worked as a general manager, head trainer, and personal chef and now owns One Hot Mama's restaurant in Hilton Head Island, South Carolina. This outspoken mother of three prides herself on her southern barbecue and is well known locally for her wings and ribs.

12. **Penny Davidi.** A mother of two teenagers, Penny grew up learning the art of cooking from the women in her family and used this knowledge as a launching pad to fuse creativity and personality to create her own innovative recipes. Raised in California, Penny franchised Pizza Rustica and opened a popular branch in Beverly Hills that once earned the title "hottest pizza in town."

13. **Susie Jimenez.** Susie began her relationship with food picking fruit with her parents, who came to California from Mexico. To pursue her food passion, she attended the California Culinary Academy and later worked as manager, line cook, sous chef, and executive chef at several restaurants. She's now the owner of Susie's Custom Catering and Farmer's Daughter and participates in events where she teaches students how to cook with a variety of techniques and flavors.

14. **Vic "Vegas" Moea.** A self-trained restaurant chef, Vic worked his way up the culinary ladder from dishwasher to executive chef at a Las Vegas hotel restaurant. He moved from Brooklyn to Las Vegas at thirteen, but his culinary style reflects his classic New York Italian background. Learning to cook from his mother and grandmother, Vic adds his modern Vegas flair to traditional recipes from his childhood.

15. **Whitney Chen.** A former engineering consultant, Whitney quit her job and received a culinary certificate from L'Academie de Cuisine in Bethesda, Maryland, and worked her way up the culinary ladder to the line at a Three Michelin Star restaurant in New York City. A serious home cook turned professional chef, Whitney enjoys using the freshest seasonal ingredients in her cooking and believes that anyone can incorporate advanced techniques into making everyday meals that impress.

SEASON SEVEN RECAP

At press time, Season Seven was still being edited, and only a snapshot of each show was available. But it was clear that the cast assembled was the most dynamic—and at fifteen, the largest—yet. Food Network ramped up the challenges, piled on the twists, amped up the star wattage, and added an extra show to squeeze in all the drama. Plus, Giada De Laurentiis, Season Six's mentor, became a full-time member of the selection committee, which agreed and disagreed as much as ever.

In Episode One, the committee had to decide the fate of Vic "Vegas" Moea, who not only ran out of time to plate his main ingredient in the Camera Challenge but then dropped his dish at the Press Dinner when he collided with teammate Jyll Everman. Despite these hiccups, dark horse Vic cooked strongly enough to be one of the final three standing, boosting the idea that guys with tats are sweethearts under all that ink.

Whittling fifteen finalists into a group of eleven required two double eliminations this season, making the competition and the drama more intense than ever. In Episode Two, Star's all-time most in-your-face strategist, Penny Davidi, deliberately chose to work with a weak team, so she could shine. Penny clashed often with Chris Nirschel, the talented but often unfocused cook, who was this season's object of frustration for Bobby Flay. One blowup came in Episode Three (the Duff Goldman versus Robert Irvine Dueling Desserts Party Challenge) when Chef Irvine fired Chris as team leader.

The star power continued in Season Seven with Episode Four's special guests: Paula Deen and the cast of Courtney Cox's *Cougar Town*. And, of course, *Food Network Star* success story Guy Fieri made an appearance this season as well, challenging finalists to create their own mini-episodes of his popular hit show *Diners, Drive-Ins and Dives*. During this episode, Guy first identified Vic as a threat and Susie Jimenez broke out, too, emerging from a muddled POV to cook the Latin food that Susie Fogelson said was "in her bones."

The strongest and most consistent POV belonged to Jeff Mauro, the "Sandwich King," who never deviated from his message. Another of the final five, Mary Beth Albright, reached into her home life halfway through the season to create her POV of "Sunday Suppers," ideal for her warm, storytelling style. While cooking was a second career for Mary Beth, finalist Whitney Chen had the cooking chops after working at Per Se, one of the best restaurants in the world. But she would have to prove to the judges that she had what it takes to be a television star.

After *Great Food Truck Race* host Tyler Florence helmed Episode Six, an Episode Seven dinner guest, Wolfgang Puck, redefined tough love once more when he took Jyll back to the kitchen to show her how to properly make risotto. The challenges didn't ease up as the season progressed. From making cupcakes for Ina Garten to thinking on their feet live as guests on *Rachael Ray,* from getting roasted by comedians to feeling the heat in an *Iron Chef* challenge, there was no room for the finalists to make any mistakes.

The Finale twist—Cook for Your Life—cruelly eliminated one of the final three, leaving only two standing. Their pilots were directed by Guy Fieri and judged by a panel of the eliminated finalists. Finally, it came time for the Selection Committee to decide. Which finalist would they crown as the winner of *Food Network Star*? The winner, who had to compete longer and harder for the prize than any other finalist in *Food Network Star* history, would be propelled into Food Network stardom with one final ruling.

At press time the winner of Season Seven had yet to be chosen, but a sampling of recipes from the finalists are included on the following pages. Check out FoodNetwork .com/STAR to learn more about the Season Seven finale and the newest winner of *Food Network Star.*

CHICKEN APPLE SAUSAGE AND SQUASH SOUP

Recipe courtesy Jeff Mauro

Yield: 8 cups, about 6 servings ❚ Prep Time: 40 minutes ❚ Cook Time: 40 minutes ❚ Ease of Preparation: easy

3 tablespoons extra-virgin olive oil, divided

1 pound chicken apple sausage, casing removed

1 large onion, coarsely chopped

1 small butternut squash (about 1½ pounds), peeled, seeded, and coarsely chopped

1 teaspoon kosher salt

¼ teaspoon freshly ground black pepper

3 garlic cloves, chopped

¼ teaspoon crushed red pepper

½ teaspoon dried sage

5 cups chicken stock

1 red bell pepper, diced

½ cup heavy whipping cream

2 cups baby spinach

2 tablespoons brandy (optional)

1. Heat a Dutch oven over medium-high heat. Add 2 tablespoons of the oil and swirl to coat the pan. Add the sausage and cook, breaking it up with a wooden spoon, until browned, 5 to 6 minutes. Remove from the pan and set aside.

2. If the pan is dry, add the remaining 1 tablespoon of the oil. Reduce the heat to medium and sauté the onion, squash, salt, and pepper, stirring occasionally, until partially softened, about 7 minutes. Stir in the garlic, red pepper flakes, and sage and cook until aromatic, about 1 minute. Pour in the stock, bring it to a boil, then reduce the heat and simmer until the squash is softened, 15 to 20 minutes.

3. Let the mixture cool for about 5 minutes, then purée with a hand blender. Add the bell pepper and the cream. Simmer until the pepper is softened, about 5 minutes. Add the spinach, brandy, and reserved sausage and cook, stirring until the spinach wilts, about 1 minute. Adjust the seasoning to taste.

"Every emotion imaginable was pushed to the utmost extreme: Extreme anxiety before challenge reveals; extreme intensity during cooking; extreme nervousness before presenting; extreme pain and dread during evaluation; extreme homesickness; extreme boredom; and, last but not least, extreme elation during successes."

—Jeff Mauro

SAVORY BREAKFAST MUFFINS

Recipe courtesy Mary Beth Albright

Yield: 6 muffins ▌ Prep Time: 10 minutes ▌ Cook Time: 35 minutes ▌ Ease of Preparation: easy

2 tablespoons olive oil, divided

½ medium onion, finely chopped (about 1 cup)

1 cup halved cherry or grape tomatoes

1 small garlic clove, minced

½ teaspoon kosher salt, divided

¼ teaspoon freshly ground black pepper, divided

4 eggs, beaten

1 cup cooked, cooled quinoa, from ½ cup uncooked

¾ cup grated Gruyère cheese (2¼ ounces)

1 tablespoon finely chopped fresh thyme leaves

1. Preheat the oven to 350°F. Grease a 6-cup muffin tin.

2. Heat 1 tablespoon of the oil in a large skillet over medium heat. Sauté the onion, tomatoes, and garlic until the onion is light brown and tender and the tomatoes are softened, 8 to 10 minutes. Season with ¼ teaspoon of the salt and ⅛ teaspoon of the pepper. Set aside to cool slightly. Transfer to a large bowl and stir in the eggs, quinoa, Gruyère, thyme, the remaining 1 tablespoon oil, and the remaining salt and pepper. Spoon the batter into the tin, about ½ cup for each muffin, and bake until the muffins are golden brown and well risen and the eggs are set, 20 to 25 minutes. Cool the muffins in the tin for 10 minutes, then carefully remove. Serve warm or at room temperature.

"*Star* was harder than everything except motherhood, and I'm a pretty tough broad. The first days were grueling, neck-deep in extreme personalities and trash-talking."

—Mary Beth Albright

VIETNAMESE-INFLUENCED MEATBALLS

Recipe courtesy Susie Jimenez

Yield: 8 servings (as an appetizer) ▮ Prep Time: 15 minutes ▮ Cook Time: 15 minutes ▮ Ease of Preparation: easy

2 pounds ground beef

1 jalapeño pepper, chopped (remove seeds and ribs for a milder heat)

3 tablespoons soy sauce

2 tablespoons chopped fresh cilantro leaves

1 tablespoon grated fresh ginger

1 tablespoon chopped fresh mint leaves

4 large fresh basil leaves, thinly sliced

1 egg

Zest and juice of 1 lime

¼ cup canola oil

8 medium-size leaves Bibb lettuce, from 1 head

⅓ cup sweet chili sauce

1. In a bowl, combine the beef, jalapeño, soy sauce, cilantro, ginger, mint, basil, egg, and lime zest and juice and mix until well blended. Using about 2 tablespoons per meatball, shape the mixture into balls.

2. Heat the oil in two large skillets over medium-high heat. Add the meatballs and panfry, turning, until cooked through and well browned, 10 to 12 minutes. Transfer to a wire rack set over a sheet tray to drain and cool slightly. To serve, place 2 to 3 meatballs in a lettuce leaf and drizzle with the sweet chili sauce.

"I had a mentality that I was there to compete and win, but I walked away with friends that I will have a bond with for the rest of my life. I also wanted to focus only on cooking and there was so much more to worry about. The people around you, what you looked like, time, what you would be judged on and how you wanted to be perceived. It's a ton to focus on while still trying to adequately express your cooking and technique."

—Susie Jimenez

SHORT AND SWEET BRAISED BONELESS SHORT RIBS
with Brown Sugar and Butter Sweet Potato Purée

Recipe courtesy Vic "Vegas" Moea

Yield: 4 servings ▮ Prep Time: 15 minutes ▮ Cook Time: 4 hours ▮ Ease of Preparation: easy

Vegetable oil

2 pounds boneless short ribs, trimmed

Kosher salt

Freshly ground black pepper

½ pound celery, diced

1 white onion, quartered

½ pound carrots, diced

1 tomato, quartered

8 sprigs fresh thyme

8 ounces burgundy wine

8 ounces beef stock

2 pounds sweet potatoes

2 tablespoons butter

2 teaspoons brown sugar

Wild honey, for drizzling

Pinch of smoked sea salt

1. In a Dutch oven over medium-high heat, heat the vegetable oil. Season the meat generously with the salt and pepper. Add the meat to the pan and sear on all sides, about 5 to 7 minutes. Add the celery, onion, carrots, tomato, and thyme, and cook until the vegetables begin to soften, about 3 minutes. Pour in the wine and stock, reduce the heat to low, cover the pan, and simmer for 3 to 3½ hours, checking every hour to make sure there is still liquid in the pan. If the liquid is evaporating too quickly, add a little water or stock. When the meat is falling apart, carefully remove it from the pan and set aside. Strain and reserve the liquid.

2. While the meat is cooking, preheat the oven to 400°F. Bake the sweet potatoes until tender, 60 to 80 minutes. Remove from the oven and take off the skins. Mash the potatoes in a bowl, add the butter and brown sugar, and mash again. Season with salt to taste.

3. To serve, place a scoop of the potato purée on each plate, then top with a chunk of meat. Pour the strained cooking liquid over the top, then drizzle with honey and season with a pinch of smoked sea salt. *Vroooooooooooooom!* Good eats!

"Looking back at all the strides and sacrifices I made to get here, it lets me know that I need to never give up on anything. I stay humble and keep shooting for the stars. Now I incorporate the schooling I have received week after week during this competition with everything I have already molded, and I keep going and going, practicing and practicing with a camera and in the kitchen. I go eat at places and go talk to people . . . Now, that's living!"

—Vic "Vegas" Moea

FRESH CHICKPEA FALAFEL

Recipe courtesy Whitney Chen

Yield: about 3 dozen falafel balls ▌ Prep Time: 45 minutes ▌ Inactive Prep Time: overnight, soaking ▌ Cook Time: 20 minutes ▌ Ease of Preparation: intermediate

3 cups fresh garbanzo beans, raw, or 3 cups canned, rinsed and drained

1½ cups dried garbanzo beans, soaked for several hours

½ large onion, coarsely chopped

¼ cup oat bran

¼ cup wheat germ

3 garlic cloves, coarsely chopped

1 tablespoon ground cumin

1 tablespoon ground allspice

1 tablespoon kosher salt

1 teaspoon freshly ground black pepper

¼ cup finely chopped fresh parsley leaves

1 tablespoon chopped fresh dill

Zest from 2 lemons (preferably Meyer), 1 tablespoon

Canola oil, for frying

1. In a large bowl, toss the fresh and the soaked beans, onion, oat bran, wheat germ, garlic, cumin, allspice, salt, and pepper. Run the ingredients through a meat grinder using the smallest grinding die. Add the parsley, dill, and lemon zest. Using 2-tablespoon portions, firmly shape the dough into balls and place them on a parchment-lined baking sheet.

2. Fill a large pot with 3 to 4 inches of canola oil and heat to 375°F. Fry the falafel balls, in batches of about 6, until dark brown, 2 to 3 minutes. Transfer to a wire rack set over a baking sheet to drain.

"To up the ante on any meal, you only need to apply a single exciting element. I don't think people want to make three-Michelin-star food at home, but I think they occasionally want to make a pot roast in a crock pot and somehow serve it with three-Michelin-star flair."

—Whitney Chen

On Their Plate Now

What are your favorite finalists up to? Read on to find out . . .

Season One

Deborah Fewell became a Maven on TLC's *Home Made Simple* series ★ **Brook Harlan** is a teacher and author of "Cooking with Brook" for *Inside Columbia* magazine ★ **Susannah Locketti** is a food expert on Momlogic.com ★ **Hans Rueffert** is the author of *Eat Like There's No Tomorrow* ★ in Chicago, **Dan Smith and Steve McDonagh** are the Hearty Boys, restaurateurs and caterers ★ **Michael Thomas** is cooking, surfing, and continuing to be ridiculous, and has launched a surf company Dr. Wilbur's ★ **Eric Warren** owns Mean Cuisine Foods, a catering company in Los Angeles

Season Two

Jess Dang is working as a business analyst while experimenting in her kitchen in the Bay Area ★ **Guy Fieri**'s *Guy Fieri Food: Cookin' It, Livin' It, Lovin' It* was published in 2011 ★ **Carissa Giacalone (Seward)** writes recipes and is senior banquet chef at the Hilton San Diego Bayfront ★ **Nathan Lyon** is a host of PBS's *Growing a Greener World* ★ **Beth Raynor** is chef/owner of a restaurant in San Francisco ★ **Evette Rodriguez** is catering locally and employed by the state college in her area

Season Three

Vivien Cunha is a private chef and caterer in Los Angeles ★ **Tommy Grella** is a financial planner in northeastern Massachusetts ★ **Amy Finley** is the author of the memoir *How to Eat a Small Country* ★ visit **Joshua Adam Garcia** at chefjag.com ★ **Colombe Jacobsen** welcomed a baby boy in 2011 and cooks healthy and seasonal food for individuals and corporate events ★ **Paul McCullough** is chef/owner of Paul's Kitchen catering and event company in Los Angeles ★ **Patrick Rolfe** is Executive Kitchen Manager for Ling and Louie's Asian Bar and Grill in Boise, Idaho ★ **Michael Salmon** runs foodservice operations at Macy's Herald Square in New York ★ **Rory Schepisi** is chef/owner of Boot Hill Saloon and Grill in Vega, Texas ★ **Adrien Sharp** is host of JTV's *Food Circus* ★ **Nikki Shaw** is a celebrity chef and caterer in Los Angeles

Season Four

Jennifer Cochrane is manager at a restaurant in Providence ★ **Lisa Garza** operates her food and fashion business Lisa Garza Taste Studio in Dallas ★ **Adam Gertler** is host of Food Network's *Kid in a Candy Store* ★ Comedian **Cory Kahaney** appears frequently onstage and on national television ★ **Shane Lyons** is Executive Chef at Nosh in Colorado Springs ★ **Aaron McCargo, Jr.,** is the author of *Simply Done, Well Done* ★ **Kelsey Nixon** is host of Cooking Channel's *Kelsey's Essentials* ★ **Kevin Roberts** is chef/owner of four San Diego restaurants and host of TLC's *BBQ Pitmasters* ★ **Jeffrey Vaden** is chef/owner of Soul/Luxe caterers in White Plains, New York

Season Five

Brett August is head chef at Agua Dulce in New York City ★ **Katie Cavuto Boyle** is chef/owner of Healthy Bites ToGo Market and Cafe in Philadelphia ★ **Melissa d'Arabian** is host of Food Network's *Ten Dollar Dinners* ★ **Teddy Folkman** is Executive Chef at Granville Moore's in Washington, D.C. ★ **Jen Isham** is a manager at a major hotel in Orlando ★ **Debbie Lee** is a restaurant consultant and operates the Ahn-Joo Food Truck in L.A. and is the author of cookbook *Seoultown Kitchen* ★ **Jamika Pessoa** operates personal chef service Life of the Party ★ **Michael Proietti** is Food and Beverage Director at a hotel in New Rochelle, New York ★ **Jeffrey Saad** is host of Cooking Channel's *United Tastes of America*

Season Six

Dzintra Dzenis is chef/owner of Plate by Dzintra in Austin ★ Traveling chef **Doreen Fang** is author of the blog *Dining with Doreen* ★ **Alexis Hernandez** grows produce and cooks on his sixty-five-acre family farm ★ **Aria Kagan** has been working hard on Eats Good, her meal delivery service in Hollywood, Florida ★ **Brianna Jenkins** is chef/owner of her own catering company ★ **Herb Mesa** is a personal trainer and personal chef in Atlanta ★ **Serena Palumbo** is an attorney and creator of the webisode series Cooking in Manhattan ★ **Tom Pizzica** is host of Food Network's *Outrageous Food* ★ **Aarti Sequeira** is host of Food Network's *Aarti Party* ★ **Darrel A. Smith** teaches the Culinary Arts program at Beverly Hills High School ★ **Brad Sorenson** is a chef at ASTI Trattoria in Austin ★ **Paul Young** is the executive chef at Stubby's Pub & Grub in Milwaukee

Do you have what it takes to be the
next Food Network Star?

If you think you can battle it out in the kitchen and shine in front of the cameras, there's nothing standing between you and the chance to fulfill your dream. For information on how you can enter to become a finalist and to learn more about your favorite *Food Network Star* personalities, please visit FoodNetwork.com/STAR.

★ INDEX